CLEP Pre-Calculus FOR BEGINNERS

The Ultimate Step by Step Guide to Acing CLEP Precalculus

By

Reza Nazari

Copyright © 2024
Effortless Math Education Inc.

All rights reserved. No part of this publication may be reproduced, stored in a retrieval system, or transmitted in any form or by any means, electronic, mechanical, photocopying, recording, scanning, or otherwise, except as permitted under Section 107 or 108 of the 1976 United States Copyright Act, without permission of the author.

All inquiries should be addressed to:
info@effortlessMath.com
www.EffortlessMath.com

ISBN: 978-1-63719-638-0

Published by: **Effortless Math Education Inc.**

for Online Math Practice Visit www.EffortlessMath.com

Welcome to
CLEP Precalculus Prep

Thank you for choosing Effortless Math for your CLEP Precalculus preparation and congratulations on making the decision to take the CLEP Precalculus test! It's a remarkable move you are taking, one that shouldn't be diminished in any capacity.

That's why you need to use every tool possible to ensure you succeed on the final exam with the highest possible score, and this extensive study guide is one such tool.

CLEP Pre-Calculus for Beginners is designed to be comprehensive and cover all the topics that are typically covered in the CLEP Precalculus test. It provides clear explanations and examples of the concepts and includes practice problems and quizzes to test your understanding of the material. The textbook also provides step-by-step solutions to the problems, so you can check your work and understand how to solve similar problems on your own.

Additionally, this book is written in a user-friendly way, making it easy to follow and understand even if you have struggled with math in the past. It also includes a variety of visual aids such as diagrams, graphs, and charts to help you better understand the concepts.

CLEP Pre-Calculus for Beginners is flexible and can be used to supplement a traditional classroom setting, or as a standalone resource for self-study. With the help of this comprehensive textbook, you will have the necessary foundation to master the material and succeed in the CLEP Precalculus course.

EffortlessMath.com

Effortless Math's Precalculus Online Center

Effortless Math Online Precalculus Center offers a complete study program, including the following:

- ✓ Step-by-step instructions on how to prepare for the CLEP Precalculus test

- ✓ Numerous Precalculus worksheets to help you measure your math skills

- ✓ Complete list of Precalculus formulas

- ✓ Video lessons for all Precalculus topics

- ✓ Full-length Precalculus practice tests

- ✓ And much more…

No Registration Required

Visit **EffortlessMath.com/Precalculus** to find your online Precalculus resources.

How to Use This Book Effectively?

Look no further when you need a study guide to improve your math skills to succeed on the CLEP Precalculus test. Each chapter of this comprehensive guide to the Precalculus will provide you with the knowledge, tools, and understanding needed for every topic covered on the course.

It's very important that you understand each topic before moving onto another one, as that's the way to guarantee your success. Each chapter provides you with examples and a step-by-step guide of every concept to better understand the content that will be on the course. To get the best possible results from this book:

> **Begin studying long before your test date.** This provides you ample time to learn the different math concepts. The earlier you begin studying for the test, the sharper your skills will be. Do not procrastinate! Provide yourself with plenty of time to learn the concepts and feel comfortable that you understand them when your test date arrives.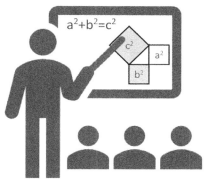

> **Practice consistently.** Study Precalculus concepts at least 30 to 40 minutes a day. Remember, slow and steady wins the race, which can be applied to preparing for the Precalculus test. Instead of cramming to tackle everything at once, be patient and learn the math topics in short bursts.

> Whenever you get a math problem wrong, **mark it off, and review it later** to make sure you understand the concept.

> Start each session by **looking over the previous material.**

> Once you've reviewed the book's lessons, **take a practice test at the back of the book** to gauge your level of readiness. Then, review your results. Read detailed answers and solutions for each question you missed.

> **Take another practice test** to get an idea of how ready you are to take the actual exam. Taking the practice tests will give you the confidence you need on test day. Simulate the CLEP Precalculus testing environment by sitting in a quiet room free from distraction. Make sure to clock yourself with a timer.

Looking for more?

Visit EffortlessMath.com/Precalculus to find hundreds of CLEP Precalculus worksheets, video tutorials, practice tests, CLEP Precalculus formulas, and much more.

Or scan this QR code.

No Registration Required.

Contents

1 Polynomial and Rational Functions

Chapter: Equations and Inequalities — 1

Solving Multi–Step Equations	2
Slope and Intercepts	3
Using Intercepts	4
Transforming Linear Functions	5
Solving Inequalities	6
Graphing Linear Inequalities	7
Solving Compound Inequalities	8
Solving Absolute Value Equations	9
Solving Absolute Value Inequalities	10
Graphing Absolute Value Inequalities	11
Solving Systems of Equations	12
Solving Special Systems	13
Systems of Equations Word Problems	14
Solve Systems of Non-linear Equations (by Graph)	15
Solve Systems of Non-linear Equations (by Substitution)	16
Solve Systems of Non-linear Equations (by Elimination)	17
Chapter 1: Practices	18
Chapter 1: Answers	22

Chapter: Functions — 25

Evaluating Functions: Function Notation	26
Modeling Real-world Situations with Functions	27
Adding and Subtracting Functions	28
Multiplying and Dividing Functions	29
Composite Functions	30
Real Zeros	31
Average Rate of Changes	32
Codomain	33
Chapter 2: Practices	34
Chapter 2: Answers	38

Contents

Chapter 3: Polynomial and Rational Functions — 39

- The Simplest Functions: Constant and Identity 40
- Polynomial Functions 41
- Graphing Polynomial Functions 42
- Writing Polynomials in Standard Form 43
- Simplifying Polynomials 44
- Factoring Trinomials 45
- Solving a Quadratic Equation 46
- Graphing Quadratic Functions 47
- Solving Quadratic Inequalities 48
- Graphing Quadratic Inequalities 49
- Polynomial Functions and Complex Zeros 50
- Rational Equations 51
- Multiplying and Dividing Rational Expressions 52
- Simplifying Rational Expressions 53
- Rational Functions 54
- Graphing Rational Expressions 55
- Chapter 3: Practices 56
- Chapter 3: Answers 60

2 Exponential and Logarithmic Functions

Chapter 4: Exponential Functions and Logarithms — 63

- Exponential Functions: Definition and Properties 64
- Solving Exponential Equations 65
- Logarithmic Functions: Definition and Properties 66
- Evaluating Logarithms 67
- Properties of Logarithms 68
- Natural Logarithms 69
- Solving Logarithmic Equations 70
- Chapter 4: Practices 71
- Chapter 4: Answers 74

Chapter 5: Radical and absolute value Functions — 75

- Simplifying Radical Expressions 76
- Simplifying Radical Expressions Involving Fractions 77
- Adding and Subtracting Radical Expressions 78
- Multiplying Radical Expressions 79
- Radical Equations 80
- Solving Radical Inequalities 81

Chapter 5

- Radical Functions 82
- Graphing Radical Functions 83
- Absolute Value Functions.. 84
- Graphing Absolute Value Functions 85
- Absolute Value Properties 86
- Floor Value... 87
- Floor Function 88
- Graphing Floor Function 89
- Chapter 5: Practices 90
- Chapter 5: Answers 94

Chapter 6: Functions Operations — 99

- Positive, Negative, Increasing and Decreasing Functions on Intervals... 100
- Transformations of Functions 101
- Function Symmetry: Even and Odd 102
- End Behavior of Polynomial Functions................................ 103
- One-to-One Function 104
- Identifying the Function One-by-One from the Graph......... 105
- Onto (Surjective) Functions.. 106
- Function Inverses 107
- Inverse Function Graph 108
- Inverse Variation 109
- Piecewise-defined Functions 110
- Chapter 6: Practices 111
- Chapter 6: Answers 114

Chapter 7: Sequences and Series — 117

- Sequence 118
- Recursive Formula.. 119
- Write a Formula for a Recursive Sequence.......................... 120
- Arithmetic Sequences 121
- Geometric Sequences 122
- Sigma Notation 123
- Arithmetic Series 124
- Finite Geometric Series 125
- Infinite Geometric Series.. 126
- Convergent and Divergent Series 127
- The nth Term Test for Divergence 128
- Introduction to the Integral Test 129
- Comparison, Ratio, and Root Tests 130
- Alternating Series and Absolute Convergence 131
- Pascal's Triangle 132
- The Binomial Theorem 133
- Chapter 7: Practices 134
- Chapter 7: Answers 138

3 Trigonometric and Polar Functions

Chapter 8: Trigonometry — 139

- Degrees, Radians and Angle Conversions 140
- Coterminal and Reference Angles 141
- Angles of Rotation and Unit Circle 142
- Arc Length and Sector Area 143
- Sine, Cosine, and Tangent 144
- Reciprocal Functions: Cosecant, Secant, and Cotangent 145
- Domain and Range of Trigonometric Functions 146
- Arcsine, Arccosine, and Arctangent 147
- Applications of Inverse Trigonometric Function 148
- Fundamental Trigonometric Identities 149
- Pythagorean Trigonometric Identities 150
- Co-Function, Even-Odd, and Periodicity Identities 151
- Double Angle and Half-Angle Formulas 152
- Sum and Difference Formulas 153
- Product-to-Sum and Sum-to-Product Formulas 154
- Chapter 8: Practices 155
- Chapter 8: Answers 160

Chapter 9: Trigonometric Functions and Graphs — 163

- Graph of the Sine Function 164
- Graph of the Cosine Function 165
- Amplitude, Period, and Phase Shift 166
- Writing the Equation of a Sine Graph 167
- Writing the Equation of a Cosine Graph 168
- Graph of the Tangent Function 169
- Graph of the Cosecant Function 170
- Graph of the Secant Function 171
- Graph of the Cotangent Function 172
- Graph of Inverse of the Sine Function 173
- Graph of Inverse of the Cosine Function 174
- Graph of Inverse of the Tangent Function 175
- Sketching Trigonometric Graphs 176
- Chapter 9: Practices 177
- Chapter 9: Answers 182

Contents

Chapter 10: Trigonometric Equations — 185
- Basic Techniques for Solving Trigonometric Equations 186
- Factoring and Simplifying Trigonometric Expressions 187
- Solving Equations with Multiple Angles 188
- Chapter 10: Practices 189
- Chapter 10: Answers 190

Chapter 11: Trigonometric Applications — 191
- Law of Sines: Definition and Applications 192
- Law of Cosines: Definition and Applications 193
- Area of a Triangle Using Trigonometry 194
- Chapter 11: Practices 195
- Chapter 11: Answers 198

Chapter 12: Complex Numbers — 199
- Polar Coordinate System 200
- Converting Between Polar and Rectangular Coordinates 201
- Introduction to Complex Numbers 202
- Adding and Subtracting Complex Numbers 203
- Multiplying and Dividing Complex Numbers 204
- Rationalizing Imaginary Denominators 205
- Polar Form of Complex Numbers 206
- Multiplying and Dividing in Polar Form 207
- Powers and Roots in Polar Form 208
- Graphs of Polar Equations 209
- Rate of Change in Polar Functions 210
- Chapter 12: Practices 211
- Chapter 12: Answers 216

4 Functions Involving Parameters, Vectors, and Matrices

Chapter 13: Real Numbers and Relation — 215
- Real Numbers 216
- Real Numbers Line 217
- Coordinate Plane 218
- Relation 219
- Showing the Relation in the Coordinate Plane 220
- Domain and Range of Relation 221

Chapter 13

- Functions 222
- Identifying the Function from the Graph 223
- Graphs of Basic Functions.. 224
- Chapter 13: Practices 225
- Chapter 13: Answers 228

Chapter 14: Vectors in Two Dimension — 231

- Introduction to Vectors: Vectors in Two Dimensions 232
- Equality of Vectors in Two Dimensions 233
- Scalar Multiplication 234
- Vector Addition and Subtraction.. 235
- Representation of Addition and Subtraction 236
- Length of a Vector 237
- Dot Product and Cross Product 238
- Parallel Vectors 239
- Orthogonal Vectors 240
- Parametric Equations and Graphs 241
- Applications of Vectors 242
- Chapter 14: Practices 243
- Chapter 14: Answers 246

Chapter 15: Analytic Geometry — 249

- Distance and Midpoint Formulas... 250
- Circles 251
- Finding the Center and the Radius of Circles 252
- Parabolas 253
- Finding the Focus, Vertex, and Directrix of a Parabola 254
- Ellipses... 255
- Hyperbolas 256
- Classifying a Conic Section (in Standard Form).................................... 257
- Rotation of Axes and General Form of Conic Sections 258
- Chapter 15: Practices 259
- Chapter 15: Answers 262

Chapter 16: Matrices — 265

- Introduction to Matrices... 266
- Matrix Addition and Subtraction... 267
- Scalar Multiplication 268
- Matrix Multiplication 269
- Determinants of Matrices... 270
- Inverse of a Matrix 271
- Solving Systems of Equations with Matrices... 272
- Chapter 16: Practices 273
- Chapter 16: Answers 276

Contents

CLEP Precalculus Practice Test 1	281
CLEP Precalculus Practice Test 2	299
CLEP Precalculus Practice Tests Answer Keys	318
CLEP Precalculus Practice Tests 1 Explanations	320
CLEP Precalculus Practice Tests 2 Explanations	336

1 Polynomial and Rational Functions

CHAPTER 1: Equations and Inequalities

Math topics that you'll learn in this chapter:

- ☑ Solving Multi–Step Equations
- ☑ Slope and Intercepts
- ☑ Using Intercepts
- ☑ Transforming Linear Functions
- ☑ Solving Inequalities
- ☑ Graphing Linear Inequalities
- ☑ Solving Compound Inequalities
- ☑ Solving Absolute Value Equations
- ☑ Solving Absolute Value Inequalities
- ☑ Graphing Absolute Value Inequalities
- ☑ Solving Systems of Equations
- ☑ Solving Special Systems
- ☑ Systems of Equations Word Problems
- ☑ Solve Systems of Nonlinear Equations (by Graph)
- ☑ Solve Systems of Nonlinear Equations (by Substitution)
- ☑ Solve Systems of Nonlinear Equations (by Elimination)

Solving Multi−Step Equations

- To solve a multi-step equation, combine "like" terms on one side.
- Bring variables to one side by adding or subtracting.
- Simplify using the inverse of addition or subtraction.
- Simplify further by using the inverse of multiplication or division.
- Check your solution by plugging the value of the variable into the original equation.

Examples:

Example 1. Solve this equation for x. $4x + 8 = 20 - 2x$

Solution: First, bring variables to one side by adding $2x$ to both sides. Then:

$4x + 8 + 2x = 20 - 2x + 2x \Rightarrow 4x + 8 + 2x = 20$.

Simplify: $6x + 8 = 20$.

Now, subtract 8 from both sides of the equation:

$6x + 8 - 8 = 20 - 8 \Rightarrow 6x = 12$.

Divide both sides by 6:
$6x = 12 \Rightarrow \frac{6x}{6} = \frac{12}{6} \Rightarrow x = 2$.

Let's check this solution by substituting the value of 2 for x in the original equation: $x = 2 \Rightarrow 4x + 8 = 20 - 2x \Rightarrow 4(2) + 8 = 20 - 2(2) \Rightarrow 16 = 16$.

The answer $x = 2$ is correct.

Example 2. Solve this equation for x. $-5x + 4 = 24$

Solution: Subtract 4 from both sides of the equation.

$-5x + 4 = 24 \Rightarrow -5x + 4 - 4 = 24 - 4 \Rightarrow -5x = 20$.

Divide both sides by -5, then:
$-5x = 20 \Rightarrow \frac{-5x}{-5} = \frac{20}{-5} \Rightarrow x = -4$.

Now, check the solution: $x = -4 \Rightarrow -5x + 4 = 24 \Rightarrow -5(-4) + 4 = 24 \Rightarrow 24 = 24$. The answer $x = -4$ is correct.

Slope and Intercepts

- The slope of a line represents the direction of a line on the coordinate plane.
- A coordinate plane contains two perpendicular number lines. The horizontal line is x and the vertical line is y. The point at which the two axes intersect is called the origin. An ordered pair (x, y) shows the location of a point.
- A line on a coordinate plane can be drawn by connecting two points.
- To find the slope of a line, we need the equation of the line or two points on the line.
- The slope of a line with two points $A(x_1, y_1)$ and $B(x_2, y_2)$ can be found by using this formula: $\frac{y_2 - y_1}{x_2 - x_1} = \frac{rise}{run}$.
- The equation of a line is typically written as $y = mx + b$ where m is the slope and b is the y-intercept.

Examples:

Example 1. Find the slope of the line through these two points: $A(1, -6)$ and $B(3, 2)$.

Solution: Slope $= \frac{y_2 - y_1}{x_2 - x_1}$. Let (x_1, y_1) be $A(1, -6)$ and (x_2, y_2) be $B(3, 2)$.

(Remember, you can choose any point for (x_1, y_1) and (x_2, y_2).)

Then:
Slope $= \frac{y_2 - y_1}{x_2 - x_1} = \frac{2 - (-6)}{3 - 1} = \frac{8}{2} = 4$.

The slope of the line through these two points is 4.

Example 2. Find the slope of the line with equation $y = -2x + 8$.

Solution: when the equation of a line is written in the form of $y = mx + b$, the slope is m. In this line: $y = -2x + 8$, the slope is -2.

Using Intercepts

- The cartesian plane is the 2−dimensional coordinate plane that consists of a horizontal number line that is called the x−axis, and a perpendicular number line through the point 0 on the first number line which is called the y−axis.
- Intercepts are points where a graph passes through an axis. An x−intercept is where the graph passes through the x−axis. A y−intercept is where the graph passes through the y−axis.
- The y−axis is the line where x is equal to zero and the x−axis is the line where y is equal to zero. An x−intercept can be considered as a point on the graph where the value of y is zero, and a y−intercept can be considered as a point on the graph where the x−value is zero.
- When the equation is represented in the slope−intercept form $y = mx + b$, the y−intercept is equal to the value of b. When you consider the $x = 0$, then mx becomes equal to 0, so when the value of x is equal to 0, $y = b$.
- When you want to find the x−intercept, you can put the value of y equal to 0 and solve the equation for x. In this way, when the value of y is equal to 0, the line passes through the x−axis.
- When the given equation isn't in $y = mx + b$ form, you can find the value of the intercepts by putting in 0 where needed and solving for the other variable.

Examples:

Example 1. Find the x−intercept and y−intercept of the following line:
$$5x + 4y = 40$$
Solution: Find the x−intercept by replacing y with 0 and solve for x:
$5x + 4y = 40 \Rightarrow 5x + 4(0) = 40 \Rightarrow 5x + 0 = 40 \Rightarrow 5x = 40 \Rightarrow x = \frac{40}{5} = 8 \Rightarrow x = 8$.
So, the x−intercept is 8. Find the y−intercept by replacing x with 0 and solve for y: $5x + 4y = 40 \Rightarrow 5(0) + 4y = 40 \Rightarrow 0 + 4y = 40 \Rightarrow y = \frac{40}{4} = 10$.
So, the y−intercept is 10.

Example 2. Find the x−intercept and y−intercept of the following line:
$$8x^2 + 2y^2 = 32.$$
Solution: Find the x−intercept by replacing y with 0 and solve for x: $8x^2 + 2y^2 = 32 \Rightarrow 8x^2 + 2(0)^2 = 32 \Rightarrow 8x^2 + 0 = 32 \Rightarrow 8x^2 = 32 \Rightarrow x^2 = \frac{32}{8} = 4 \Rightarrow x = \pm 2$.
So, the x−intercept is ± 2. Then find the y−intercept by replacing x with 0 and solve for y: $8x^2 + 2y^2 = 32 \Rightarrow 8(0)^2 + 2y^2 = 32 \Rightarrow 0 + 2y^2 = 32 \Rightarrow y^2 = \frac{32}{2} = 16 \Rightarrow y = \pm 4$. So, the y−intercept is ± 4.

bit.ly/3DcysRE
Find more at

Transforming Linear Functions

- Transformation of linear functions means moving the graphs of linear functions by changing the position of the y-intercept or the line's slope without changing the line's shape. The transformed linear function still follows the slope-intercept form ($y = mx + b$). The three types of linear function transformations are translation, rotation, and reflection. In fact, a transformation of the linear function is a change in the position or size of a linear function.
- A group of functions whose graphs have basic common features is called a family of functions.
- The most basic function in a family of functions is called the parent function. The parent function of linear functions is $f(x) = x$.
- All the graphs of linear functions are transformed shapes of the parent function's graph ($f(x) = x$).
- The graph is translated vertically when you change the y-intercept (b) in the function $f(x) = mx + b$. If the value of b rises up, the graph is translated up. If the value of b reduces, the graph is translated down.
- The rotation of the graph about the point $(0, b)$ occurs when you change the slope m in the function $f(x) = mx + b$. In this case, the rotation of the graph changes the steepness of the line.
- The reflection of the graph across the y-axis occurs when you multiply the slope m of function $f(x) = mx + b$ by -1.

Example:

Graph $f(x) = x$ and find $g(x) = x + 2$.

Solution: Here, the parent function is $f(x) = x$ which passes through the origin $(0,0)$. You should change y-intercept (b) in the function. $f(x) = mx + b$:
$f(x) = x + 0 \Rightarrow f(x) = x + 2$.
In fact, the value of b rises up 2 units, and the graph is translated up.

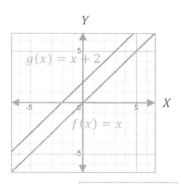

Solving Inequalities

- An inequality compares two expressions using an inequality sign.
- Inequality signs are: "less than" <, "greater than" >, "less than or equal to" ≤, and "greater than or equal to" ≥.
- You only need to perform one Math operation to solve the one-step inequalities.
- To solve one-step inequalities, find the inverse (opposite) operation is being performed.
- For dividing or multiplying both sides by negative numbers, flip the direction of the inequality sign.

Examples:

Example 1. Solve this inequality for x. $x + 5 \geq 4$

Solution: The inverse (opposite) operation of addition is subtraction. In this inequality, 5 is added to x. To isolate x we need to subtract 5 from both sides of the inequality. Then: $x + 5 \geq 4 \Rightarrow x + 5 - 5 \geq 4 - 5 \Rightarrow x \geq -1$.

The solution is: $x \geq -1$.

Example 2. Solve the inequality. $x - 3 > -6$

Solution: 3 is subtracted from x. Add 3 to both sides.

$x - 3 > -6 \Rightarrow x - 3 + 3 > -6 + 3 \Rightarrow x > -3$.

Example 3. Solve. $4x \leq -8$

Solution: 4 is multiplied by x. Divide both sides by 4.
Then: $4x \leq -8 \Rightarrow \frac{4x}{4} \leq \frac{-8}{4} \Rightarrow x \leq -2$.

Example 4. Solve. $-3x \leq 6$

Solution: -3 is multiplied by x. Divide both sides by -3. Remember when dividing or multiplying both sides of an inequality by negative numbers, flip the direction of the inequality sign. Then: $-3x \leq 6 \Rightarrow \frac{-3x}{-3} \geq \frac{6}{-3} \Rightarrow x \geq -2$.

Graphing Linear Inequalities

- To graph a linear inequality, first draw a graph of the "equals" line.
- Use a dashed line for "less than" (<) and "greater than" (>) signs and a solid line for "less than and equal to" (≤) and "greater than and equal to" (≥).
- Choose a testing point. (It can be any point on both sides of the line.)
- Put the value of (x, y) of that point in the inequality. If that works, that part of the line is the solution. If the values don't work, then the other part of the line is the solution.

Example:

Sketch the graph of inequality: $y < 2x + 4$.

Solution: To draw the graph of $y < 2x + 4$, you first need to graph the line:
$$y = 2x + 4$$

Since there is a "less than" (<) sign, draw a dashed line.

The slope is 2 and the y-intercept is 4.

Then, choose a testing point and substitute the value of x and y from that point into the inequality.

The easiest point to test is the origin, (0,0):
$$(0,0) \Rightarrow y < 2x + 4 \Rightarrow 0 < 2(0) + 4 \Rightarrow 0 < 4$$

This is correct! 0 is less than 4.

So, this part of the line (on the right side) is the solution of this inequality.

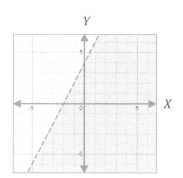

Solving Compound Inequalities

- To solve a multi-step inequality, combine "like" terms on one side.
- Bring variables to one side by adding or subtracting.
- Isolate the variable.
- Simplify using the inverse of addition or subtraction.
- Simplify further by using the inverse of multiplication or division.
- For dividing or multiplying both sides by negative numbers, flip the direction of the inequality sign.

Examples:

Example 1. Solve this inequality. $8x - 2 \leq 14$

Solution: In this inequality, 2 is subtracted from $8x$. The inverse of subtraction is addition. Add 2 to both sides of the inequality:

$8x - 2 + 2 \leq 14 + 2 \Rightarrow 8x \leq 16$.

Now, divide both sides by 8. Then:

$8x \leq 16 \Rightarrow \frac{8x}{8} \leq \frac{16}{8} \Rightarrow x \leq 2$.

The solution of this inequality is $x \leq 2$.

Example 2. Solve this inequality. $3x + 9 < 12$

Solution: First, subtract 9 from both sides: $3x + 9 - 9 < 12 - 9$.

Then simplify: $3x + 9 - 9 < 12 - 9 \Rightarrow 3x < 3$.

Now divide both sides by 3: $\frac{3x}{3} < \frac{3}{3} \Rightarrow x < 1$.

Example 3. Solve this inequality. $-5x + 3 \geq 8$

Solution: First, subtract 3 from both sides:

$-5x + 3 - 3 \geq 8 - 3 \Rightarrow -5x \geq 5$.

Divide both sides by -5. Remember that you need to flip the direction of the inequality sign. $-5x \geq 5 \Rightarrow \frac{-5x}{-5} \leq \frac{5}{-5} \Rightarrow x \leq -1$.

Solving Absolute Value Equations

- Isolate the absolute value.
- Take off the absolute value sign and solve the equation.
- Write another equation with the negative sign of the answer of the absolute value equation.
- Plug in the value of the variable into the original equation and check your answer.

Examples:

Example 1. Solve this equation. $|x + 1| = 2$

Solution: First take off the absolute value sign: $x + 1 = 2$ or $x + 1 = -2$. Then:

$x = 2 - 1 = 1$ or $x = -2 - 1 = -3$.

Example 2. Solve this equation. $|x + 2| = 5$

Solution: First take off the absolute value sign $x + 2 = 5$ or $x + 2 = -5$. Then:

$x = 5 - 2 = 3$ or $x = -5 - 2 = -7$.

Example 3. Solve this equation. $|x + 3| = 8$

Solution: First take off the absolute value sign $x + 3 = 8$ or $x + 3 = -8$. Then:

$x = 8 - 3 = 5$ or $x = -8 - 3 = -11$.

Example 4. Solve this equation. $|2 - x| = 1$

Solution: First take off the absolute value sign $2 - x = 1$ or $2 - x = -1$.

Then: $x = 2 - 1 = 1$ or $x = 2 + 1 = 3$.

Solving Absolute Value Inequalities

- An Absolute value can never be negative. Therefore, the absolute value cannot be less than a negative number.
- To solve an absolute value inequality, first isolate it on one side of the inequality. Then, if the inequality sign is greater (or greater and equal), write the value inside the absolute value greater than the value provided and less than the negative of the value provided and solved. If the sign is less than, then do the opposite.

Examples:

Example 1. Solve this equation. $|2x| \geq 24$

Solution: Since the inequality sign is greater and equal:

$2x \geq 24$ or $2x \leq -24$.

Then: $x \geq 12$ or $x \leq -12$.

Example 2. Solve this equation. $|x + 2| > 5$

Solution: Since the inequality sign is greater than:

$x + 2 > 5$ or $x + 2 < -5$.

Then: $x > 3$ or $x < -7$.

Example 3. Solve this equation. $|1 - x| < 4$

Solution: Since the inequality sign is less than:

$-4 < 1 - x < 4 \Rightarrow -5 < -x < 3$.

Then: $-3 < x < 5$.

Graphing Absolute Value Inequalities

- Solve the absolute value inequality using the Properties of Inequality.
- Find two key values.
- Represent absolute value inequalities on a number line.

Examples:

Example 1. Solve and graph this equation $|-8x| < 32$.

Solution: Use absolute rule: if $|u| < a, a > 0$, then: $-a < u < a$.

Therefore: $-32 < -8x < 32$, in other words $-8x > -32$ and $-8x < 32$.

So, we have: $-8x > -32 \Rightarrow x < 4$ and $-8x < 32 \Rightarrow x > -4$.

Then: $-4 < x < 4$.

Example 2. Solve and graph this equation $|10 + 4x| < 14$.

Solution: Use absolute rule: if $|u| < a, a > 0$, then: $-a < u < a$.

Then: $-14 < 10 + 4x < 14$, $10 + 4x > -14$ and $10 + 4x < 14$.

Thus: $10 + 4x > -14 \Rightarrow x > -6$ and $10 + 4x < 14 \Rightarrow x < 1$.

Then: $-6 < x < 1$.

Example 3. Solve and graph this equation $|2x - 3| \geq 5$.

Solution: Use absolute rule: if $|u| \geq a, a > 0$, then: $u \geq a$ or $u \leq -a$.

Therefore: $2x - 3 \geq 5$ or $2x - 3 \leq -5$.

So: $x \geq 4$ or $x \leq -1$.

Solving Systems of Equations

- A system of equations contains two equations and two variables. For example, consider the system of equations: $x - y = 1$, $x + y = 5$.
- The easiest way to solve a system of equations is using the elimination method. The elimination method uses the addition property of equality. You can add the same value to each side of an equation.
- For the first equation above, you can add $x + y$ to the left side and 5 to the right side of the first equation: $x - y + (x + y) = 1 + 5$. Now, if you simplify, you get: $x - y + (x + y) = 1 + 5 \Rightarrow 2x = 6 \Rightarrow x = 3$. Now, substitute 3 for the x in the first equation: $3 - y = 1$. By solving this equation, $y = 2$.

Examples:

Example 1. What is the value of $x + y$ in this system of equations?
$$\begin{cases} 2x + 4y = 12 \\ 4x - 2y = -16 \end{cases}$$

Solution: Solving a system of equations by elimination:

Multiply the first equation by (-2), then add it to the second equation.
$$\begin{array}{l} -2(2x + 4y = 12) \\ 4x - 2y = -16 \end{array} \Rightarrow \begin{array}{l} -4x - 8y = -24 \\ 4x - 2y = -16 \end{array} \Rightarrow -10y = -40 \Rightarrow y = 4.$$

Plug in the value of y into one of the equations and solve for x.

$2x + 4(4) = 12 \Rightarrow 2x + 16 = 12 \Rightarrow 2x = -4 \Rightarrow x = -2$.

Thus: $x + y = -2 + 4 = 2$.

Example 2. What is the value of y in the following system of equations?
$$\begin{cases} 2x + 5y = 11 \\ 2x - y = -7 \end{cases}$$

Solution: Solving systems of equations by elimination: multiply the first equation by (-1), then add it to the second equation.

$$\begin{array}{l} (-1)(2x + 5y = 11) \\ 2x - y = -7 \end{array} \Rightarrow \begin{array}{l} -2x - 5y = -11 \\ 2x - y = -7 \end{array} \Rightarrow -6y = -18 \Rightarrow y = 3.$$

Solving Special Systems

- Two linear equations whose graph consists of parallel lines or have an infinite number of solutions may make a special system. For solving the system, you should add or subtract the two linear equations and find the value of the variables x and y.
- System of equations with no solution: When the system of equations graph consists of parallel lines or there is no intersection point, the system of the equation has no solution.
- System of equations with infinite number solutions: When the system of equations graph consists of straight lines overlapping each other or there are infinite points as a solution set, the equations system has an infinite number of solutions.
- Three ways for solving special systems of linear equations with two variables:
  - Substitution Method: In this method, you have 2 linear equations in x and y; you can represent y in terms of x in one of the equations and then substitute that equation in the second equation.
  - Elimination Method: In this method, you should eliminate one variable. For this purpose, multiply equations by suitable numbers and make one of the variables coefficients the same.
  - Graphical Method: In the graphical method, you can find the solution to the system of equations by plotting their graphs. If your graph consists of parallel lines or straight lines overlapping each other, your system of equations is a special one.

Example:

Determine if the following system of equations has a solution or not:
$$\begin{cases} y - 2x = 6 \\ \frac{1}{2}y - x = 8 \end{cases}$$

Solution: You can write both equations in the form $y = mx + b$:
$y - 2x = 6 \Rightarrow y = 2x + 6$ and $\frac{1}{2}y - x = 8 \Rightarrow \frac{1}{2}y = x + 8 \Rightarrow y = 2x + 16$.

Now, use the substitution method and substitute the first equation ($y = 2x + 6$) for y in the second equation $\frac{1}{2}y - x = 8$: $\frac{1}{2}(2x + 6) - x = 8 \Rightarrow x + 3 - x = 8 \Rightarrow 3 \neq 8$. This system has no solution so it's a special system.

Systems of Equations Word Problems

- Define your variables, write two equations, and use the elimination method for solving systems of equations.

Examples:

Example 1. Tickets to a movie cost $8 for adults and $5 for students. A group of friends purchased 20 tickets for $115.00. How many adults' tickets did they buy?

Solution: Let x be the number of adult tickets and y be the number of student tickets. There are 20 tickets. Then: $x + y = 20$. The cost of adult tickets is $8 and for students it is $5, and the total cost is $115. So, $8x + 5y = 115$.

Now, we have a system of equations: $\begin{cases} x + y = 20 \\ 8x + 5y = 115 \end{cases}$.

Multiply the first equation by -5 and add to the second equation:

$-5(x + y = 20) \Rightarrow -5x - 5y = -100$.

$8x + 5y + (-5x - 5y) = 115 - 100 \Rightarrow 3x = 15 \Rightarrow x = 5 \Rightarrow 5 + y = 20 \Rightarrow y = 15$.

There are 5 adult tickets and 15 student tickets.

Example 2. A group of 38 graduates of a high school are going to a picnic in 8 cars. Some of the cars can hold 4 students, and the rest can hold 6 students each. Assuming all the cars are filled, how many of the cars can hold 4 students?

Solution: Let a be the number of cars with 4 people capacity and b the number of cars with 6 people capacity. There are 8 cars. Then: $a + b = 8$.

All students are 38, to go with 4 and 6 capacity cars. This means that: $4a + 6b = 38$. Now, we have: $\begin{cases} a + b = 8 \\ 4a + 6b = 38 \end{cases}$.

Solving by elimination method: multiply the first equation by (-4), then add it to the second equation.

$\begin{array}{c}(-4)(a+b=8) \\ 4a+6b=38\end{array} \Rightarrow \begin{array}{c}-4a-4b=-32 \\ 4a+6b=38\end{array} \Rightarrow 2b = 6 \Rightarrow b = 3$.

Plug in the value of b into one of the equations and solve for a.

$a + 3 = 8 \Rightarrow a = 5$.

bit.ly/3vEOOhy
Find more at

EffortlessMath.com

Solve Systems of Non-linear Equations (by Graph)

- A system of nonlinear equations is a system in which at least one of its equations is not linear.
- In order to solve a system of two nonlinear equations, one of the following three methods can be used:
    1. Solving a system of non-linear equations using a graph: In this method, by graphing two graphs and finding their intersection points with each other, the obtained ordered pairs form the solution set of the equation.
    2. Solving a system of non-linear equations using substitution:
    3. Solving a system of nonlinear equations using elimination:

Example:

Solve the system of nonlinear equations below: $\begin{cases} x - y = 2 \\ y = x^2 - 4 \end{cases}$.

Solution: Graphically, by graphing two functions and finding the points of intersection of the two graphs, we can find the answer in the set of order pairs.

First, we graph two functions in a coordinate system.

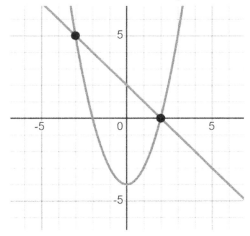

In the above coordinate system, two ordered pairs $(-3, 5)$ and $(2, 0)$ are the coordinates of the intersection of two graphs. The set consisting of these two ordered pairs is the answer to this system of equations.

Solve Systems of Non-linear Equations (by Substitution)

- Solving a system of non-linear equations using substitution: To solve the system of equations in this way, we follow the following steps:

  Step 1: Solve one of the equations in terms of one of the variables.
  Step 2: Substitute the obtained equation in another equation.
  Step 3: Solve the resulting equation.
  Step 4: Substitute each solution in step 3 into one of the original equations to find the other variable.
  Step 5: Write each solution as an ordered pair.
  Step 6: Check that each ordered pair is a solution to both original equations.

Example:

Solve the system by using substitution: $\begin{cases} 9x^2 + y^2 = 9 \\ y - 3x + 3 = 0 \end{cases}$.

Solution: To solve the system of equations by elimination method, we have these steps:

Step 1: Solve one of the equations in terms of one of the variables. The equation $y - 3x + 3 = 0 \Rightarrow y = 3x - 3$ is solved for y.

Step 2: Substitute the obtained equation $y = 3x - 3$ in the equation $9x^2 + y^2 = 9$. Then: $9x^2 + (3x - 3)^2 = 9$.

Step 3: Solve the equation $9x^2 + 9x^2 - 18x + 9 = 9$. So, we get:

$18x^2 - 18x = 0 \Rightarrow 18x(x - 1) = 0 \Rightarrow x = 0$ and $x = 1$.

Step 4: Substitute $x = 0$ and $x = 1$ into the equation $y = 3x - 3$. To find y. Therefore, $x = 0 \Rightarrow y = 3 \times 0 - 3 \Rightarrow y = -3 \Rightarrow (0, -3)$,

$x = 1 \Rightarrow y = 3 \times 1 - 3 \Rightarrow y = 0 \Rightarrow (1, 0)$.

Check that each ordered pair is a solution to both original equations. The solutions are $(0, -3)$, and $(1, 0)$.

EffortlessMath.com

Solve Systems of Non-linear Equations (by Elimination)

- Solving a system of nonlinear equations using elimination:

  Step 1: Write the equations in standard form.
  Step 2: Decide which variable you will delete.
  Step 3: Opposite the variable coefficients selected in step 2 in the two equations.
  Step 4: Add the equations from step 3 to eliminate one variable.
  Step 5: Obtain the remaining variable in the equation obtained from the previous step.
  Step 6: By putting the solution of the obtained variable in one of the equations, obtain the other variable.
  Step 7: Write each solution as an ordered pair.
  Step 8: Check that each ordered pair is a solution to both original equations.

Example:

Solve the system by elimination: $\begin{cases} x^2 + y^2 = 4 \\ x^2 - y = 4 \end{cases}$.

Solution: To solve the system of equations by elimination method, we perform the following steps.

Step 1: Both equations are in standard form. Equation $x^2 + y^2 = 4$ is a circle and equation $x^2 - y = 4$ is a parabola.

Step 2: According to the equations, we want to remove variable x, which appeared as x^2.

Step 3: To get opposite coefficients of x^2, we will multiply the second equation by -1. Then simplify: $\begin{cases} x^2 + y^2 = 4 \\ x^2 - y = 4 \end{cases} \Rightarrow \begin{cases} x^2 + y^2 = 4 \\ -1(x^2 - y) = -1(4) \end{cases} \Rightarrow \begin{cases} x^2 + y^2 = 4 \\ -x^2 + y = -4 \end{cases}$.

Step 4: Add the equations from step 3 to eliminate variable x. So, we have: $y^2 + y = 0$

Step 5: Obtain the remaining variable in the equation obtained from the step 5. $y^2 + y = 0 \Rightarrow y(y+1) = 0 \Rightarrow y = 0$ and $y = -1$.

Step 6: Substitute $y = 0$ and $y = -1$ into one of the two equations. Then solve for x: $y = 0 \Rightarrow x^2 - 0 = 4 \Rightarrow x^2 = 4 \Rightarrow x = \pm 2 \Rightarrow (-2, 0)$ and $(2, 0)$, $y = -1 \Rightarrow x^2 - (-1) = 4 \Rightarrow x^2 = 3 \Rightarrow x = \pm\sqrt{3} \Rightarrow (-\sqrt{3}, -1)$ and $(\sqrt{3}, -1)$.

Check that each ordered pair is a solution to both original equations. The solutions are $(-2, 0)$, $(2, 0)$, $(-\sqrt{3}, -1)$, and $(\sqrt{3}, -1)$.

Chapter 1: Practices

✎ Solve each equation.

1) $-3(2 + x) = 3$
2) $-2(4 + x) = 4$
3) $20 = -(x - 8)$
4) $2(2 - 2x) = 20$
5) $-12 = -(2x + 8)$
6) $5(2 + x) = 5$
7) $2(x - 14) = 4$
8) $-28 = 2x + 12x$
9) $3x + 15 = -x - 5$
10) $2(3 + 2x) = -18$
11) $12 - 2x = -8 - x$
12) $10 - 3x = 14 + x$

✎ Find the slope of the line through each pair of points.

13) $(1,1), (2,3)$
14) $(-1,2), (0,3)$
15) $(3,-1), (2,3)$
16) $(-2,-1), (0,5)$
17) $(5,1), (2,4)$
18) $(-3,1), (-2,4)$
19) $(6,2), (7,4)$
20) $(6,-5), (3,4)$
21) $(12,-9), (11,-8)$
22) $(7,4), (5,-2)$
23) $(1,1), (3,5)$
24) $(7,-12), (5,10)$

✎ Solve each inequality and graph it.

25) $2x \geq 12$

26) $4 + x \leq 5$

27) $x + 3 \leq -3$

28) $4x \geq 16$

Effortless Math Education

EffortlessMath.com

29) $9x \leq 18$

✎ Find the x-intercepts and y-intercepts of the line.

30) $2x + 8y = -8$

   x-intercepts: _____

   y-intercepts: _____

31) $3x - 2y = 24$

   x-intercepts: _____

   y-intercepts: _____

32) $-3x + 5y = -15$

   x-intercepts: _____

   y-intercepts: _____

33) $8x - 2y = 10$

   x-intercepts: _____

   y-intercepts: _____

✎ Graph $f(x)$ and find $g(x)$.

34) $f(x) = x$, $g(x) = x - 3$

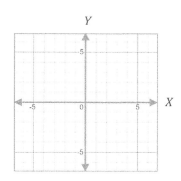

35) $f(x) = x$, $g(x) = x + 1$

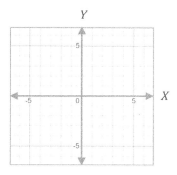

✎ Sketch the group of each linear inequality.

36) $y > 3x - 1$

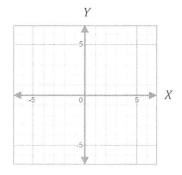

37) $y < -x + 4$

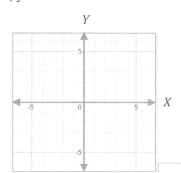

38) $y \leq -5x + 8$

39) $y \geq 2x - 1$

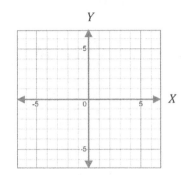
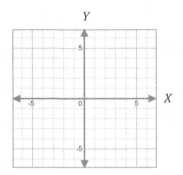

✎ Solve each inequality.

40) $2x - 8 \leq 6$

41) $4x - 21 < 19$

42) $8x - 2 \leq 14$

43) $2x - 3 < 21$

44) $-5 + 3x \leq 10$

45) $17 - 3x \geq -13$

46) $2(x - 3) \leq 6$

47) $2 - 3x > -7$

48) $7x - 5 \leq 9$

49) $3 + 2x \geq 19$

✎ Solve each equation.

50) $|a| + 12 = 22$

51) $-2|x + 2| = -12$

52) $3|x + 4| = 45$

53) $|6x| + 4 = 70$

54) $-2|x| = -24$

55) $|-5m| = 30$

56) $|5 + x| = 5$

57) $|-4 + 5x| = 16$

58) $|-4x| = 16$

59) $\left|\frac{x}{4}\right| = 5$

✎ Solve each inequality.

60) $|x| + 4 \geq 6$

61) $|x - 2| - 6 < 5$

62) $3 + |2 + x| < 5$

63) $|x + 7| - 9 < -6$

64) $|x| - 3 > 2$

65) $|x| - 2 > 0$

66) $|3x| \leq 15$

67) $|x + 4| \leq 8$

68) $|3x| \leq 24$

69) $|x - 8| - 10 < -6$

✎ Solve each inequality and graph its solution.

70) $|2x - 2| \geq 10$

71) $|\frac{1}{3}x - 1| \leq 3$

72) $|x| - 2 < 6$

✎ Solve each system of equations.

73) $\begin{array}{l} -4x - 6y = 7 \\ x - 2y = 7 \end{array}$ $\begin{array}{l} x = \cdots \\ y = \cdots \end{array}$

74) $\begin{array}{l} 3y = -6x + 12 \\ 8x - 9y = -10 \end{array}$ $\begin{array}{l} x = \cdots \\ y = \cdots \end{array}$

75) $\begin{array}{l} 3x - 2y = 15 \\ 3x - 5y = 15 \end{array}$ $\begin{array}{l} x = \cdots \\ y = \cdots \end{array}$

76) $\begin{array}{l} -5x + y = -3 \\ 3x - 7y = 21 \end{array}$ $\begin{array}{l} x = \cdots \\ y = \cdots \end{array}$

77) $\begin{array}{l} x + 15y = 50 \\ x + 10y = 40 \end{array}$ $\begin{array}{l} x = \cdots \\ y = \cdots \end{array}$

78) $\begin{array}{l} 3x - 6y = -12 \\ -x - 3y = -6 \end{array}$ $\begin{array}{l} x = \cdots \\ y = \cdots \end{array}$

✎ Determine if the following system of equations has a solution or not:

79) $\begin{cases} 2y - 4x = 8 \\ y - 2x = 16 \end{cases}$

✎ Solve each word problems.

80) A theater is selling tickets for a performance. Mr. Smith purchased 8 senior tickets and 5 child tickets for $150 for his friends and family. Mr. Jackson purchased 4 senior tickets and 6 child tickets for $96. What is the price of a senior ticket? $_____

81) The difference of two numbers is 6. Their sum is 14. What is the bigger number? _____

82) The sum of the digits of a certain two−digit number is 7. Reversing its digits increase the number by 9. What is the number? _____

83) The difference of two numbers is 18. Their sum is 66. What are the numbers? _____

Effortless Math Education

Chapter 1: Answers

1) -3 13) 2
2) -6 14) 1
3) -12 15) -4
4) -4 16) 3
5) 2 17) -1
6) -1 18) 3
7) 16 19) 2
8) -2 20) -3
9) -5 21) -1
10) -6 22) 3
11) 20 23) 2
12) -1 24) -11

25) Number line with point at 6

26) Number line with point at 1

27) Number line with point at -6

28) Number line with point at 4

29) Number line with point at 2

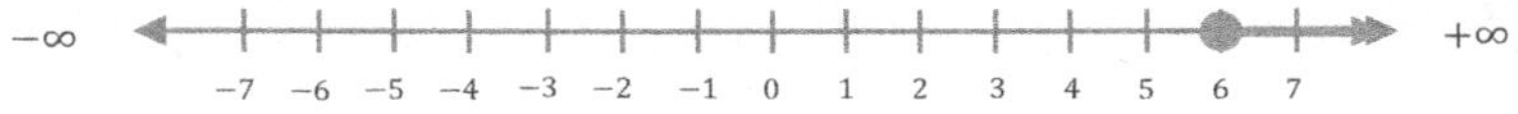

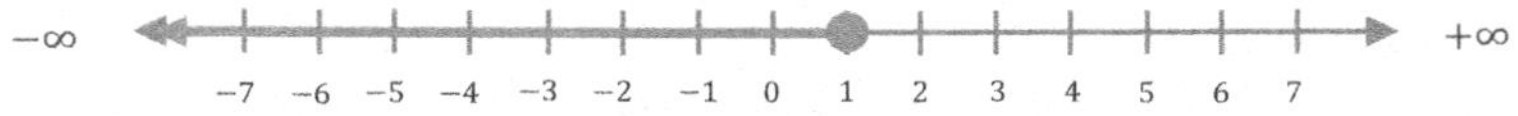

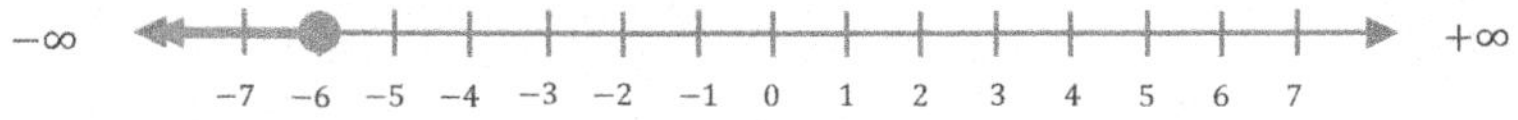

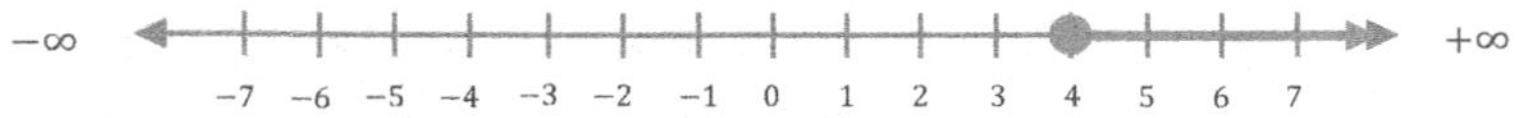

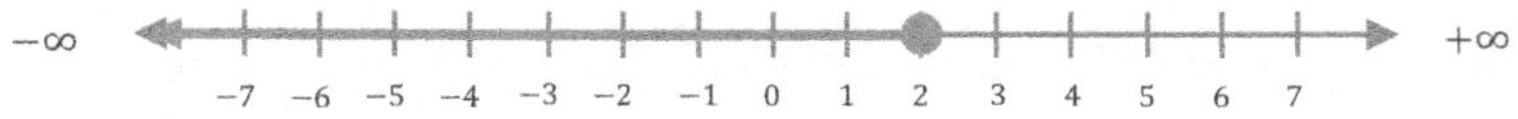

30) x −intercepts: $(-4,0)$, y −intercepts: $(0,-1)$

31) x −intercepts: $(8,0)$, y −intercepts: $(0,-12)$

32) x −intercepts: $(5,0)$, y −intercepts: $(0,-3)$

33) x −intercepts: $\left(\frac{5}{4},0\right)$, y −intercepts: $(0,-5)$

34)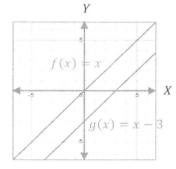

35)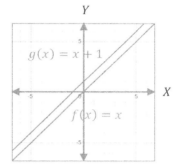

36)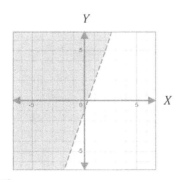

37)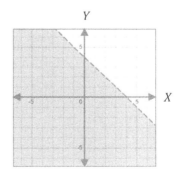

38)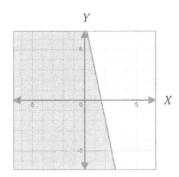

39)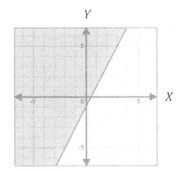

Effortless Math Education

40) $x \leq 7$
41) $x < 10$
42) $x \leq 2$
43) $x < 12$
44) $x \leq 5$
45) $x \leq 10$
46) $x \leq 6$
47) $x < 3$
48) $x \leq 2$
49) $x \geq 8$
50) $\{10, -10\}$
51) $\{4, -8\}$
52) $\{11, -19\}$
53) $\{11, -11\}$
54) $\{-12, 12\}$
55) $\{6, -6\}$

56) $\{0, -10\}$
57) $\left\{-\frac{12}{5}, 4\right\}$
58) $\{4, -4\}$
59) $\{20, -20\}$
60) $x \geq 2$ or $x \leq -2$
61) $x < 13$ and $x > -9$
62) $x < 0$ and $x > -4$
63) $x < -4$ and $x > -10$
64) $x > 5$ or $x < -5$
65) $x > 2$ or $x < -2$
66) $x \leq 5$ and $x \geq -5$
67) $-12 \leq x \leq 4$
68) $x \leq 8$ and $x \geq -8$
69) $4 < x < 12$

70)

71)

72)

73) $x = 2, y = -\frac{5}{2}$
74) $x = 1, y = 2$
75) $x = 5, y = 0$

76) $x = 0, y = -3$
77) $x = 20, y = 2$
78) $x = 0, y = 2$

79) This system has no solution so it's a special system.

80) $15
81) 10
82) 34
83) 42, 24

CHAPTER 2: Functions

Math topics that you'll learn in this chapter:

- ☑ Evaluating Functions: Function Notation
- ☑ Modeling Real-world Situations with Functions
- ☑ Adding and Subtracting Functions
- ☑ Multiplying and Dividing Functions
- ☑ Composite Functions
- ☑ Real Zeros
- ☑ Average Rate of Changes
- ☑ Codomain

Evaluating Functions: Function Notation

- Functions are mathematical operations that assign unique outputs to given inputs.
- Function notation is the way a function is written. It is meant to be a precise way of giving information about the function without a rather lengthy written explanation.
- The most popular function notation is $f(x)$ which is read as "f of x". Any letter can name a function. For example: $g(x)$, $h(x)$, etc.
- To evaluate a function, plug in the input (the given value or expression) for the function's variable (place holder, x).

Examples:

Example 1. Evaluate: $f(x) = x + 6$, find $f(2)$.

Solution: Substitute x with 2:

Then: $f(x) = x + 6 \Rightarrow f(2) = 2 + 6 \Rightarrow f(2) = 8$.

Example 2. Evaluate: $w(x) = 3x - 1$, find $w(4)$.

Solution: Substitute x with 4:

Then: $w(x) = 3x - 1 \Rightarrow w(4) = 3(4) - 1 = 12 - 1 = 11$.

Example 3. Evaluate: $f(x) = 2x^2 + 4$, find $f(-1)$.

Solution: Substitute x with -1:

Then: $f(x) = 2x^2 + 4 \Rightarrow f(-1) = 2(-1)^2 + 4 \Rightarrow f(-1) = 2 + 4 = 6$.

Example 4. Evaluate: $h(x) = 4x^2 - 9$, find $h(2a)$.

Solution: Substitute x with $2a$:

Then: $h(x) = 4x^2 - 9 \Rightarrow h(2a) = 4(2a)^2 - 9 \Rightarrow h(2a) = 4(4a^2) - 9 = 16a^2 - 9$.

Modeling Real-world Situations with Functions

- A function is a kind of relationship between variables, and it shows how 2 things are related to each other. It can take various forms, like an equation.
- Every function consists of inputs and outputs. The input is a variable that goes into the function it is also called the independent variable or domain. The output is a variable that comes out of the function, and it is also called the dependent variable or range.
- The function rule is an algebraic statement that specifies a function. The function determines which inputs are suitable, and the outputs will be determined by the inputs. 3 methods to show functions are graphs, tables, and algebraic expressions.
- A table that shows a function usually includes a column of inputs, a column of outputs, and a third column between the input and output to present how the outputs can be made by the inputs.

Examples:

Example 1. According to the values of x and y in the following relationship, find the right equation. $\{(1,4), (2,8), (3,12), (4,16)\}$

Solution: Find the relationship between the first x-value and first y-value: $(1,4)$. The value of y is 4 times the value of x: $1 \times 4 = 4$. The equation is $y = 4x$. Now draw the input-output table of the values to make sure the relationship is correct:

x	$y = 4x$	y
1	$4(1) = 4$	4
2	$4(2) = 8$	8
3	$4(3) = 12$	12
4	$4(4) = 16$	16

Example 2. According to the values of x and y in the following relationship, find the right equation. $\{(1,3), (2,4), (3,5), (4,6)\}$

Solution: Find the relationship between the first x-value and first y-value: $(1,3)$. The value of y is 2 more than the x-value: $1 + 2 = 3$. So, the equation is $y = x + 2$. Now check the other values: $2 + 2 = 4$, $3 + 2 = 5$, $4 + 2 = 6$. Therefore each x-value and y-value satisfies the equation $y = x + 2$.

Adding and Subtracting Functions

- Just like we can add and subtract numbers and expressions, we can add or subtract two functions and simplify or evaluate them. The result is a new function.
- For two functions $f(x)$ and $g(x)$, we can create two new functions:
$$(f + g)(x) = f(x) + g(x) \text{ and } (f - g)(x) = f(x) - g(x)$$

Examples:

Example 1. If $g(x) = 2x - 2$, $f(x) = x + 1$. Find: $(g + f)(x)$.

Solution: We know that:

$(g + f)(x) = g(x) + f(x)$.

Then:

$(g + f)(x) = (2x - 2) + (x + 1) = 2x - 2 + x + 1 = 3x - 1$.

Example 2. If $f(x) = 4x - 3$, $g(x) = 2x - 4$. Find: $(f - g)(x)$.

Solution: Considering that:

$(f - g)(x) = f(x) - g(x)$.

Then:

$(f - g)(x) = (4x - 3) - (2x - 4) = 4x - 3 - 2x + 4 = 2x + 1$.

Example 3. If $g(x) = x^2 + 2$, and $f(x) = x + 5$. Find: $(g + f)(x)$.

Solution: According to the:

$(g + f)(x) = g(x) + f(x)$.

Then:

$(g + f)(x) = (x^2 + 2) + (x + 5) = x^2 + x + 7$.

Example 4. If $f(x) = 5x^2 - 3$, and $g(x) = 3x + 6$. Find: $(f - g)(3)$.

Solution: Use this: $(f - g)(x) = f(x) - g(x)$.

Then: $(f - g)(x) = (5x^2 - 3) - (3x + 6) = 5x^2 - 3 - 3x - 6 = 5x^2 - 3x - 9$.

Substitute x with 3: $(f - g)(3) = 5(3)^2 - 3(3) - 9 = 45 - 9 - 9 = 27$.

EffortlessMath.com

Multiplying and Dividing Functions

- Just like we can multiply and divide numbers and expressions, we can multiply and divide two functions and simplify or evaluate them.
- For two functions $f(x)$ and $g(x)$, we can create two new functions:
$$(f \cdot g)(x) = f(x) \cdot g(x) \text{ and } \left(\frac{f}{g}\right)(x) = \frac{f(x)}{g(x)}$$

Examples:

Example 1. If $g(x) = x + 3$, $f(x) = x + 4$. Find: $(g \cdot f)(x)$.

Solution: According to:

$(f \cdot g)(x) = f(x) \cdot g(x)$.

Therefore:

$(x + 3)(x + 4) = x^2 + 4x + 3x + 12 = x^2 + 7x + 12$.

Example 2. If $f(x) = x + 6$, and $h(x) = x - 9$. Find: $\left(\frac{f}{h}\right)(x)$.

Solution: Use this:
$\left(\frac{f}{g}\right)(x) = \frac{f(x)}{g(x)}$.
We have: $\left(\frac{f}{h}\right)(x) = \frac{x+6}{x-9}$.

Example 3. If $g(x) = x + 7$, and $f(x) = x - 3$. Find: $(g \cdot f)(2)$.

Solution: Considering that:

$(f \cdot g)(x) = f(x) \cdot g(x)$.

We have:

$(g \cdot f)(x) = (x + 7)(x - 3) = x^2 - 3x + 7x - 21 = x^2 + 4x - 21$.

Substitute x with 2:

$(g \cdot f)(x) = (2)^2 + 4(2) - 21 = 4 + 8 - 21 = -9$.

Example 4. If $f(x) = x + 3$, and $h(x) = 2x - 4$. Find: $\left(\frac{f}{h}\right)(3)$.

Solution: We have: $\left(\frac{f}{h}\right)(x) = \frac{f(x)}{h(x)} = \frac{x+3}{2x-4}$.
Substitute x with 3: $\left(\frac{f}{h}\right)(3) = \frac{3+3}{2(3)-4} = \frac{6}{2} = 3$.

Composite Functions

- "Composition of functions" simply means combining two or more functions in a way where the output from one function becomes the input for the next function.
The notation used for composition is: $(fog)(x) = f(g(x))$ and is read "f composed with g of x" or "f of g of x".

Examples:

Example 1. Using $f(x) = 2x + 3$ and $g(x) = 5x$, find: $(fog)(x)$.
Solution: Using definition:
$(fog)(x) = f(g(x))$.
Then:
$(fog)(x) = f(g(x)) = f(5x)$.
Now, find $f(5x)$ by substituting x with $5x$ in $f(x)$ function.
Then:
$f(x) = 2x + 3; (x \to 5x) \Rightarrow f(5x) = 2(5x) + 3 = 10x + 3$.

Example 2. Using $f(x) = 3x - 1$ and $g(x) = 2x - 2$, find: $(gof)(5)$.
Solution: $(fog)(x) = f(g(x))$.
Then: Using by: $(gof)(x) = g(f(x)) = g(3x - 1)$.
Now, substitute x in $g(x)$ by $(3x - 1)$.
Then: $g(3x - 1) = 2(3x - 1) - 2 = 6x - 2 - 2 = 6x - 4$.
Substitute x with 5: $(gof)(5) = g(f(5)) = 6(5) - 4 = 30 - 4 = 26$.

Example 3. Using $f(x) = 2x^2 - 5$ and $g(x) = x + 3$, find: $f(g(3))$.
Solution: First, find $g(3)$: $g(x) = x + 3 \Rightarrow g(3) = 3 + 3 = 6$.
Then: $f(g(3)) = f(6)$.
Now, find $f(6)$ by substituting x with 6 in $f(x)$ function.
$f(g(3)) = f(6) = 2(6)^2 - 5 = 2(36) - 5 = 67$.

Real Zeros

- The real zeros (or roots) of a function are the values of x for which the function $f(x)$ equals zero. In graphical terms, real zeros correspond to the $x-$intercepts of the function, which are the points where the graph of the function crosses or touches the $x-$axis.
    - The real zeros can be found by setting the function equal to zero and solving for x.
    - A polynomial function of degree n can have up to n real zeros.
    - The graph of the function will cross the $x-$axis at each of its real zeros.
- These zeros are vital in sketching the graph of the polynomial and understanding its behavior. For each zero, the graph of the polynomial will cross or touch the $x-$axis.

Examples:

Example 1. Find the zeros of $f(x) = x^2 - 4$.

Solution: This is a difference of squares: $f(x) = (x-2)(x+2)$. The zeros are $x = 2$ and $x = -2$.

Example 2. What are the real zeros of $f(x) = x^3 - x^2 - 4x + 4$?

Solution: Factoring by grouping, $f(x) = x^2(x-1) - 4(x-1) = (x^2 - 4)(x-1)$. Further factoring the difference of squares, we get $(x+2)(x-2)(x-1)$. The zeros are $x = -2, 2, 1$.

Example 3. For the function $h(p) = p^3 - 3p^2 - 4p$, identify the real zeros.

Solution: Factoring out the common term, we get: $h(p) = p(p-4)(p+1)$.

The real zeros are $p = 0, 4,$ and -1.

Example 4. Determine the zeros of the function shown in the graph below.

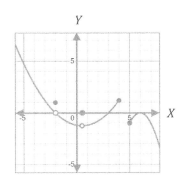

Solution: The zeros of the displayed function are the intersection of the graph and $x-$axis. That is, points $x = \frac{1}{2}$, 3 and 6.

Average Rate of Changes

- The rate of change signifies how one quantity changes in relation to another quantity. The average rate of change of a function between two points is the slope of the secant line that passes through those points.
  - The rate of change is essentially the change in the output (or the y-values) of a function divided by the change in the input (or the x-values).
  - Algebraically, for a function $f(x)$, the average rate of change between $x = a$ and $x = b$ is given by:

  $$\text{Average rate of change} = \frac{f(b) - f(a)}{b - a}$$

  - Graphically, the average rate of change is the slope of the secant line passing through the points $(a, f(a))$ and $(b, f(b))$.
  - In the context of real-world applications, rate of change can represent speed, acceleration, growth rate, and more.
  - The concept of rate of change is foundational for the study of derivatives in calculus.

Examples:

Example 1. Determine the average rate of change of the function $f(x) = 3x^2 + 2$ from $x = 1$ to $x = 4$.
Solution: Using the formula, $\frac{f(4)-f(1)}{4-1} = \frac{50-5}{3} = \frac{45}{3} = 15$.

Example 2. What is the average rate of change of $g(t) = 3t + 2$ over the interval $[-2, 2]$.
Solution: $\frac{g(2)-g(-2)}{2-(-2)} = \frac{8-(-4)}{4} = 3$.
The average rate of change is 3.

Example 3. Determine the average rate of change of $f(x) = x^2$ over the interval $[1, 3]$ and represent it graphically.
Solution: Using the formula, we get: $\frac{f(3)-f(1)}{3-1} = \frac{9-1}{2} = 4$.
The average rate of change is 4.

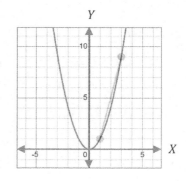

Codomain

- In the context of functions, two main sets are often discussed: the domain (set of inputs) and the codomain (a set that includes the possible outputs). Understanding the difference between codomain and range is essential for a deeper comprehension of functions.
- **Definition**: For a function $f: A \to B$, where A is the domain and B is the codomain, the codomain contains all possible outputs of the function. The range is a subset (or possibly equal to) the codomain and consists of actual outputs that the function produces.
- **Note that**:
  - Every function has a domain, codomain, and range.
  - The range is always a subset of the codomain.
  - The codomain is not necessarily equal to the range, but it can be.
- In mathematics, especially when working with functions, specifying the domain and codomain is important for clarity. While the range gives the actual outputs, the codomain gives an overarching set of possible outputs. Not every element in the codomain must be an output of the function, but every output (element in the range) must belong to the codomain.

Examples:

Example 1. Let $f: \mathbb{R} \to \mathbb{R}$ be defined as $f(x) = x^2$. What is the domain, codomain, and range of f?

Solution: Domain: $\mathbb{R}$ (all real numbers) and codomain: $\mathbb{R}$.

Range: Since x^2 always produces non-negative values, the range is $[0, \infty)$.

Example 2. Define $g: \mathbb{R} \to [0, +\infty)$, where $g(x) = e^x$. Identify the domain, codomain, and range of g.

Solution: Domain: $\mathbb{R}$. Codomain: $[0, +\infty)$ (all positive real numbers).

Range: Since e^x is always positive for any real number x, the range is also $[0, +\infty)$. In this case, the range matches the codomain.

Example 3. Given $h: \mathbb{R} \to \mathbb{R}$ with $h(x) = sin(x)$, determine the domain, codomain, and range.

Solution: Domain: $\mathbb{R}$. Codomain: $\mathbb{R}$. Range: Since $sin(x)$ oscillates between -1 and 1 inclusive, the range is $[-1, 1]$.

Chapter 2: Practices

✎ Evaluate each function.

1) $g(n) = 2n + 5$, find $g(2)$

2) $h(n) = 5n - 9$, find $h(4)$

3) $k(n) = 10 - 6n$, find $k(2)$

4) $g(n) = -5n + 6$, find $g(-2)$

5) $k(n) = -8n + 3$, find $k(-6)$

6) $w(n) = -2n - 95$, find $w(-5)$

✎ According to the values of x and y in the following relationship, find the right equation.

7) $\{(1,3), (2,6), (3,9), (4,12)\}$

8) $\{(1,5), (2,7), (3,9), (4,11)\}$

✎ Perform the indicated operation.

9) $f(x) = x + 6$

$g(x) = 3x + 2$

Find $(f - g)(x)$

10) $g(x) = x - 9$

$f(x) = 2x - 1$

Find $(g - f)(x)$

11) $h(x) = 5x + 6$

$g(x) = 2x + 4$

Find $(h + g)(x)$

12) $g(x) = -6x + 1$

$f(x) = 3x^2 - 3$

Find $(g + f)(5)$

13) $g(x) = 7x - 1$

$h(x) = -4x^2 + 2$

Find $(g - h)(-3)$

14) $h(x) = -x^2 - 1$

$g(x) = -7x - 1$

Find $(h - g)(-5)$

Effortless Math Education

EffortlessMath.com

Perform the indicated operation.

15) $g(x) = x + 3$
    $f(x) = x + 1$
    Find $(g.f)(x)$

16) $f(x) = 4x$
    $h(x) = x - 6$
    Find $(f.h)(x)$

17) $g(a) = a - 8$
    $h(a) = 4a - 2$
    Find $(g.h)(3)$

18) $f(x) = 6x + 2$
    $h(x) = 5x - 1$
    Find $\left(\frac{f}{h}\right)(-2)$

19) $f(x) = 7x - 1$
    $g(x) = -5 - 2x$
    Find $\left(\frac{f}{g}\right)(-4)$

20) $g(a) = a^2 - 4$
    $f(a) = a + 6$
    Find $\left(\frac{g}{f}\right)(-3)$

Using $f(x) = 4x + 3$ and $g(x) = x - 7$, find:

21) $g(f(2)) =$

22) $g(f(-2)) =$

23) $f(g(4)) =$

24) $f(f(7)) =$

25) $g(f(5)) =$

26) $g(f(-5)) =$

Perform the indicated operation.

27) $p(x) = x^3 - 6x^2 + 9x$

28) $r(x) = 9 - x^4$

29) $s(x) = \left(\frac{1}{2}\right)^x$

30) $q(x) = x^3 - 4x^2 - x + 4$

31)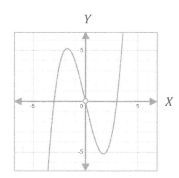

32)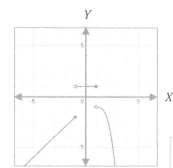

Determine the average rate of change of the following.

33) $f(x) = 2x^2$

from $x = 1$ to $x = 3$

34) $g(x) = 5t^2 - 3t + 1$

from $x = 2$ to $x = 4$

35) $h(x) = \frac{1}{x}$

from $x = 4$ to $x = 8$

36) $k(x) = 2^x$

from $x = -1$ to $x = 1$

37) from $x = -2$ to $x = 2$

38) from $x = 1$ to $x = 4$

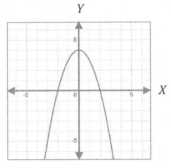 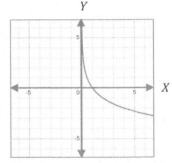

39) from $x = 9$ to $x = 81$

x	$s(x)$
1	1
4	2
9	3
25	5
81	9

40) from $x = -3$ to $x = 5$

x	$r(x)$
−3	0
−1	−2
0	−3
2	−1
5	2

Effortless Math Education

Chapter 2: Answers

1) 9
2) 11
3) −2
4) 16
5) 51
6) 1
7) $y = 3x$
8) $y = 2x + 3$
9) $-2x + 4$
10) $-x - 8$
11) $7x + 10$
12) 43
13) 12
14) −60
15) $x^2 + 4x + 3$
16) $4x^2 - 24x$
17) −50
18) $\frac{10}{11}$
19) $-\frac{29}{3}$
20) $\frac{5}{3}$
21) 4
22) −12
23) −9
24) 127
25) 16
26) −24
27) 0 and 3
28) $-\sqrt{3}$ and $\sqrt{3}$
29) No Solution
30) −1, 1 and 4
31) −3 and 3
32) No Solution
33) 8
34) 27
35) $-\frac{1}{32}$
36) $\frac{3}{4}$
37) 0
38) $-\frac{2}{3}$
39) $\frac{1}{12}$
40) $\frac{1}{4}$

CHAPTER 3
Polynomial and Rational Functions

Math topics that you'll learn in this chapter:

- ☑ The Simplest Functions: Constant and Identity
- ☑ Polynomial Functions
- ☑ Graphing Polynomial Functions
- ☑ Writing Polynomials in Standard Form
- ☑ Simplifying Polynomials
- ☑ Factoring Trinomials
- ☑ Solving a Quadratic Equation
- ☑ Graphing Quadratic Functions
- ☑ Solving Quadratic Inequalities
- ☑ Graphing Quadratic Inequalities
- ☑ Polynomial Functions and Complex Zeros
- ☑ Rational Equations
- ☑ Multiplying and Dividing Rational Expressions
- ☑ Simplifying Rational Expressions
- ☑ Rational Functions
- ☑ Graphing Rational Expressions

The Simplest Functions: Constant and Identity

- Two of the simplest functions are the constant function and the identity function. These functions serve as basic building blocks and are important for understanding more complex functions and their transformations.
    1. **Constant Function**: A constant function is a function that always has the same output, regardless of the input. It is represented as $f(x) = c$, where c is a constant. Graphically, it appears as a horizontal line at the height of the constant value c.
    2. **Identity Function**: The identity function is a function where the output is equal to the input. It is represented as $f(x) = x$. Graphically, it appears as a straight line at a 45° angle with the origin as its intercept.
- The constant and identity functions serve as fundamental concepts in the study of vectors. Understanding these simple functions helps in analyzing more complex vector functions, vector spaces, and transformations. These functions are also crucial for understanding concepts such as basis vectors, linear independence, and the span of a vector space.

Examples:

Example1. The function $f(x) = 5$ is a constant function.
Solution: Regardless of the input, the output is always 5. The graph of this function is a horizontal line at $y = 5$.

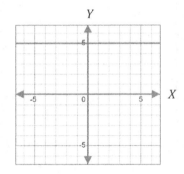

Example2. The function $f(x) = x$ is an identity function.
Solution: If the input is 2, the output is 2; if the input is -3, the output is -3. The graph of this function is a straight line with a slope of 1 that passes through the origin.

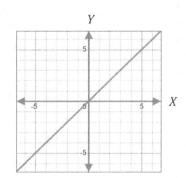

Polynomial Functions

- **Definition**: A polynomial function is a function that can be expressed in the form $P(x) = a_n x^n + a_{n-1} x^{n-1} + \cdots + a_2 x^2 + a_1 x + a_0$ where $a_n, a_{n-1}, \cdots, a_1, a_0$ are constants and n is a non-negative integer. The highest power of x (i.e., n) is called the degree of the polynomial.
- **Graph**: The graph of a polynomial is smooth and continuous, without breaks, jumps, or holes.
- **Types based on degree**:
  - Constant (Degree 0): $P(x) = a$
  - Linear (Degree 1): $P(x) = ax + b$
  - Quadratic (Degree 2): $P(x) = ax^2 + bx + c$
  - Cubic (Degree 3): $P(x) = ax^3 + bx^2 + cx + d$ and so on.
- **Domain**: The domain of a polynomial function is all real numbers, $(-\infty, \infty)$.
- **Range**: The range of a function represents all possible output values. For polynomial functions, determining the range can be a bit more nuanced compared to other functions, particularly due to the nature of polynomial functions, their degrees, and leading coefficients.
  - Polynomial functions of **odd degree** will have a range of $(-\infty, \infty)$ since they exhibit opposite end behaviors.
  - Polynomial functions of **even degree** can have either a maximum or a minimum value depending on their leading coefficient. The range could be limited to values greater than or less than a certain number.

Examples:

Example 1. What is the degree and leading coefficient of $P(x) = 2x^3 - 5x^2 + 7$?
Solution: Degree = 3; Leading coefficient = 2.
Example 2. What type of polynomial is $P(x) = 3x^2 - 4x$?
Solution: It is a binomial and also a quadratic polynomial.
Example 3. Given the polynomial $P(x) = x^4 - 2x^2 + 1$, what is the domain?
Solution: Domain: $(-\infty, \infty)$. Since it's an even degree and leading coefficient is positive, the range is $[0, \infty]$.
Example 4. Classify $P(x) = 5x - 3$.
Solution: It is a binomial and also a linear polynomial.

Graphing Polynomial Functions

- Polynomial functions are algebraic expressions with non-negative integer exponents. Their graphs are smooth, continuous curves. The shape, number of turning points, and behavior of the graph depend on the degree and coefficients of the polynomial.
  - **Degree**: Determines the general shape of the graph. Odd-degree polynomials exhibit opposite end behaviors, while even-degree polynomials have the same end behaviors.
  - **Sign of Leading Coefficient**: Determines whether the polynomial opens up or down.
  - **Roots or Zeros**: Points where the graph intersects or touches the x-axis.
  - **Turning Points**: The graph changes direction at these points. A polynomial of degree n will have at most $n-1$ turning points.
  - **End Behavior**: Describes the direction of the graph as x approaches positive or negative infinity.

Examples:

Example 1. Graph the polynomial $P(x) = x^3 - 4x$.
Solution: Factor as $P(x) = x(x^2 - 4) = x(x-2)(x+2)$. Roots are 0, 2, and -2. The graph crosses the x-axis at these points. Being an odd-degree polynomial with a positive leading coefficient, the left side goes to negative infinity and the right side to positive infinity.

Example 2. Graph the polynomial $Q(x) = x^2 - 6x + 9$.
Solution: This is a perfect square trinomial, $P(x) = (x-3)^2$. It has a vertex at $(3,0)$ and opens upwards, touching but not crossing the x-axis at $x = 3$.

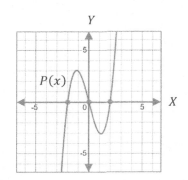
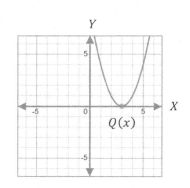

Writing Polynomials in Standard Form

- A polynomial function $f(x)$ of degree n is of the form:
$$f(x) = a_n x^n + a_{n-1} x^{n-1} + \cdots + a_1 x + a_0$$
- The first term is the one with the biggest power!

Examples:

Example 1. Write this polynomial in standard form.
$$8 + 5x^2 - 3x^3 =$$
Solution: The highest exponent is the 3, so that entire term must be written first: $-3x^3$.

The next highest exponent is the 2, so that term comes next. So, we have: $-3x^3 + 5x^2$.

The constant term always comes last so the final answer is: $-3x^3 + 5x^2 + 8$.

Example 2. Write this polynomial in standard form.
$$5x^2 - 9x^5 + 8x^3 - 11 =$$
Solution: The first term is the one with the biggest power:
$5x^2 - 9x^5 + 8x^3 - 11 = -9x^5 + 8x^3 + 5x^2 - 11$.

Example 3. Write this polynomial in standard form.
$$7x^2 - 2x^6 - x^3 - 11 + 3x =$$
Solution: The first term is the one with the biggest power:
$7x^2 - 2x^6 - x^3 - 14 + 3x = -2x^6 - x^3 + 7x^2 + 3x - 14$.

Example 4. Write this polynomial in standard form. $1 - 4a =$

Solution: The first term is the one with the biggest power:
$1 - 4a = -4a + 1$.

Example 5. Write this polynomial in standard form.
$$-2 + 5y^3 - 4y =$$
Solution: The first term is the one with the biggest power:
$-2 + 5y^3 - 4y = 5y^3 - 4y - 2$.

Simplifying Polynomials

- To simplify Polynomials, find "like" terms. (They have the same variables with same power).
- Use "FOIL". (First–Out–In–Last) for binomials:
$$(x + a)(x + b) = x^2 + (b + a)x + ab$$
- Add or subtract "like" terms using order of operation.

Examples:

Example 1. Simplify this expression. $x(4x + 7) - 2x =$

Solution: Use the Distributive Property:

$x(4x + 7) = 4x^2 + 7x$.

Now, combine like terms:

$x(4x + 7) - 2x = 4x^2 + 7x - 2x = 4x^2 + 5x$.

Example 2. Simplify this expression. $(x + 3)(x + 5) =$

Solution: First, apply the FOIL method:

$(a + b)(c + d) = ac + ad + bc + bd$.

Now, we have:

$(x + 3)(x + 5) = x^2 + 5x + 3x + 15$.

Now combine like terms:

$x^2 + 5x + 3x + 15 = x^2 + 8x + 15$.

Example 3. Simplify this expression. $2x(x - 5) - 3x^2 + 6x =$

Solution: Use the Distributive Property:

$2x(x - 5) = 2x^2 - 10x$.

Then:

$2x(x - 5) - 3x^2 + 6x = 2x^2 - 10x - 3x^2 + 6x$.

Now combine like terms:

$2x^2 - 3x^2 = -x^2$, and $-10x + 6x = -4x$.

The simplified form of the expression:

$$2x^2 - 10x - 3x^2 + 6x = -x^2 - 4x.$$

bit.ly/3rnAcj8

Factoring Trinomials

To factor trinomials, you can use following methods:
- "FOIL": $(x + a)(x + b) = x^2 + (b + a)x + ab$.
- "Difference of Squares":
$$a^2 - b^2 = (a + b)(a - b)$$
$$a^2 + 2ab + b^2 = (a + b)(a + b)$$
$$a^2 - 2ab + b^2 = (a - b)(a - b)$$
- "Reverse FOIL": $x^2 + (b + a)x + ab = (x + a)(x + b)$.

Examples:

Example 1. Factor this trinomial. $x^2 - 2x - 8$

Solution: Break the expression into groups. You need to find two numbers that their product is -8 and their sum is -2.

(remember "Reverse FOIL": $x^2 + (b + a)x + ab = (x + a)(x + b)$).

Those two numbers are 2 and -4. Then:

$x^2 - 2x - 8 = (x^2 + 2x) + (-4x - 8)$.

Now factor out x from $x^2 + 2x$: $x(x + 2)$, and factor out -4 from $-4x - 8$: $-4(x + 2)$;

Then: $(x^2 + 2x) + (-4x - 8) = x(x + 2) - 4(x + 2)$

Now factor out like term: $(x + 2)$. Then:

$(x + 2)(x - 4)$.

Example 2. Factor this trinomial. $x^2 - 2x - 24$

Solution: Break the expression into groups:

$(x^2 + 4x) + (-6x - 24)$.

Now factor out x from $x^2 + 4x$: $x(x + 4)$, and factor out -6 from $-6x - 24$: $-6(x + 4)$;

Then: $x(x + 4) - 6(x + 4)$,

now factor out like term:

$(x + 4) \Rightarrow x(x + 4) - 6(x + 4) = (x + 4)(x - 6)$.

Solving a Quadratic Equation

- Write the equation in the form of: $ax^2 + bx + c = 0$.
- Factorize the quadratic, set each factor equal to zero and solve.
- Use quadratic formula if you couldn't factorize the quadratic.
- Quadratic formula: $x_{1,2} = \frac{-b \pm \sqrt{b^2 - 4ac}}{2a}$.

Examples:

Find the solutions of each quadratic function.

Example 1. $x^2 + 7x + 12 = 0$.

Solution: Factor the quadratic by grouping. We need to find two numbers whose sum is 7 (from $7x$) and whose product is 12. Those numbers are 3 and 4. Then:

$$x^2 + 7x + 12 = 0 \Rightarrow x^2 + 3x + 4x + 12 = 0 \Rightarrow (x^2 + 3x) + (4x + 12) = 0.$$

Now, find common factors:

$$(x^2 + 3x) = x(x + 3) \text{ and } (4x + 12) = 4(x + 3).$$

We have two expressions $(x^2 + 3x)$ and $(4x + 12)$ and their common factor is $(x + 3)$. Then:

$$(x^2 + 3x) + (4x + 12) = 0 \Rightarrow x(x + 3) + 4(x + 3) = 0 \Rightarrow (x + 3)(x + 4) = 0.$$

The product of two expressions is 0. Then:

$$(x + 3) = 0 \Rightarrow x = -3 \text{ or } (x + 4) = 0 \Rightarrow x = -4.$$

Example 2. $x^2 + 5x + 6 = 0$.

Solution: Use quadratic formula:

$x_{1,2} = \frac{-b \pm \sqrt{b^2 - 4ac}}{2a}$, $a = 1$, $b = 5$ and $c = 6$.

We have $x = \frac{-5 \pm \sqrt{5^2 - 4 \times 1(6)}}{2(1)}$, therefore:

$$x_1 = \frac{-5 + \sqrt{5^2 - 4 \times 1(6)}}{2(1)} = -2,$$

$$x_2 = \frac{-5 - \sqrt{5^2 - 4 \times 1(6)}}{2(1)} = -3.$$

Graphing Quadratic Functions

- Quadratic functions in vertex form: $y = a(x-h)^2 + k$ where (h,k) is the vertex of the function. The axis of symmetry is $x = h$.
- Quadratic functions in standard form: $y = ax^2 + bx + c$ where $x = -\frac{b}{2a}$ is the value of x in the vertex of the function.
- To graph a quadratic function, first find the vertex, then substitute some values for x and solve for y. (Remember that the graph of a quadratic function is a U-shaped curve, and it is called "parabola".)

Example:

Sketch the graph of $y = (x+2)^2 - 3$.

Solution: Quadratic functions in vertex form:

$$y = a(x-h)^2 + k,$$

where (h,k) is the vertex.

In addition, the axis of symmetry is:

$$x = h.$$

Then, the vertex of $y = (x+2)^2 - 3$ is:

$$(-2, -3).$$

And the axis of symmetry is:

$$x = -2.$$

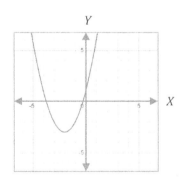

Now, substitute zero for x and solve for y: $y = (0+2)^2 - 3 = 1$.

The y-intercept is $(0,1)$.

Now, you can simply graph the quadratic function.

Notice that quadratic function is a U-shaped curve.

Solving Quadratic Inequalities

- A quadratic inequality is one that can be written in the standard form of
- $ax^2 + bx + c > 0$. (Or substitute $<$, $\leq$, or $\geq$ for $>$)
- Solving a quadratic inequality is like solving equations. We need to find the solutions (the zeroes).
- To solve quadratic inequalities, first find quadratic equations. Then choose a test value between zeroes. Finally, find interval(s), such as > 0 or < 0.

Examples:

Example 1. Solve quadratic inequality. $x^2 + x - 6 > 0$

Solution: First solve $x^2 + x - 6 = 0$ by factoring. Then:
$x^2 + x - 6 = 0 \Rightarrow (x - 2)(x + 3) = 0$.
The product of two expressions is 0. Then:
$(x - 2) = 0 \Rightarrow x = 2$ or $(x + 3) = 0 \Rightarrow x = -3$.
Now, choose a value between 2 and -3. Let's choose 0. Then:
$x = 0 \Rightarrow x^2 + x - 6 > 0 \Rightarrow (0)^2 + (0) - 6 > 0 \Rightarrow -6 > 0$.
-6 is not greater than 0. Therefore, all values between 2 and -3 are NOT the solution of this quadratic inequality.
The solution is: $x > 2$ or $x < -3$. To represent the solution, we can use interval notation, in which solution sets are indicated with parentheses or brackets. The solutions $x > 2$ or $x < -3$ represented as: $(-\infty, -3) \cup (2, \infty)$.

Example 2. Solve quadratic inequality. $x^2 - 2x - 8 \geq 0$

Solution: First solve: $x^2 - 2x - 8 = 0$, Factor:
$x^2 - 2x - 8 = 0 \Rightarrow (x - 4)(x + 2) = 0$.
-2 and 4 are the solutions. Choose a point between -2 and 4. Let's choose 0.
Then: $x = 0 \Rightarrow x^2 - 2x - 8 \geq 0 \Rightarrow (0)^2 - 2(0) - 8 \geq 0 \Rightarrow -8 \geq 0$. This is NOT true.
So, the solution is: $x \leq -2$ or $x \geq 4$ (using interval notation the solution is: $(-\infty, -2] \cup [4, \infty)$.

Graphing Quadratic Inequalities

- A quadratic inequality is in the form:

  $y > ax^2 + bx + c$ (Or substitute $<, \leq$ or $\geq$ for $>$).

- To graph a quadratic inequality, start by graphing the quadratic parabola. Then fill in the region either inside or outside of it, depending on the inequality.

- Choose a testing point and check the solution section.

Example:

Sketch the graph of $y > 2x^2$.

Solution: First, graph the quadratic:

$y = 2x^2$.

Quadratic functions in vertex form:

$y = a(x - h)^2 + k,$

where (h, k) is the vertex.

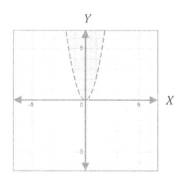

Then, the vertex of $y = 2x^2$ is:

$(h, k) = (0, 0)$.

Since the inequality sing is $>$, we need to use dash lines.

Now, choose a testing point inside the parabola. Let's choose $(0, 2)$.

$y > 2x^2 \Rightarrow 2 > 2(0)^2 \Rightarrow 2 > 0$.

This is true. So, inside the parabola is the solution section.

Polynomial Functions and Complex Zeros

- A polynomial function is of the form $P(x) = a_n x^n + a_{n-1} x^{n-1} + \ldots + a_1 x + a_0$, where n is a non-negative integer, and $a\_n, a_{n-1}, \cdots, a_0$ are constants with $a_n \neq 0$.
- Complex zeros are solutions to the polynomial equation $P(x) = 0$ that are not real numbers but have the form $a + bi$ where a and b are real numbers, and i is the imaginary unit.
- Complex zeros always occur in conjugate pairs if coefficients of the polynomial are real.
- Every degree n polynomial has n root. These answers include real and complex numbers.

Examples:

Example 1. Find the zeros of the following polynomial $P(x) = x^2 + 1$:

Solution: Zeros are solutions to $x^2 + 1 = 0$, which are i and $-i$. Because,
$x^2 + 1 = 0 \Rightarrow x^2 = -1 \Rightarrow |x| = \sqrt{-1} \Rightarrow |x| = i \Rightarrow x = i$ or $x = -i$.
These are complex because they involve the imaginary unit i.

Example 2. Determine the roots of the polynomial $Q(x) = x^2 - 2x + 5$:

Solution: Zeros can be found using the quadratic formula, yielding complex numbers.

The zeros are complex conjugates. Rewrite the polynomial as $x^2 - 2x + 5 = (x^2 - 2x + 1) + 4 = (x - 1)^2 + 4$. So, we get:
$(x - 1)^2 + 4 = 0 \Rightarrow (x - 1)^2 = -4 \Rightarrow |x - 1| = \sqrt{-4}$
Since we know that $i = \sqrt{-1}$. Therefore, by simplifying we have:
$|x - 1| = \sqrt{4 \times (-1)} \Rightarrow |x - 1| = 2i \Rightarrow x - 1 = 2i$ or $x - 1 = -2i$
Thus, the roots of $P(x)$ are $1 + 2i$ and $1 - 2i$.

Rational Equations

- For solving rational equations, we can use following methods:
- **Converting to a common denominator:** In this method, you need to get a common denominator for both sides of the equation. Then, make numerators equal and solve for the variable.
- **Cross-multiplying:** This method is useful when there is only one fraction on each side of the equation. Simply multiply the first numerator by the second denominator and make the result equal to the product of the second numerator and the first denominator.

Examples:

Example 1. Solve. $\frac{x-2}{x+1} = \frac{x+4}{x-2}$

Solution: Use cross multiply method: if $\frac{a}{b} = \frac{c}{d}$, then: $a \times d = b \times c$.
$\frac{x-2}{x+1} = \frac{x+4}{x-2} \Rightarrow (x-2)(x-2) = (x+4)(x+1)$.

Expand: $(x-2)^2 = x^2 - 4x + 4$ and $(x+4)(x+1) = x^2 + 5x + 4$.

Then:

$x^2 - 4x + 4 = x^2 + 5x + 4$.

Now, simplify:

$x^2 - 4x = x^2 + 5x$.

Subtract both sides $(x^2 + 5x)$, Then:

$x^2 - 4x - (x^2 + 5x) = x^2 + 5x - (x^2 + 5x) \Rightarrow -9x = 0 \Rightarrow x = 0$.

Example 2. Solve. $\frac{2x}{x-3} = \frac{2x+2}{2x-6}$

Solution: Multiply the numerator and denominator of the rational expression on the left by 2 to get a common denominator $(2x - 6)$:
$\frac{2(2x)}{2(x-3)} = \frac{4x}{2x-6}$.

Now, the denominators on both side of the equation are equal. Therefore, their numerators must be equal too.
$\frac{4x}{2x-6} = \frac{2x+2}{2x-6} \Rightarrow 4x = 2x + 2 \Rightarrow 2x = 2 \Rightarrow x = 1$.

Multiplying and Dividing Rational Expressions

- Multiplying rational expressions is the same as multiplying fractions. First, multiply numerators and then multiply denominators. Then, simplify as needed.
- To divide rational expressions, use the same method we use for dividing fractions. (Keep, Change, Flip)
- Keep the first rational expression, change the division sign to multiplication, and flip the numerator and denominator of the second rational expression. Then, multiply numerators and multiply denominators. Simplify as needed.

Examples:

Example 1. Solve: $\frac{x+6}{x-1} \times \frac{x-1}{5} =$

Solution: Multiply numerators and denominators: $\frac{a}{b} \times \frac{c}{d} = \frac{a \times c}{b \times d}$.

Then: $\frac{x+6}{x-1} \times \frac{x-1}{5} = \frac{(x+6)(x-1)}{5(x-1)}$.

Cancel the common factor: $(x-1)$.

Therefore: $\frac{(x+6)(x-1)}{5(x-1)} = \frac{(x+6)}{5}$.

Example 2. Solve. $\frac{x+2}{3x} \div \frac{x^2+5x+6}{3x^2+3x} =$

Solution: Use fractions division rule: $\frac{a}{b} \div \frac{c}{d} = \frac{a}{b} \times \frac{d}{c} = \frac{a \times d}{b \times c}$.

Therefore:
$\frac{x+2}{3x} \div \frac{x^2+5x+6}{3x^2+3x} = \frac{x+2}{3x} \times \frac{3x^2+3x}{x^2+5x+6} = \frac{(x+2)(3x^2+3x)}{(3x)(x^2+5x+6)}$.

Now, factorize the expressions $3x^2 + 3x$ and $(x^2 + 5x + 6)$. Then:

$3x^2 + 3x = 3x(x+1)$ and $x^2 + 5x + 6 = (x+2)(x+3)$.

Simplify: $\frac{(x+2)(3x^2+3x)}{(3x)(x^2+5x+6)} = \frac{(x+2)(3x)(x+1)}{(3x)(x+2)(x+3)}$, cancel common factors.

Then: $\frac{(x+2)(3x)(x+1)}{(3x)(x+2)(x+3)} = \frac{x+1}{x+3}$.

Example 3. Solve. $\frac{5x}{x+3} \div \frac{x}{2x+6} =$

Solution: Use fractions division rule: $\frac{a}{b} \div \frac{c}{d} = \frac{a}{b} \times \frac{d}{c} = \frac{a \times d}{b \times c}$

Then: $\frac{5x}{x+3} \div \frac{x}{2x+6} = \frac{5x}{x+3} \times \frac{2x+6}{x} = \frac{5x(2x+6)}{x(x+3)} = \frac{5x \times 2(x+3)}{x(x+3)}$.

Cancel common factor: $\frac{5x \times 2(x+3)}{x(x+3)} = \frac{10x(x+3)}{x(x+3)} = 10$.

Simplifying Rational Expressions

- Factorize numerator and denominator if they are factorable.
- Find common factors of both numerator and denominator.
- Remove the common factor in both numerator and denominator.
- Simplify if needed.

Examples:

Example 1. Simplify. $\frac{9x^2y}{3y^2}$

Solution: Cancel the common factor 3: $\frac{9x^2y}{3y^2} = \frac{3x^2y}{y^2}$.
Cancel the common factor y: $\frac{3x^2y}{y^2} = \frac{3x^2}{y}$.

Then:
$$\frac{9x^2y}{3y^2} = \frac{3x^2}{y}.$$

Example 2. Simplify. $\frac{x^2+5x-6}{x+6}$

Solution: Factor $x^2 + 5x - 6 = (x - 1)(x + 6)$.
Then: $\frac{x^2+5x-6}{x+6} = \frac{(x-1)(x+6)}{x+6}$.

Cancel the common factor: $(x + 6)$,

Then:
$$\frac{(x-1)(x+6)}{x+6} = x - 1.$$

Example 3. Simplify. $\frac{18a^3(b+1)c^2}{6a^2c(b^2-1)}$

Solution: Cancel common factor in numerator and denominator: a^2, c and 6.
Then: $\frac{18a^3(b+1)c^2}{6a^2c(b^2-1)} = \frac{3a(b+1)c}{(b^2-1)}$.

Now, by factoring $b^2 - 1 = (b + 1)(b - 1)$, and cancel common factor $(b + 1)$, we have:
$\frac{3a(b+1)c}{(b^2-1)} = \frac{3a(b+1)c}{(b+1)(b-1)} = \frac{3ac}{b-1} \Rightarrow \frac{18a^3(b+1)c^2}{6a^2c(b^2-1)} = \frac{3ac}{b-1}.$

Rational Functions

- **Rational Function**: A function of the form $R(x) = \frac{P(x)}{Q(x)}$, where $P(x)$ and $Q(x)$ are polynomial functions and $Q(x) \neq 0$.
- **Vertical Asymptote**: A vertical line $x = a$ where the function approaches infinity (or negative infinity) as x approaches a. It represents values of x where the denominator is zero, but the numerator isn't.
- **Horizontal Asymptote**: A horizontal line $y = b$ which the graph of the function approaches as x approaches positive or negative infinity.
- **Note that**:
    - The domain of a rational function is all real numbers except where the denominator is zero.
    - Holes occur at values of x where both the numerator and denominator are zero.
    - The behavior around vertical asymptotes and the presence or absence of horizontal asymptotes can determine the range of the function.

Examples:

Example 1. Given $R(x) = \frac{x}{x^2-4}$, find the domain and vertical asymptotes.

Solution: The domain is all real numbers except where the denominator is zero.
$$x^2 - 4 = (x+2)(x-2)$$
So, $x = 2$ and $x = -2$ are excluded from the domain. These are also vertical asymptotes.

Example 2. Determine the horizontal asymptote of $R(x) = \frac{3x^2+x-5}{x^2+4}$.

Solution: The degrees of the numerator and denominator are the same. The horizontal asymptote is $y = \frac{3}{1} = 3$.

Example 3. For $R(x) = \frac{5x-4}{x^2+x-6}$, identify any holes.

Solution: Factoring the denominator gives $x^2 + x - 6 = (x+3)(x-2)$. Since the numerator doesn't have factors of $x + 3$ or $x - 2$, there are no holes.

Graphing Rational Expressions

- A rational expression is a fraction in which the numerator and/or the denominator are polynomials. Examples: $\frac{1}{x}, \frac{x^2}{x-1}, \frac{x^2-x+2}{x^2+5x+1}, \frac{m^2+6m-5}{m-2m}$.
- To graph a rational function:
  - Find the vertical asymptotes of the function if there is any. (Vertical asymptotes are vertical lines which correspond to the zeroes of the denominator. The graph will have a vertical asymptote at $x = a$ if the denominator is zero at $x = a$ and the numerator isn't zero at $x = a$.)
  - Find the horizontal or slant asymptote. (If the numerator has a bigger degree than the denominator, there will be a slant asymptote. To find the slant asymptote, divide the numerator by the denominator using either long division or synthetic division.)
  - If the denominator has a bigger degree than the numerator, the horizontal asymptote is the x−axes or the line $y = 0$. If they have the same degree, the horizontal asymptote equals the leading coefficient (the coefficient of the largest exponent) of the numerator divided by the leading coefficient of the denominator.
  - Find intercepts and plug in some values of x and solve for y, then graph the function.

Example:

Graph rational function. $f(x) = \frac{x^2-x+2}{x-1}$.

Solution: First, notice that the graph is in two pieces. Most rational functions have graphs in multiple pieces. Find y−intercept by substituting zero for x and solving for y. $(f(x))$: $x = 0 \Rightarrow y = \frac{x^2-x+2}{x-1} = \frac{0^2-0+2}{0-1} = -2$, y−intercept: $(0, -2)$.
Asymptotes of $\frac{x^2-x+2}{x-1}$: Vertical: $x = 1$, Slant asymptote: $y = x$ (Divide the numerator by the denominator). After finding the asymptotes, you can plug in some values for x and solve for y. Here is the sketch for this function.

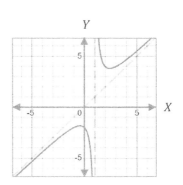

Chapter 3: Practices

✎ Write each polynomial in standard form.

1) $2x - 5x =$

2) $5 + 12x - 8x =$

3) $x^2 - 2x^3 + 1 =$

4) $2 + 2x^2 - 1 =$

5) $-x^2 + 4x - 2x^3 =$

6) $-2x^2 + 2x^3 + 12 =$

7) $18 - 5x + 9x^4 =$

8) $2x^2 + 13x - 2x^3 =$

✎ Determine the degree, type, and range of polynomials.

9) $f(x) = 7 - 2x$

10) $g(x) = -x^2 + 3x^3 + 4$

11) $h(x) = x^3 - 3x$

12) $m(x) = -2x^2 - 3x + 1$

✎ Graph polynomials.

13) $y = x^4 - 4x^3 + 4x^2$

14) $y = -2x^3$

✎ Simplify each expression.

15) $2(4x - 6) =$

16) $5(3x - 4) =$

17) $x(2x - 5) =$

18) $4(5x + 3) =$

19) $2x(6x - 2) =$

20) $x(3x + 8) =$

21) $(x - 2)(x + 4) =$

22) $(x + 3)(x + 2) =$

✎ Factor each trinomial.

23) $x^2 + 3x - 10 =$

24) $x^2 - x - 6 =$

25) $x^2 + 8x + 15 =$

26) $x^2 - 7x + 12 =$

27) $x^2 - x - 20 =$

28) $x^2 + 11x + 18 =$

Effortless Math Education

Solve each equation.

29) $x^2 - 5x - 14 = 0$

30) $x^2 + 8x + 15 = 0$

31) $x^2 - 5x - 36 = 0$

32) $x^2 - 12x + 35 = 0$

33) $x^2 + 12x + 32 = 0$

34) $5x^2 + 27x + 28 = 0$

35) $8x^2 + 26x + 15 = 0$

36) $3x^2 + 10x + 8 = 0$

37) $12x^2 + 30x + 12 = 0$

38) $9x^2 + 57x + 18 = 0$

Sketch the graph of each function. Identify the vertex and axis of symmetry.

39) $y = 3(x - 5)^2 - 2$

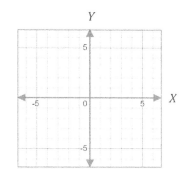

40) $y = x^2 - 3x + 15$

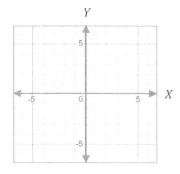

Solve each quadratic inequality.

41) $x^2 + 7x + 10 < 0$

42) $x^2 + 9x + 20 > 0$

43) $x^2 - 8x + 16 > 0$

44) $x^2 - 8x + 12 \leq 0$

45) $x^2 - 11x + 30 \leq 0$

46) $x^2 - 12x + 27 \geq 0$

47) $x^2 - 16x + 64 \geq 0$

48) $x^2 - 36 \leq 0$

49) $x^2 - 13x + 36 \geq 0$

50) $x^2 + 15x + 36 \leq 0$

51) $4x^2 - 6x - 9 > x^2$

52) $5x^2 - 15x + 10 < 0$

Effortless Math Education

Sketch the graph of each function.

53) $y < -2x^2$

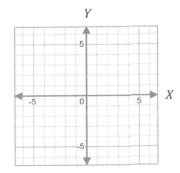

54) $y \geq 4x^2$

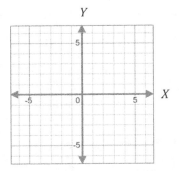

Simplify.

55) $\frac{16x^3}{20x^3} =$

56) $\frac{64x^3}{24x} =$

57) $\frac{25x^5}{15x^3} =$

58) $\frac{16}{2x-2} =$

59) $\frac{15x-3}{24} =$

60) $\frac{4x+16}{28} =$

61) $\frac{x^2-10x+25}{x-5} =$

62) $\frac{x^2-49}{x^2+3x-28} =$

Simplify each expression.

63) $\frac{79x}{25} \cdot \frac{85}{27x^2} =$

64) $\frac{96}{38x} \cdot \frac{25}{45} =$

65) $\frac{84}{3} \cdot \frac{48x}{95} =$

66) $\frac{53}{43} \cdot \frac{46x^2}{31} =$

67) $\frac{93}{21x} \cdot \frac{34x}{51x} =$

68) $\frac{5x+50}{x+10} \cdot \frac{x-2}{5} =$

69) $\frac{x-7}{x+6} \cdot \frac{10x+60}{x-7} =$

70) $\frac{1}{x+10} \cdot \frac{10x+30}{x+3} =$

Solve each equation.

71) $x^2 + 9 = 0$

72) $x^3 + 4x^2 + 5x = 0$

73) $x^4 - 16 = 0$

74) $x^3 - x^2 + x - 1 = 0$

Divide.

75) $\frac{12x}{3} \div \frac{5}{8} =$

76) $\frac{10x^2}{7} \div \frac{3x}{12} =$

77) $\frac{x+5}{5x^2-10x} \div \frac{1}{5x} =$

78) $\frac{x-2}{x+6x-12} \div \frac{x}{x+3} =$

79) $\frac{5x}{x-10} \div \frac{5x}{x-5} =$

80) $\frac{x^2+10x+16}{x^2+6x+8} \div \frac{1}{x+4} =$

81) $\frac{x^2-2x-15}{8x+20} \div \frac{2}{4x+10} =$

82) $\frac{x-4}{x^2-2x-8} \div \frac{1}{x-5} =$

Solve each equation. Remember to check for extraneous solutions.

83) $\frac{2x-3}{x+1} = \frac{x+6}{x-2}$

84) $\frac{3x-2}{9x+1} = \frac{2x-5}{6x-5}$

85) $\frac{1}{n-8} - 1 = \frac{7}{n-8}$

86) $\frac{x+5}{x^2-2x} - 1 = \frac{1}{x^2-2x}$

87) $\frac{x-2}{x+3} - 1 = \frac{1}{x+2}$

88) $\frac{1}{6x^2} = \frac{1}{x^2-x} - \frac{1}{x}$

89) $\frac{x+5}{x^2-x} = \frac{1}{x^2-x} - \frac{x-6}{x-1}$

90) $1 = \frac{1}{x^2-2x} + \frac{x-1}{x}$

Find the domain and asymptotes.

91) $f(x) = \frac{x^2-4}{x-2}$

92) $g(x) = \frac{2x}{x^2-9}$

93) $h(x) = \frac{3}{x-1}$

94) $k(x) = \frac{4x^2+3x+1}{x^2+5}$

Graph rational expressions.

95) $f(x) = \frac{x^2+2x-4}{x-2}$

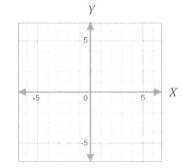

96) $f(x) = \frac{4x^3-16x+64}{x^2-2x-4}$

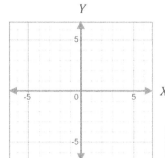

Effortless Math Education

Chapter 3: Answers

1) $-3x$

2) $4x + 5$

3) $-2x^3 + x^2 + 1$

4) $2x^2 + 1$

5) $-2x^3 - x^2 + 4x$

6) $2x^3 - 2x^2 + 12$

7) $9x^4 - 5x + 18$

8) $-2x^3 + 2x^2 + 13x$

9) One, Linear and $\mathbb{R}$

10) Three, Cubic and $\mathbb{R}$

11) Three, Cubic and $\mathbb{R}$

12) Two, Quadratic and $\left(-\infty, -\frac{3}{4}\right]$

13)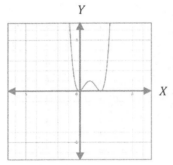

14)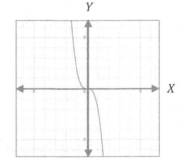

15) $8x - 12$

16) $15x - 20$

17) $2x^2 - 5x$

18) $20x + 12$

19) $12x^2 - 4x$

20) $3x^2 + 8x$

21) $x^2 + 2x - 8$

22) $x^2 + 5x + 6$

23) $(x - 2)(x + 5)$

24) $(x + 2)(x - 3)$

25) $(x + 5)(x + 3)$

26) $(x - 3)(x - 4)$

27) $(x - 5)(x + 4)$

28) $(x + 2)(x + 9)$

29) $-2, 7$

30) $-3, -5$

31) $9, -4$

32) $7, 5$

33) $-4, -8$

34) $-\frac{7}{5}, -4$

35) $-\frac{5}{2}, -\frac{3}{4}$

36) $-\frac{4}{3}, -2$

37) $-\frac{1}{2}, -2$

38) $-\frac{1}{3}, -6$

39) $y = 3(x-5)^2 - 2$

40) $y = x^2 - 3x + 15$

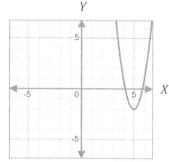

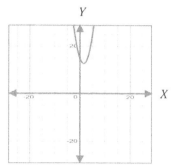

41) $-5 < x < -2$

42) $x < -5$ or $x > -4$

43) $x < 4$ or $x > 4$

44) $2 \leq x \leq 6$

45) $5 \leq x \leq 6$

46) $x \leq 3$ or $x \geq 9$

47) All real numbers

48) $-6 \leq x \leq 6$

49) $x \leq 4$ or $x \geq 9$

50) $-12 \leq x \leq -3$

51) $x < -1$ or $x > 3$

52) $1 < x < 2$

53)

54)

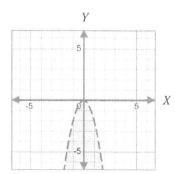

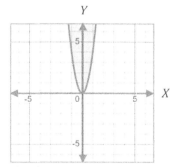

55) $\frac{4}{5}$

56) $\frac{8x^2}{3}$

57) $\frac{5x^2}{3}$

58) $\frac{8}{x-1}$

59) $\frac{5x-1}{8}$

60) $\frac{x+4}{7}$

61) $x - 5$

62) $\frac{x-7}{x-4}$

63) $\frac{1,343}{135x}$

64) $\frac{80}{57x}$

65) $\frac{1,344x}{95}$

66) $\frac{2,438x^2}{1,333}$

67) $\frac{62}{21x}$

68) $x - 2$

69) 10

70) $\frac{10}{x+10}$

71) $3i$ and $-3i$

72) $0, -2 + i$ and $-2 - i$

73) $2, -2, 2i,$ and $-2i$

74) $1, i,$ and $-i$

75) $\frac{32}{5}x$

76) $\frac{40x}{7}$

77) $\frac{x+5}{x-2}$

78) $\frac{(x-2)(x+3)}{x(7x-12)}$

79) $\frac{(x-5)}{(x-10)}$

80) $x + 8$

81) $\frac{(x+3)(x-5)}{4}$

82) $\frac{x-5}{x+2}$

83) $\{0, 14\}$

84) $\left\{-\frac{15}{16}\right\}$

85) $\{2\}$

86) $\{4, -1\}$

87) $\left\{-\frac{13}{6}\right\}$

88) $\left\{\frac{1}{6}\right\}$

89) $\{4\}$

90) $\{3\}$

91) $\mathbb{R} - \{2\}$, No asymptotes

92) $\mathbb{R} - \{-3, 3\}$
    $x = -3, x = 3$ and $y = 0$

93) $\mathbb{R} - \{1\}$
    $x = 1$ and $y = 0$

94) $\mathbb{R}, y = 4$

95)
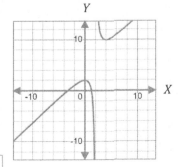

96)
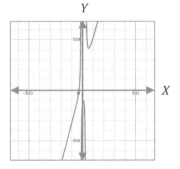

2 Exponential and Logarithmic Functions

CHAPTER 4: Exponential Functions and Logarithms

Math topics that you'll learn in this chapter:

- ☑ Exponential Functions: Definition and Properties
- ☑ Graphing Exponential Functions
- ☑ Solving Exponential Equations
- ☑ Logarithmic Functions: Definition and Properties
- ☑ Converting Between Exponential and Logarithmic Forms
- ☑ Graphing Logarithmic Functions
- ☑ Evaluating Logarithms
- ☑ Properties of Logarithms
- ☑ Natural Logarithms
- ☑ Solving Logarithmic Equations

Exponential Functions: Definition and Properties

- An exponential function with a base a is shown as $f(x) = a^x$, where a is a positive real number and $a \neq 1$, and $a \in \mathbb{R}$.
- Exponential Growth and Decay:
  - If $a > 1$, the function $f(x) = a^x$ is exponential growth.
  - If $0 < a < 1$, the function $f(x) = a^x$ is exponential decay.
- All exponent functions of the form $f(x) = a^x$ have the same domain, range and y-intercept. As follow: Domain: $\mathbb{R}$, Range: $(0, +\infty)$, y-intercept: 1

Example:

Graph $f(x) = 2^x$, and $g(x) = -5f(x) + 1$. Which one is exponential decay? Then give domain, range and y-intercept.

Solution: Since the base of the $f(x) = 2^x$ is 2 and greater than 1, then $f(x)$ is growth with domain $\mathbb{R}$, range $(0, +\infty)$, and y-intercept 1.

We know that the function $y = h(x)$ is symmetric to the function $y = -kf(x)$ with respect to the x-axis, and all values of function $y = kf(x)$, where $k > 0$ are k times of function $y = h(x)$. Now, all values of $y = 5f(x)$ are 5 times the function $y = f(x)$, and the function $y = 5f(x)$ is symmetric to the function $y = -5f(x)$ with respect to the x-axis. As follow:

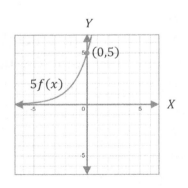

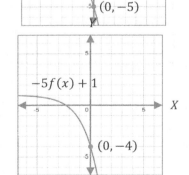

On the other hand, $y = -5f(x) + 1$ is shifted 1 unit to the up, therefore, according to the graph of $y = -5f(x) + 1$, the y-intercept is -4, the domain is $\mathbb{R}$, and the range is $(-\infty, 1)$.

Solving Exponential Equations

- Exponential equations involve variables in the exponent. They can be solved using various methods, such as logarithms, equalizing bases, or graphically.
- **Methods**:
  - **Equalizing Bases**: If bases are equal, their exponents must be equal. For $b^m = b^n$, $m = n$.
  - **Logarithms**: Taking the logarithm of both sides can simplify the equation. Use properties of logarithms to solve.
- **Steps to Solve Using Logarithms**:
  Step 1: Take the natural logarithm (ln) or logarithm (base 10, log) of both sides.
  Step 2: Use log properties to bring down the exponent.
  Step 3: Solve for the variable.

Examples:

Example 1. Solve $2^x = 8$.
Solution: Using the equal bases method, rewrite 8 as 2^3. Therefore, $x = 3$.
Example 2. Solve $3^{2x} = 9$.
Solution: Rewrite 9 as 3^2. So, $2x = 2$. Thus, $x = 1$.
Example 3. Solve $e^x = 5$.
Solution: Taking ln of both sides, $ln(e^x) = ln(5)$.
By properties of logarithms, $x \cdot ln(e) = ln(5)$. Since $ln(e) = 1$, $x = ln(5)$.
Example 4. Solve $10^x = 100$.
Solution: Taking log of both sides, $x \cdot log(10) = log(100)$.
Since $log(10) = 1$, $x = 2$.

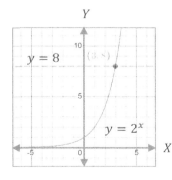
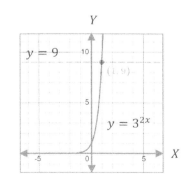
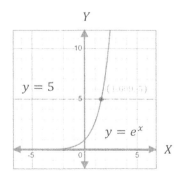

Logarithmic Functions: Definition and Properties

- **Definition**: A logarithmic function is defined as $f(x) = \log_b x$, where b is the base of the logarithm and $b > 0$, $b \neq 1$. The logarithm gives the exponent to which the base must be raised to produce x.
- **Graph**: The graph of $y = \log_b x$ is a curve that:
  - Passes through the point $(1,0)$ since any base raised to the power of 0 equals 1.
  - Has a vertical asymptote at $x = 0$.
  - Is increasing for all $x > 0$.
- **Domain**: The domain of the logarithmic function is $x > 0$. Logarithms are undefined for values $x \leq 0$.
- **Range**: The range of a logarithmic function is all real numbers $(-\infty, \infty)$.
- For the graph of the logarithmic function, imagine a curve that starts from the lower left, touches the y-axis (but never crosses or meets it), moves through the point $(1,0)$, and then extends infinitely to the upper right. This general shape illustrates the increasing nature of the logarithm and its domain and range properties.

Examples:

Example 1. Sketch the graph of $f(x) = \log_2 x$.
Solution: The graph is a curve that passes through $(1,0)$, has a vertical asymptote at $x = 0$, and increases to the right. (Visualize a curve starting from the bottom-left, curving upwards and rightwards.)

Example 2. Determine the domain and range of $f(x) = \log_5 x$.
Solution: Domain: $x > 0$. Range: $(-\infty, \infty)$.

Example 3. For what values of x is $\log_3 x$ defined?
Solution: For all $x > 0$.

Example 4. Find the x-intercept of $y = \log_4 x$.
Solution: The x-intercept is where $y = 0$. So, $\log_4 x = 0$ gives $x = 1$. Hence, the x-intercept is $(1,0)$.

Evaluating Logarithms

- Logarithm is another way of writing exponent. $log_b y = x$ is equivalent to $y = b^x$.
- Learn some logarithms rules: ($a > 0$, $a \neq 0$, $M > 0$, $N > 0$, and k is a real number.)

  Rule 1: $log_a(M \cdot N) = log_a M + log_a N$,   Rule 4: $log_a a = 1$,

  Rule 2: $log_a \frac{M}{N} = log_a M - log_a N$,   Rule 5: $log_a 1 = 0$,

  Rule 3: $log_a M^k = k \, log_a M$,   Rule 6: $a^{log_a k} = k$.

Examples:

Example 1. Evaluate: $log_2 32$.

Solution: Rewrite 32 in power base form: $32 = 2^5$, then:

$log_2 32 = log_2 (2)^5$.

Use log rule: $log_a M^k = k \, log_a M \Rightarrow log_2(2)^5 = 5 \, log_2 2$.

Use log rule: $log_a a = 1 \Rightarrow log_2 2 = 1 \Rightarrow 5 \, log_2 2 = 5$.

Therefore: $log_2 32 = 5$.

Example 2. Evaluate: $3 \, log_5 125$.

Solution: Rewrite 125 in power base form: $125 = 5^3$,

then: $log_5 125 = log_5 (5)^3$.

Use log rule: $log_a M^k = k \, log_a M \Rightarrow log_5(5)^3 = 3 \, log_5 5$.

Use log rule: $log_a a = 1 \Rightarrow log_5 5 = 1 \Rightarrow 3 \, log_5 5 = 3$.

Therefore: $3 \, log_5 125 = 3 \times 3 = 9$.

Example 3. Evaluate: $log_3(3)^5$

Solution: Use log rule: $log_a M^k = k \, log_a M \Rightarrow log_3(3)^5 = 5 \, log_3 3$.

Use log rule: $log_a a = 1 \Rightarrow log_3 3 = 1 \Rightarrow 5 \, log_3 3 = 5 \times 1 = 5$.

Properties of Logarithms

- Using some of the properties of logs, (the product rule, quotient rule, and power rule) sometimes we can expand a logarithm expression (expanding) or convert some logarithm expressions into a single logarithm (condensing).
- Let's review some logarithms properties:

$a^{\log_a b} = b$ $\qquad\qquad\qquad\qquad\qquad \log_a \frac{1}{x} = -\log_a x$

$\log_a 1 = 0$ $\qquad\qquad\qquad\qquad\qquad \log_a x^p = p \log_a x$

$\log_a a = 1$ $\qquad\qquad\qquad\qquad\qquad \log_{a^k} x = \frac{1}{k} \log_a x$, for $k \neq 0$

$\log_a(x \cdot y) = \log_a x + \log_a y$ $\qquad\quad \log_a x = \log_{a^c} x^c$

$\log_a \frac{x}{y} = \log_a x - \log_a y$ $\qquad\qquad \log_a x = \frac{1}{\log_x a}$

Examples:

Example 1. Expand this logarithm. $\log_a(3 \times 5) =$

Solution: Use log rule: $\log_a(x \cdot y) = \log_a x + \log_a y$.

Then:

$\log_a(3 \times 5) = \log_a 3 + \log_a 5$.

Example 2. Condense this expression to a single logarithm. $\log_a 2 - \log_a 7$

Solution: Use log rule: $\log_a x - \log_a y = \log_a \frac{x}{y}$.

Then: $\log_a 2 - \log_a 7 = \log_a \frac{2}{7}$.

Example 3. Expand this logarithm. $\log\left(\frac{1}{7}\right) =$

Solution: Use log rule: $\log_a \frac{1}{x} = -\log_a x$.

Then: $\log\left(\frac{1}{7}\right) = -\log 7$.

Natural Logarithms

- A natural logarithm is a logarithm that has a special base of the mathematical constant e, which is an irrational number approximately equal to 2.71.
- The natural logarithm of x is generally written as $\ln x$, or $\log_e x$.

Examples:

Example 1. Expand this natural logarithm. $\ln 4x^2 =$

Solution: Use *log* rule: $\log_a(x.y) = \log_a x + \log_a y$.

Therefore:

$\ln 4x^2 = \ln 4 + \ln x^2$.

Now, use *log* rule: $\log_a(M)^k = k.\log_a(M)$.

Then:

$\ln 4 + \ln x^2 = \ln 4 + 2\ln x$.

Example 2. Condense this expression to a single logarithm. $\ln x - \log_e 2y$

Solution: Use *log* rule: $\log_a x - \log_a y = \log_a \frac{x}{y}$.

Then:

$\ln x - \log_e 2y = \ln \frac{x}{2y}$.

Example 3. Solve this equation for x: $e^x = 6$.

Solution: If $f(x) = g(x)$, then: $\ln(f(x)) = \ln(g(x)) \Rightarrow \ln(e^x) = \ln(6)$.

Use *log* rule: $\log_a x^b = b \log_a x \Rightarrow \ln(e^x) = x \ln(e) \Rightarrow x \ln(e) = \ln(6)$.

We know that: $\ln(e) = 1$, then:

$x = \ln(6)$.

Example 4. Solve this equation for x: $\ln(4x - 2) = 1$.

Solution: Use *log* rule: $a = \log_b(b^a) \Rightarrow 1 = \ln(e^1) = \ln(e) \Rightarrow \ln(4x - 2) = \ln(e)$.

When the *log*s have the same base: $\log_b(f(x)) = \log_b(g(x)) \Rightarrow f(x) = g(x)$.

$\ln(4x - 2) = \ln(e)$, then: $4x - 2 = e \Rightarrow x = \frac{e+2}{4}$.

Solving Logarithmic Equations

To solve a logarithm equation:
- Convert the logarithmic equation to an exponential equation when it's possible. (If no base is indicated, the base of the logarithm is 10.)
- Condense logarithms if you have more than one *log* on one side of the equation.
- Plug the answers back into the original equation and check to see if the solution works.

Examples:

Example 1. Find the value of x in this equation. $log_2(36 - x^2) = 4$

Solution: Use *log* rule: $log_b x = log_b y$, then: $x = y$.

We can write number 4 as a logarithm: $4 = log_2(2^4)$.

Then:

$log_2(36 - x^2) = log_2(2^4) = log_2 16$.

Then: $36 - x^2 = 16 \Rightarrow 36 - 16 = x^2 \Rightarrow x^2 = 20 \Rightarrow x = \pm\sqrt{20} = \pm 2\sqrt{5}$.

You can plug in back the solutions into the original equation to check your answer.

$x = \sqrt{20} \Rightarrow log_2\left(36 - \left(\sqrt{20}\right)^2\right) = 4 \Rightarrow log_2(36 - 20) = 4 \Rightarrow log_2 16 = 4$.

$x = -\sqrt{20} \Rightarrow log_2\left(36 - \left(-\sqrt{20}\right)^2\right) = 4 \Rightarrow log_2(36 - 20) = 4 \Rightarrow log_2 16 = 4$.

Both solutions work in the original equation.

Example 2. Find the value of x in this equation. $log(5x + 2) = log(3x - 1)$

Solution: When the *log*s have the same base: $f(x) = g(x)$, then:
$ln(f(x)) = ln(g(x))$, $log(5x + 2) = log(3x - 1) \Rightarrow 5x + 2 = 3x - 1$. Then:
$5x + 2 - 3x + 1 = 0 \Rightarrow 2x + 3 = 0 \Rightarrow 2x = -3 \Rightarrow x = -\frac{3}{2}$.

Verify Solution: $log\left(5\left(-\frac{3}{2}\right) + 2\right) = log(-5.5)$.

Logarithms of negative numbers are not defined. Therefore, there is no solution for this equation.

Chapter 4: Practices

✎ **Sketch the graph of each function.**

1) $y = 2 \cdot \left(\frac{1}{2}\right)^x$

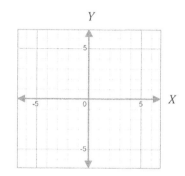

2) $y = 4 \cdot (2)^x$

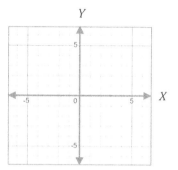

✎ **Solve.**

3) $7^{2x} = 49$

4) $2^{x-4} = 16$

5) $8^{\frac{x}{2}} = 32$

6) $9^{x+1} = 3$

7) $\left(\frac{1}{2}\right)^x = 4$

8) $10^x = 0.01$

9) $4^x = 64$

10) $6^x = 1$

✎ **Graph.**

11) $y = \log_4(x) + 2$

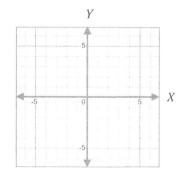

12) $y = \log_2(x - 1)$

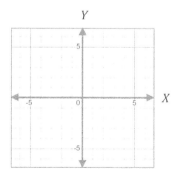

Expand each logarithm.

13) $\log_b(2 \times 9) =$

14) $\log_b(5 \times 7) =$

15) $\log_b(xy) =$

16) $\log_b(2x^2 \times 3y) =$

Evaluate each logarithm.

17) $2 \log_9(9) =$

18) $3 \log_2(8) =$

19) $2 \log_5(125) =$

20) $\log_{100}(1) =$

21) $\log_{10}(100) =$

22) $3 \log_4(16) =$

23) $\frac{1}{2} \log_3(81) =$

24) $\log_7(343) =$

Reduce the following expressions to simplest form.

25) $e^{\ln 4 + \ln 5} =$

26) $e^{\ln\left(\frac{9}{e}\right)} =$

27) $e^{\ln 2 + \ln 7} =$

28) $6 \ln(e^5) =$

Find the value of the variables in each equation.

29) $\log_3 8x = 3 \Rightarrow x =$

30) $\log_4 2x = 5 \Rightarrow x =$

31) $\log_5 5x = 0 \Rightarrow x =$

32) $\log 4x = \log 5 \Rightarrow x =$

Chapter 4: Answers

1)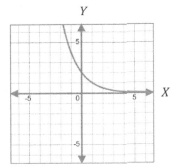

2)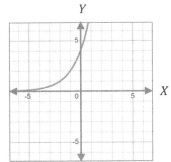

3) 1
4) 8
5) $\frac{10}{3}$
6) $-\frac{1}{2}$

7) -2
8) -2
9) 3
10) 0

11) $y = \log_4(x) + 2$

12) $y = \log_2(x - 1)$

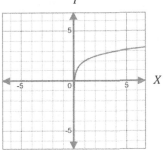

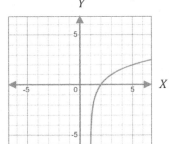

13) $\log_b 2 + 2 \log_b 3$
14) $\log_b 5 + \log_b 7$
15) $\log_b x + \log_b y$
16) $\log_b 6 + 2 \log_b x + \log_b y$
17) 2
18) 9
19) 6
20) 0
21) 2
22) 6

23) 2
24) 3
25) 20
26) $\frac{9}{e}$
27) 14
28) 30
29) $\frac{27}{8}$
30) 512
31) $\frac{1}{5}$
32) $\frac{5}{4}$

Effortless Math Education

CHAPTER
5 Radical and absolute value Functions

Math topics that you'll learn in this chapter:

- ☑ Simplifying Radical Expressions
- ☑ Simplifying Radical Expressions Involving Fractions
- ☑ Adding and Subtracting Radical Expressions
- ☑ Multiplying Radical Expressions
- ☑ Radical Equations
- ☑ Solving Radical Inequalities
- ☑ Radical Functions
- ☑ Graphing Radical Functions
- ☑ Absolute Value Functions
- ☑ Graphing Absolute Value Functions
- ☑ Absolute Value Properties
- ☑ Floor Value
- ☑ Floor Function
- ☑ Graphing Floor Function

Simplifying Radical Expressions

- Find the prime factors of the numbers or expressions inside the radical.
- Use radical properties to simplify the radical expression:

$$\sqrt[n]{x^a} = x^{\frac{a}{n}}, \sqrt[n]{xy} = x^{\frac{1}{n}} \times y^{\frac{1}{n}}, \sqrt[n]{\frac{x}{y}} = \frac{x^{\frac{1}{n}}}{y^{\frac{1}{n}}}, \text{ and } \sqrt[n]{x} \times \sqrt[n]{y} = \sqrt[n]{xy}$$

Examples:

Example 1. Find the square root of $\sqrt{144x^2}$.

Solution: Find the factor of the expression $144x^2$: $144 = 12 \times 12$ and $x^2 = x \times x$.

Now use the radical rule: $\sqrt[n]{a^n} = a$.

Then: $\sqrt{12^2} = 12$ and $\sqrt{x^2} = x$.

Finally:

$\sqrt{144x^2} = \sqrt{12^2} \times \sqrt{x^2} = 12 \times x = 12x$.

Example 2. Write this radical in exponential form. $\sqrt[3]{x^4}$

Solution: To write a radical in exponential form, use this rule: $\sqrt[n]{x^a} = x^{\frac{a}{n}}$.

Then:

$\sqrt[3]{x^4} = x^{\frac{4}{3}}$.

Example 3. Simplify. $\sqrt{8x^3}$

Solution: First factor the expression $8x^3$: $8x^3 = 2^3 \times x \times x \times x$.

We need to find perfect squares: $8x^3 = 2^2 \times 2 \times x^2 \times x = 2^2 \times x^2 \times 2x$.

Then: $\sqrt{8x^3} = \sqrt{2^2 \times x^2} \times \sqrt{2x}$.

Now use the radical rule: $\sqrt[n]{a^n} = a$. Then:

$\sqrt{2^2 \times x^2} \times \sqrt{2x} = 2x \times \sqrt{2x} = 2x\sqrt{2x}$.

Example 4. Simplify. $\sqrt{27a^5b^4}$

Solution: First factor the expression $27a^5b^4$: $27a^5b^4 = 3^3 \times a^5 \times b^4$.

We need to find perfect squares: $27a^5b^4 = 3^2 \times 3 \times a^4 \times a \times b^4$. Then:

$\sqrt{27a^5b^4} = \sqrt{3^2 \times a^4 \times b^4} \times \sqrt{3a}$.

Now use the radical rule: $\sqrt[n]{a^n} = a$. Then:

$\sqrt{3^2 \times a^4 \times b^4} \times \sqrt{3a} = 3 \times a^2 \times b^2 \times \sqrt{3a} = 3a^2b^2\sqrt{3a}$.

Simplifying Radical Expressions Involving Fractions

- Radical expressions cannot be in the denominator. (Number in the bottom)
- To get rid of the radical in the denominator, multiply both the numerator and denominator by the radical in the denominator.
- If there is a radical and another integer in the denominator, multiply both the numerator and denominator by the conjugate of the denominator.
- The conjugate of $a + b$ is $a - b$ and vice versa.

Examples:

Example 1. Simplify. $\frac{2}{\sqrt{3}-2}$

Solution: Multiply by the conjugate:
$\frac{\sqrt{3}+2}{\sqrt{3}+2} \Rightarrow \frac{2}{\sqrt{3}-2} \times \frac{\sqrt{3}+2}{\sqrt{3}+2}$.

Since $(\sqrt{3}-2)(\sqrt{3}+2) = -1$,

Then:
$\frac{2}{\sqrt{3}-2} = \frac{2(\sqrt{3}+2)}{-1}$.

Use the fraction rule:
$\frac{a}{-b} = -\frac{a}{b} \Rightarrow \frac{2(\sqrt{3}+2)}{-1} = -\frac{2(\sqrt{3}+2)}{1} = -2(\sqrt{3}+2)$.

Example 2. Simplify. $\frac{3}{\sqrt{7}-2}$

Solution: Multiply by the conjugate: $\frac{\sqrt{7}+2}{\sqrt{7}+2}$.
$\frac{\sqrt{7}+2}{\sqrt{7}+2} \Rightarrow \frac{3}{\sqrt{7}-2} \times \frac{\sqrt{7}+2}{\sqrt{7}+2}$.

Therefore:
$\frac{3}{\sqrt{7}-2} \times \frac{\sqrt{7}+2}{\sqrt{7}+2} = \frac{3(\sqrt{7}+2)}{3} \Rightarrow \frac{3(\sqrt{7}+2)}{3} = \sqrt{7} + 2$.

Finally:
$\frac{3}{\sqrt{7}-2} = \sqrt{7} + 2$.

Adding and Subtracting Radical Expressions

- Only numbers that have the same radical part can be added or subtracted.
- Remember, combining "unlike" radical terms is not possible.
- For numbers with the same radical part, just add or subtract factors outside the radicals.

Examples:

Example 1. Simplify. $4\sqrt{5} + 3\sqrt{5} =$

Solution: Add like terms:

$4\sqrt{5} + 3\sqrt{5} = 7\sqrt{5}$.

Example 2. Simplify. $2\sqrt{7} + 4\sqrt{7} =$

Solution: Add like terms:

$2\sqrt{7} + 4\sqrt{7} = 6\sqrt{7}$.

Example 3. Simplify. $5\sqrt{3} + 2\sqrt{3} =$

Solution: Add like terms:

$5\sqrt{3} + 2\sqrt{3} = 7\sqrt{3}$.

Example 4. Simplify. $3\sqrt{2} + 2\sqrt{5} + 5\sqrt{2} =$

Solution: Add like terms:

$3\sqrt{2} + 5\sqrt{2} = 8\sqrt{2}$.

Therefore:

$3\sqrt{2} + 2\sqrt{5} + 5\sqrt{2} = 8\sqrt{2} + 2\sqrt{5}$.

Example 5. Simplify. $2\sqrt{3} + \sqrt{3} + 5 =$

Solution: Add like terms:

$2\sqrt{3} + \sqrt{3} = 3\sqrt{3}$.

Therefore:

$2\sqrt{3} + \sqrt{3} + 5 = 3\sqrt{3} + 5$.

Multiplying Radical Expressions

- To multiply radical expressions:
  - Multiply the numbers outside of the radicals.
  - Multiply the numbers inside the radicals.
  - Simplify if needed.

Examples:

Example 1. Evaluate. $\sqrt{16} \times \sqrt{9} =$

Solution: First factor the numbers: $16 = 4^2$ and $9 = 3^2$.

Then:

$\sqrt{16} \times \sqrt{9} = \sqrt{4^2} \times \sqrt{3^2}$.

Now use the radical rule: $\sqrt[n]{a^n} = a$.

Then:

$\sqrt{4^2} \times \sqrt{3^2} = 4 \times 3 = 12$.

Example 2. Evaluate. $2\sqrt{5} \times 3\sqrt{2} =$

Solution: Multiply the numbers: $2 \times 3 = 6$.

$2\sqrt{5} \times 3\sqrt{2} = 6\sqrt{5}\sqrt{2}$.

Use the radical rule:

$\sqrt{a}\sqrt{b} = \sqrt{ab} \Rightarrow 6\sqrt{5}\sqrt{2} = 6\sqrt{5 \times 2} = 6\sqrt{10}$.

Example 3. Evaluate. $5\sqrt{12a^3b^3} \cdot \sqrt{3ab^2}$

Solution: First multiply the expression inside the radicals:

$12a^3b^3 \times 3ab^2 = 36a^4b^5$.

Now factor the expression:

$36a^4b^5 = 3^2 \times 2^2 \times a^4 \times b^5$.

We need to find the perfect square: $36a^4b^5 = 3^2 \times 2^2 \times a^4 \times b^4 \times b$.

Therefore: $\sqrt{12a^3b^3} \cdot \sqrt{3ab^2} = \sqrt{36a^4b^5} = \sqrt{3^2 \times 2^2 \times a^4 \times b^4 \times b} = 6a^2b^2\sqrt{b}$.

Finally:

$5\sqrt{12a^3b^3} \cdot \sqrt{3ab^2} = 30a^2b^2\sqrt{b}$.

Radical Equations

- Isolate the radical on one side of the equation.
- Square both sides of the equation to remove the radical.
- Solve the equation for the variable.
- Plugin the answer into the original equation to avoid extraneous values.

Examples:

Example 1. Solve. $\sqrt{x} - 8 = 12$

Solution: Add 8 to both sides:

$\sqrt{x} - 8 + 8 = 12 + 8 \Rightarrow \sqrt{x} = 20.$

Square both sides:

$(\sqrt{x})^2 = 20^2 \Rightarrow x = 400.$

Example 2. Solve. $\sqrt{x + 2} = 6$

Solution: Square both sides:

$(\sqrt{x+2})^2 = 6^2 \Rightarrow x + 2 = 36.$

Subtract 2 to both sides:

$x + 2 - 2 = 36 - 2 \Rightarrow x = 34.$

Example 3. Solve. $2\sqrt{x - 5} + 1 = 4$

Solution: Subtract 1 to both sides:

$2\sqrt{x-5} + 1 - 1 = 4 - 1 \Rightarrow 2\sqrt{x-5} = 3.$

Divide 2 to both sides:

$(2\sqrt{x-5}) \div 2 = 3 \div 2 \Rightarrow \sqrt{x-5} = \frac{3}{2}.$

Square both sides:

$(\sqrt{x-5})^2 = \left(\frac{3}{2}\right)^2 \Rightarrow x - 5 = \frac{9}{4} \Rightarrow x = \frac{29}{4}.$

Solving Radical Inequalities

- Radical inequality is an inequality that contains rational expressions.
- To solve a radical inequality, follow these steps:
  Step 1: Step1: Write radical expressions on one side of the inequality and other expressions on the other side.
  Step 2: Step2: Raise both sides of the inequality to the power equal to the index of the radical.
  Step 3: Step3: Simplify the obtained inequality and solve.
- You can solve radical inequalities by graphing.

Examples:

Example 1. Solve: $2\sqrt[3]{1-x} - 3 \geq 0$.

Solution: First, rewrite the inequality as follows:
$2\sqrt[3]{1-x} - 3 \geq 0 \Rightarrow 2\sqrt[3]{1-x} \geq 3 \Rightarrow \sqrt[3]{1-x} \geq \frac{3}{2}$.

Raise both sides of the inequality to the power of 3:
$\sqrt[3]{1-x} \geq \frac{3}{2} \Rightarrow (\sqrt[3]{1-x})^3 \geq (\frac{3}{2})^3 \Rightarrow 1-x \geq \frac{27}{8}$.

Simplify and solve: $1 - x \geq \frac{27}{8} \Rightarrow 1 - \frac{27}{8} \geq x \Rightarrow x \leq -\frac{19}{8}$.

The final answer to this problem is $\left(-\infty, -\frac{19}{8}\right]$.

Example 2. Solve: $1 - \sqrt{x+3} < 0$.

Solution: First, rewrite the inequality as follows:
$1 - \sqrt{x+3} < 0 \Rightarrow 1 < \sqrt{x+3} \Rightarrow \sqrt{x+3} > 1$.

Raise both sides of the inequality to the power of 2:
$\sqrt{x+3} > 1 \Rightarrow (\sqrt{x+3})^2 > (1)^2 \Rightarrow x + 3 > 1$.

Simplify and solve: $x + 3 > 1 \Rightarrow x > -2$. On the other hand, for a radical expression with an even index in the form $\sqrt[2k]{f(x)}$ where $k \in N$, is $f(x) \geq 0$. It means that:

$x + 3 \geq 0 \Rightarrow x \geq -3$.

The final answer to this problem is $(-2, +\infty) \cap [-3, +\infty) = (-2, +\infty)$.

Radical Functions

Radical functions of the form $f(x) = \sqrt[n]{g(x)}$ involve an nth root (a radical) of a function $g(x)$. Here, n represents the degree of the root (square root, cube root, etc.), and $g(x)$ can be any real-valued function. For the function $f(x) = \sqrt[n]{g(x)}$, "n" is the index of the root, and "$g(x)$" is the radicand.

- **Domain**: The domain of the function depends on both the index "n" and the radicand "$g(x)$":
  - If "n" is even, $g(x) \geq 0$, meaning the radicand must be non-negative.
  - If "n" is odd, there's no restriction, so $g(x)$ can be any real number.
- **Range**:
  - For even roots (e.g., square roots, fourth roots), if $g(x) \geq 0$, then $f(x) \geq 0$.
  - For odd roots (e.g., cube roots), the range is all real numbers.
- To find the domain of the function, find all possible values of the variable inside radical.
- To find the range, plugin the minimum and maximum values of the variable inside radical.

Examples:

Example 1. What is the domain of the function $f(x) = \sqrt{x^2 - 4}$?

Solution: The radicand, $x^2 - 4$, must be non-negative. Therefore, $x^2 - 4 \geq 0 \Rightarrow x^2 \geq 4$. This means $x \leq -2$ or $x \geq 2$. The domain is $(-\infty, -2] \cup [2, \infty)$.

Example 2. Determine the domain of $g(x) = \sqrt[3]{x^3 - x - 6}$.

Solution: Since it's a cube root (odd degree), the domain is all real numbers because the radicand can take any value.

Example 3. Find the domain and range of the radical function.
$$y = 3\sqrt{2x - 3} + 1$$

Solution: For the domain, find non-negative values for radicals: $2x - 3 \geq 0$. The domain of functions: $2x - 3 \geq 0 \Rightarrow 2x \geq 3 \Rightarrow x \geq \frac{3}{2}$.
Domain of the function $y = 3\sqrt{2x - 3} + 1$: $x \geq \frac{3}{2}$.

For the range, the range of a radical function of the form $c\sqrt{ax + b} + k$ is: $f(x) \geq k$.
For the function $y = 3\sqrt{2x - 3} + 1$, the value of k is 1. Then: $f(x) \geq 1$. Range of the function $y = 3\sqrt{2x - 3} + 1$: $f(x) \geq 1$.

Graphing Radical Functions

- Radical functions of the form $f(x) = \sqrt[n]{g(x)}$, those involving roots, can be graphed by understanding the behavior of the function based on its degree and radicand.
    - The index "n" determines the degree: if "n" is even (like square roots), the function will only produce non-negative outputs. If "n" is odd (like cube roots), the function can produce both positive and negative outputs.
    - The radicand "$g(x)$" determines the domain of the function. If "n" is even, $g(x) \geq 0$. If "n" is odd, there's no domain restriction for "$g(x)$".
- **Steps for Graphing**:
  Step 1: Find the domain.
  Step 2: Identify key points, particularly where $g(x) = 0$ since those give x −intercepts.
  Step 3: Plot the points and sketch the graph. For even roots, the curve typically starts from a point and rises, while for odd roots, it can cross the x −axis.
- The graph's basic shape is influenced by the radical, but it may be transformed based on the behavior of $g(x)$.
- Like other functions, radical functions of this form can undergo transformations such as shifts, stretches, and reflections based on the inner function $g(x)$.

Examples:

Example 1. Graph $f(x) = \sqrt{x}$.
Solution: The domain is $x \geq 0$. For key points: $f(0) = 0, f(1) = 1, f(4) = 2$, etc. Plot these points and sketch a curve rising to the right.

Example 2. Graph $g(x) = \sqrt[3]{x}$.
Solution: There's no domain restriction. For key points: $g(-1) = -1, g(0) = 0, g(1) = 1$. Plot and sketch.

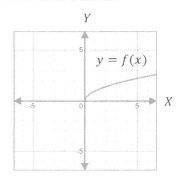
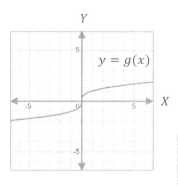

Absolute Value Functions

- Absolute value functions in the form $f(x) = |g(x)|$ measure the "distance" a number has from zero, regardless of its sign. When the function $g(x)$ is nested inside an absolute value, the resulting graph and properties exhibit unique traits due to the nature of the absolute value.
    - **Domain**: The domain of $f(x) = |g(x)|$ is the same as that of $g(x)$, as the absolute value doesn't restrict input values.
    - **Range**: Since absolute values are always non-negative, the minimum value of $f(x) = |g(x)|$ is always 0, unless there's a vertical shift.
    - **Graph Transformations**: The portion of $g(x)$ below the $x-$axis is reflected to lie above. Other transformations of $g(x)$ also affect $f(x)$.
    - **Intercepts and Behavior**: The $x-$intercepts of $f(x)$ are the same as $g(x)$, but $y-$intercepts can differ.
- The function $f(x) = |g(x)|$ takes the values of $g(x)$ and makes them non-negative, creating a characteristic "V" or "W" shape, depending on $g(x)$. The behavior, transformations, and other attributes are dictated by both the absolute value and the inner function $g(x)$. Understanding their interplay is vital for analyzing and graphing such functions.

Examples:

Example 1. What is the range of $f(x) = |x^2 - 4|$?

Solution: The minimum value of $x^2 - 4$ is -4. Because the domain of the function $g(x) = x^2 - 4$ is all real numbers. It means that $x^2 \geq 0$. So $x^2 - 4 \geq -4$. It means that the range of the function $g(x)$ is $\{-4, +\infty)$. Since the absolute value makes it positive. Thus, the range is $[0, +\infty)$.

Example 2. Find the $x-$intercepts of $f(x) = |x^3 - x^2 - 4x|$.

Solution: The $x-$intercepts occur where $g(x) = 0$. So, $x^3 - x^2 - 2x = 0 \Rightarrow x(x^2 - x - 2) = 0$. Thus, $x = 0, -1, 2$.

Example 3. Describe the behavior of $f(x) = |x(x - 3)(x + 2)|$ as x approaches $+\infty$ and $-\infty$.

Solution: As $x \to +\infty$, the expression inside the absolute value becomes positive, hence $f(x) \to +\infty$. As $x \to -\infty$, the expression inside the absolute value becomes negative, but due to the absolute value, $f(x) \to +\infty$.

Graphing Absolute Value Functions

- The absolute value function in the form $f(x) = |g(x)|$ transforms the output of $g(x)$ such that all negative values become positive. Graphically, this operation reflects portions of the graph below the x-axis to above the x-axis.
  - The absolute value function acts as a "mirror" for values of $g(x)$ that are negative.
  - The points where $g(x) = 0$ are crucial, as they serve as "hinge" or "corner" points for the absolute value graph.
- **Steps for Graphing:**
  Step 1: Sketch or identify the graph of $g(x)$.
  Step 2: Find points where $g(x) = 0$. These are the x-values where the graph of $f(x)$ will have corners.
  Step 3: For portions of $g(x)$ that are below the x-axis, reflect them above the x-axis to get the graph of $f(x) = |g(x)|$.

Examples:

Example 1. Graph $f(x) = |x|$.
Solution: The function $g(x) = x$ is a straight line passing through the origin. Since it's already non-negative for all x, the graph of $f(x)$ is identical to $g(x)$ for $x \geq 0$. For $x < 0$, the graph is reflected upwards, resulting in a V-shaped graph.

Example 2. Graph $h(x) = |x - 2|$.
Solution: First, graph $g(x) = x - 2$, a line with a y-intercept of -2 and slope of 1. The "hinge" point is at $x = 2$. For $x > 2$, $h(x) = g(x)$. For $x < 2$, reflect $g(x)$ above the x-axis.

Example 3. Graph $k(x) = |x^2 - 4|$.
Solution: The parabola $g(x) = x^2 - 4$ intersects the x-axis at $x = -2$ and $x = 2$. Since the parabola is above the x-axis everywhere except between these points, only the segment between -2 and 2 gets reflected upwards.

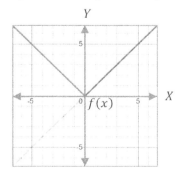
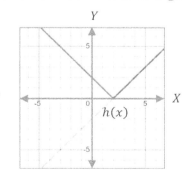
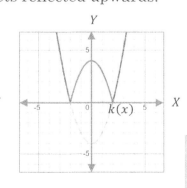

Absolute Value Properties

- The absolute value of a real number is its distance from zero on the number line, irrespective of its sign. It is denoted by $|x|$, where x is a real number.
  - $|x| \geq 0$ for all real x.
  - $|x| = x$ if $x \geq 0$ and $|x| = -x$ if $x < 0$.
  - $|-x| = |x|$ for all real x.
  - $|xy| = |x| \cdot |y|$ for all real x and y.
  - $\left|\dfrac{x}{y}\right| = \dfrac{|x|}{|y|}$ for all real x and y (with $y \neq 0$).
  - The Triangle Inequality: $|x + y| \leq |x| + |y|$ for all real x and y.
- The absolute value function captures the inherent "positivity" of numbers. Whether used in equations, inequalities, or functions, understanding its properties is essential for simplifying expressions, solving problems, and graphing.

Examples:

Example 1. Evaluate $|7|$ and $|-7|$.
Solution: $|7| = 7$ and $|-7| = 7$.

Example 2. Simplify $|3 \cdot (-5)|$.
Solution: Using property $|xy| = |x| \cdot |y|$. So, we get:
$$|3 \cdot (-5)| = |3| \cdot |-5| = 3 \cdot 5 = 15$$

Example 3. If $x = -4$ and $y = 6$, find $|x + y|$.
Solution: First, put the given value in the expression $|x + y|$. So, we have:
$$|x + y| = |(-4) + 6| = |-4 + 6| = |2| = 2$$

Example 4. For $x = -3$ and $y = 4$, prove the Triangle Inequality.
Solution: Using the Triangle Inequality: $|x + y| \leq |x| + |y|$. Plug the given value in the inequality. Next,
$$|x + y| = |(-3) + 4| = 1,$$
$$|x| + |y| = |-3| + |4| = 3 + 4 = 7.$$
Clearly, $|x + y| \leq |x| + |y|$, because $(1 \leq 7)$.

Floor Value

- In mathematics, when we want to round down to the nearest integer, we use the floor function. This function provides a way to represent the greatest integer that is less than or equal to a given value.
- **Definition**: For any real number x, the floor function, denoted by $\lfloor x \rfloor$, is defined as the largest integer less than or equal to x.
- **Properties**:
  - **Idempotence**: For any integer n, $\lfloor n \rfloor = n$.
  - **Additivity with integers**: For any real number x and any integer n, $\lfloor x + n \rfloor = \lfloor x \rfloor + n$.
  - **Floor of negative values**: $\lfloor -x \rfloor = -\lceil x + 1 \rceil$, where $\lceil x \rceil$ is the ceiling of x.
- In summary, the floor function offers a systematic way to round down real numbers. Its properties are fundamental in both theoretical mathematics and practical applications, especially in computer science.

Examples:

Example 1. What is the floor value of $\lfloor -5 \rfloor$?
Solution: -5 is an integer number. Since, for any integer n, $\lfloor n \rfloor = n$, we get: $\lfloor -5 \rfloor = -5$.

Example 2. What is the floor value of 3.72?
Solution: $\lfloor 3.72 \rfloor = 3$

Example 3. What is the floor value of -2.8?
Solution: $\lfloor -2.8 \rfloor = -3$

Example 4. Find $\lfloor 2.5 + 3 \rfloor$.
Solution: Using the property $\lfloor x + n \rfloor = \lfloor x \rfloor + n$, we get:
$$\lfloor 2.5 + 3 \rfloor = \lfloor 2.5 \rfloor + 3 = 2 + 3 = 5$$

Example 5. If $x = 4.9$, evaluate $\lfloor -x \rfloor$.
Solution: Using the property $\lfloor -x \rfloor = -\lceil x + 1 \rceil$, and substitute the value of x in the expression, we have: $\lfloor -4.9 \rfloor = -\lceil 4.9 + 1 \rceil = -\lceil 5.9 \rceil = -5$

Chapter 5: Radical and absolute value Functions

Floor Function

- The floor function in the Form $f(x) = a[g(x - b)] + k$, represented as $[x]$, is a fundamental function in mathematics that rounds a real number down to the nearest integer. When combined with linear transformations, it creates a variety of patterns and shifts in its graph.
- **Definition**: Given a function in the form $f(x) = a[g(x - b)] + k$:
  - a represents a vertical stretch or compression.
  - b represents a horizontal shift.
  - k represents a vertical shift.
- **Domain**: The domain of $f(x) = a[g(x - b)] + k$ is the domain of $g(x)$ since the floor function can handle any real number input.
- **Range**: The range of the floor function will depend on the nature of $g(x)$. If $g(x)$ is a continuous function spanning all real numbers (like a line or a parabola), the range of $f(x)$ will typically be all integers (due to the floor function) multiplied by the factor of a. But keep in mind the vertical shifts by k.

Examples:

Example 1. Given $f(x) = 2[x - 1] + 3$, determine the value at $x = 3.5$.

Solution: Plug 3.5 in the function equation and simplify. So, we have:

$x = 3.5 \Rightarrow f(3.5) = 2[3.5 - 1] + 3 = 2[2.5] + 3 = 2(2) + 3 = 7$.

Example 2. Determine the domain and range for $f(x) = -[x + 2] - 1$.

Solution: Domain: $(-\infty, \infty)$.

Range: As $g(x) = x + 2$ is linear and covers all real numbers, the range of the floor function is all integers. When multiplied by -1 and subtracting 1, the range remains all integers.

Example 3. Determine the domain and range for $h(x) = [x^2] + 1$.

Solution: Domain: $(-\infty, \infty)$.

Range: As $k(x) = x^2$ is quadratic and covers all nonnegative real numbers, the range of the floor function is all nonnegative integers. When adding 1, the range is all integers greater than 1.

EffortlessMath.com

Graphing Floor Function

- Graphing the floor function in the Form $f(x) = a[g(x - b)] + k$, particularly when combined with transformations, offers a visually insightful look into how rounding down operations interact with linear shifts, stretches, and compressions.
- **Definitions**:
  - **Floor Function** $[x]$: This is the greatest integer less than or equal to x.
  - a: This represents a vertical stretch (if $a > 1$) or compression (if $0 < a < 1$). If a is negative, it also represents a reflection across the x-axis.
  - b: Represents a horizontal shift. The graph shifts to the right if b is positive and to the left if b is negative.
  - k: Represents a vertical shift. The graph shifts upward for positive k and downward for negative k.
- **Steps to Graph** $f(x) = a[g(x - b)] + k$:
  Step 1: Start by plotting the function $y = g(x)$ without the floor operation.
  Step 2: Apply the floor operation to $g(x)$. This will create horizontal step patterns where each "step" represents an integer value.
  Step 3: Apply the vertical transformation a. This will stretch or compress the height of the steps.
  Step 4: Shift the graph horizontally by b.
  Step 5: Apply the vertical shift k to move the entire function up or down.
- **Note**: The floor function creates a non-continuous graph, with jumps at each integer value. When graphing, it's important to note that the left endpoint of each "step" is included, while the right endpoint is open (not included). This distinction is often represented with a filled dot on the left endpoint and an open circle on the right endpoint for each step.

Example:

Graph the function $f(x) = 2[x - 1] + 3$.
Solution: Begin draw the function $y = x$. Next with the base function $y = [x]$, which has steps of height 1 at every integer. The term $2[x - 1]$ stretches the graph vertically by a factor of 2 and shifts it to the right by 1 unit. The addition of 3 then shifts the entire graph up by 3 units.

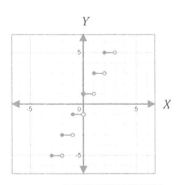

Chapter 5: Practices

✍ Simplify.

1) $\sqrt{256y} =$

2) $\sqrt{900} =$

3) $\sqrt{144a^2b} =$

4) $\sqrt{36 \times 9} =$

✍ Simplify.

5) $3\sqrt{5} + 2\sqrt{5} =$

6) $6\sqrt{3} + 4\sqrt{27} =$

7) $5\sqrt{2} + 10\sqrt{18} =$

8) $7\sqrt{2} - 5\sqrt{8} =$

✍ Evaluate.

9) $\sqrt{5} \times \sqrt{3} =$

10) $\sqrt{6} \times \sqrt{8} =$

11) $3\sqrt{5} \times \sqrt{9} =$

12) $2\sqrt{3} \times 3\sqrt{7} =$

✍ Simplify.

13) $\frac{1}{\sqrt{3}-6} =$

14) $\frac{5}{\sqrt{2}+7} =$

15) $\frac{\sqrt{3}}{1-\sqrt{6}} =$

16) $\frac{2}{\sqrt{3}+5} =$

✍ Solve for x.

17) $\sqrt{x} + 2 = 9$

18) $3 + \sqrt{x} = 12$

19) $\sqrt{x} + 5 = 30$

20) $\sqrt{x} - 9 = 27$

21) $10 = \sqrt{x+1}$

22) $\sqrt{x+4} = 3$

✍ Solve.

23) $3\sqrt{x} - 4 \geq 5$

24) $1 - \sqrt{x+8} < 0$

25) $\sqrt{x-5} < 3$

26) $4\sqrt{x} + 6 \leq 8$

27) $\sqrt[3]{x-3} \leq 6$

28) $-3\sqrt[3]{x+2} \leq 12$

Effortless Math Education

Identify the domain and range of each function.

29) $y = \sqrt{x+2} - 1$

30) $y = \sqrt{x+1}$

31) $y = \sqrt{x-4}$

32) $y = \sqrt{x-3} + 1$

Graph the functions below.

33) $y = \sqrt{x} + 3$

34) $y = 2\sqrt{x-5} + 4$

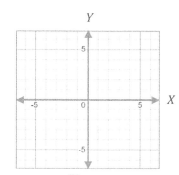
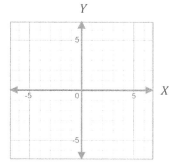

35) $y = -\sqrt{x}$

36) $y = \sqrt{x^2 - 4}$

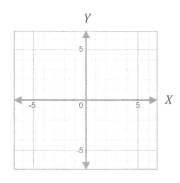
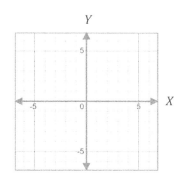

Find the domain and range of functions.

37) $y = |x+2| + |x-2|$

38) $y = |x^3 - 1| + 1$

39) $y = |x^2 - 4| - 2$

40) $y = \left|\dfrac{1}{x}\right|$

41) $y = |2x| - 3$

42) $y = 1 - |x|$

Effortless Math Education

Sketch the graphs.

43) $y = |x - 3|$

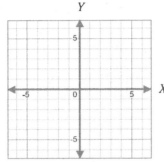

44) $y = -|x|$

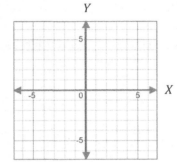

45) $y = 2|x + 1| - 3$

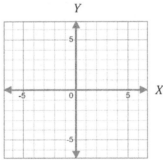

46) $y = |x^2 - 4|$

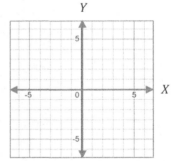

47) $y = |x - 1| + |x + 2|$

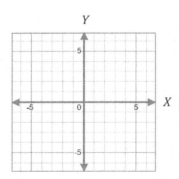

48) $y = |x^3 - x^2 - 6x|$

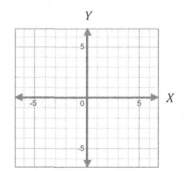

Solve for x.

49) $|x + 3| + |x - 3| = 10$

50) $|x^2 - 4| = 0$

51) $3|2x + 4| = 12$

52) $|2x - 1| = 5$

🔖 Evaluate.

53) $[4.7] - 4.7$

54) $[-2.3] + [2.3]$

55) $2[4.3 - 1]$

56) $[5 \times 0.7]$

🔖 Solve for x.

57) $[x + 1] = 2$

58) $[(x - 1)^2] = 0$

🔖 Find the domain and range of the functions.

59) $f(x) = 2[x - 1] + 1$

60) $g(x) = [x] - 1$

61) $k(x) = [x^2]$

62) $h(x) = -[x^2 + 1]$

🔖 Graph the functions.

63) $y = -\left[\dfrac{x^2}{16}\right] + 2$

64) $y = 2[x + 1] - 2$

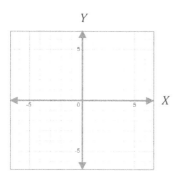

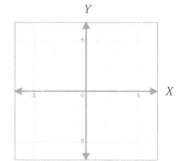

Chapter 5: Answers

1) $16\sqrt{y}$

2) 30

3) $12a\sqrt{b}$

4) 18

5) $5\sqrt{5}$

6) $18\sqrt{3}$

7) $35\sqrt{2}$

8) $-3\sqrt{2}$

9) $\sqrt{15}$

10) $4\sqrt{3}$

11) $9\sqrt{5}$

12) $6\sqrt{21}$

13) $-\frac{\sqrt{3}+9}{33}$

14) $-\frac{5(\sqrt{2}-7)}{47}$

15) $-\frac{\sqrt{3}+3\sqrt{2}}{5}$

16) $-\frac{\sqrt{3}-5}{11}$

17) $x = 49$

18) $x = 81$

19) $x = 625$

20) $x = 1,296$

21) $x = 99$

22) $x = 5$

23) $x \geq 9$

24) $x > -7$

25) $5 \leq x < 14$

26) $0 \leq x \leq \frac{1}{4}$

27) $x \leq 219$

28) $x \geq -66$

29) $x \geq -2, f(x) \geq -1$

30) $x \geq -1, f(x) \geq 0$

31) $x \geq 4, f(x) \geq 0$

32) $x \geq 3, f(x) \geq 1$

Effortless Math Education

33)
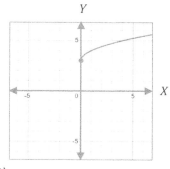

34)
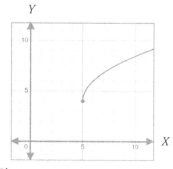

35)
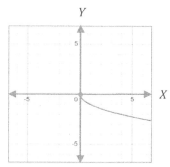

36)
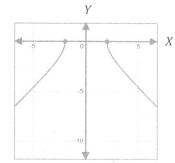

37) Domain: $\mathbb{R}$

Range: $[4, +\infty)$

38) Domain: $\mathbb{R}$

Range: $[1, +\infty)$

39) Domain: $\mathbb{R}$

Range: $[-2, +\infty)$

40) Domain: $\mathbb{R} - \{0\}$

Range: $(0, +\infty)$

41) Domain: $\mathbb{R}$

Range: $[-3, +\infty)$

42) Domain: $\mathbb{R}$

Range: $(-\infty, 1]$

Chapter 5: Radical and absolute value Functions

43)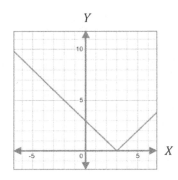

44)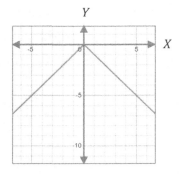

45)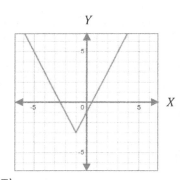

46)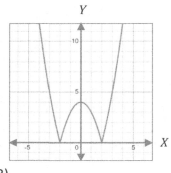

47)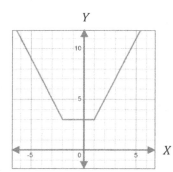

48)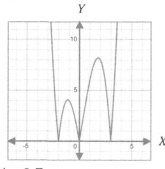

49) −5 and 5

50) −2 and 2

51) −4 and 0

52) −2 and 3

53) −0.7

54) −1

55) 6

56) 3

57) [1,2]

58) $[1,2)$

59) $\{x|x = 2n + 1, n \in \mathbb{Z}\}$

60) $\{x \in \mathbb{Z}|x \geq 0\}$

61) $\mathbb{Z}$

62) $\{x \in \mathbb{Z}|x \leq 0\}$

63)
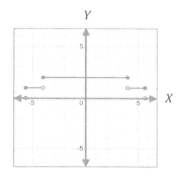

64)
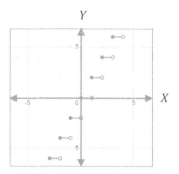

CHAPTER 6
Functions Operations

Math topics that you'll learn in this chapter:

- ☑ Positive, Negative, Increasing and Decreasing Functions
- ☑ Transformations of Functions
- ☑ Function Symmetry: Even and Odd
- ☑ End Behavior of Polynomial Functions
- ☑ One-to-One Function
- ☑ Identifying the function one by one from the graph
- ☑ Identifying functions one by one from the equation of the function
- ☑ Onto (Surjective) Functions
- ☑ Function Inverses
- ☑ Inverse Function Graph
- ☑ Inverse Variation
- ☑ Piecewise-defined Functions

Positive, Negative, Increasing and Decreasing Functions on Intervals

- For the function $f(x)$ over an arbitrary interval I:
  - f is called positive if for every x in the interval I, $f(x) > 0$. (Above the $x-$axis)
  - f is called negative if for every x in the interval I, $f(x) < 0$. (Under the $x-$axis)
- For the given function f, consider the points x and y in an arbitrary open interval of the domain. in this case:
  - The function f is increasing if for every $x < y$ in the interval, $f(x) \leq f(y)$.
  - The function f is decreasing if for every $x < y$ in the interval, $f(x) \geq f(y)$.
  - The function f is constant if for every $x < y$ in the interval, $f(x) = f(y) = C$, such that C is a constant number.

Example:

According to the graph, determine in which intervals the function is positive, negative, increasing, or decreasing.

Solution: Considering the graph, you see that:

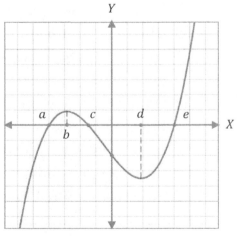

- For $(-\infty, a)$ and (c, e), the graph is under the $x-$axis. So, the function corresponding to the graph is negative.
- For (a, c) and $(e, +\infty)$, the graph is above the $x-$axis. So, the function is positive.
- Since the values of the function increase in the intervals $(-\infty, b)$ and $(d, +\infty)$, the corresponding function of the graph is increasing in each interval.

In the interval (b, d), the function is decreasing.

Transformations of Functions

- The parent function is the simplest form of representation of any function without transformations.

- The most important parent functions include constant, linear, absolute-value, polynomials, rational, radical, exponential, and logarithmic functions.

- For the function $f(x)$ and constant number $k > 0$, the transformations of functions in which the properties of the parent function are preserved is as follows:

$y = f(x) + k$	$y = f(x - k)$	$y = -f(x)$
If $k > 0$, shifted to the up. If $k < 0$, shifted to the down.	If $k > 0$, shifted to the right. If $k < 0$, shifted to the left.	is symmetric to the function $y = f(x)$ with respect to the x-axis.
$y = kf(x)$	$y = f(kx)$	$y = f(-x)$
If $k > 1$, $f(x)$ is stretch vertically. If $0 < k < 1$, $f(x)$ is compressed vertically.	If $k > 1$, $f(x)$ is compressed horizontally. If $0 < k < 1$, $f(x)$ is stretch horizontally.	is symmetric to the function $y = f(x)$ with respect to the y-axis.

Example:

What is the parent graph of the following function and what transformations have taken place on it: $y = 2x^2 - 1$.

Solution: We know that the graph $y = f(x) + k$; $k < 0$, is shifted k units to the down of the graph $y = f(x)$. Then, $y = 2x^2 - 1$, is shifted 1 unit down of the graph $y = 2x^2$.

On the other hand, $y = kf(x)$; $k > 1$ is stretched vertically then the function $y = x^2$ is stretched vertically by a factor of 2. Clearly, you can see that the function $y = x^2$ is the parent function of $y = 2x^2 - 1$.

Function Symmetry: Even and Odd

- A function f, is called even if $f(-x) = f(x)$ for all values of x in the domain of the function.
- A function f, is called odd if $f(-x) = -f(x)$ for all values of x in the domain of the function.
- An even function is symmetric relative to the x-axis and an odd function is relative to the coordinate center.

Examples:

Example 1. Identify whether the following function is even, odd, or neither:
$$f(x) = -2x^3$$
Solution: For this, it is enough to put $-x$ in the equation of the function and simplify: $f(-x) = -2(-x)^3 = -2(-x^3) = 2x^3 \Rightarrow f(-x) = -f(x)$.
This means that the function is odd.

Example 2. Identify whether the following function is even, odd, or neither:
$$g(x) = x^4 - 4x^2 + 1$$
Solution: Put $-x$ in the equation of $g(x)$:
$g(-x) = (-x)^4 - 4(-x)^2 + 1 = x^4 - 4x^2 + 1$.
Since $g(-x) = g(x)$, therefore, this function is even.

Example 3. According to the graph, determine whether the function is even, odd, or neither.

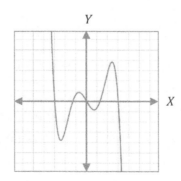

Solution: Considering that the graph is symmetric relative to the coordinate center (or in other words, relative to the x-axis and the y-axis), therefore the function corresponding to this graph is odd.

End Behavior of Polynomial Functions

- Let P be a polynomial function in the general form:
$$P(x) = a_n x^n + a_{n-1} x^{n-1} + \cdots + a_1 x + a_0.$$
- The domain of $P(x)$ is all real numbers and is continuous for any value of x.
- The end behavior of $P(x)$ is according to the following table:

End behavior of polynomial function $P(x) = a_n x^n + \cdots$		
If	$a_n > 0$	$a_n < 0$
n is even	$P(x) \to +\infty$, as $x \to +\infty$ $P(x) \to +\infty$, as $x \to -\infty$	$P(x) \to -\infty$, as $x \to +\infty$ $P(x) \to -\infty$, as $x \to -\infty$
n is odd	$P(x) \to +\infty$, as $x \to +\infty$ $P(x) \to -\infty$, as $x \to -\infty$	$P(x) \to -\infty$, as $x \to +\infty$ $P(x) \to +\infty$, as $x \to -\infty$

Examples:

Example 1. Find the end behavior of the function $f(x) = -x^4 + 3x^3 - x$.

Solution: The degree of the function is even, and the coefficient of the term with the largest degree is negative. Thus, the end behavior is:

$f(x) \to -\infty$, as $x \to +\infty$

$f(x) \to -\infty$, as $x \to -\infty$

The graph of the polynomial function $f(x)$ is as follows.

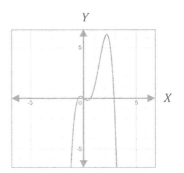

Example 2. Find the end behavior of the function $g(x) = 2x^5 - 3x^3 + x^2 - 2$.

Solution: The degree of the function is odd, and the coefficient of the term with the largest degree is positive. So, the end behavior is:

$g(x) \to +\infty$, as $x \to +\infty$

$g(x) \to -\infty$, as $x \to -\infty$

The graph of the polynomial function $g(x)$ is as follows.

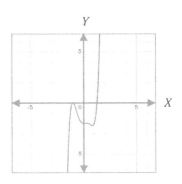

One-to-One Function

- In mathematics, a one-to-one function, also known as an injective function, is a function where every element in the domain is mapped to a unique element in the codomain. That is, if $f(x) = f(y)$, then $x = y$.
- This property ensures that no two elements of the domain share the same image in the codomain.
- Injective functions can be visualized using vectors. In the context of vectors, a one-to-one function maps every vector in the domain to a unique vector in the codomain.
- A function that is not one-to-one has at least two elements in the domain that share the same image in the codomain. In other words, there exist a and b in the domain such that $a \neq b$ but $f(a) = f(b)$.
- One-to-one functions are crucial in mathematics and its applications because they guarantee unique mapping from the domain to the codomain. They are used in solving equations, analyzing functions, and establishing one-to-one correspondence between sets.

Examples:

Example 1. Consider the function $f(x) = 2x + 3$. Is this a one-to-one function?
Solution: Assume $f(a) = f(b)$, where a and b are elements in the domain. Then $2a + 3 = 2b + 3$. Subtracting 3 from both sides gives $2a = 2b$, and dividing both sides by 2 results in $a = b$.
Since our assumption leads to $a = b$, the function is one-to-one.

Example 2. Determine whether the function $g(x) = x^2$ is a one-to-one function.
Solution: Let's assume $g(a) = g(b)$, where a and b are elements in the domain. Then $a^2 = b^2$. Taking the square root of both sides results in $|a| = |b|$.
Since the absolute values of a and b are equal, we cannot conclude that $a = b$. Therefore, the function is not one-to-one.

Identifying the Function One-by-One from the Graph

- Identifying whether a function is one-to-one (injective) from its graph is a crucial skill. A function is one-to-one if every element in the domain is mapped to a unique element in the codomain. Graphically, a function is one-to-one if no horizontal line intersects the graph of the function more than once. This property is known as the Horizontal Line Test.
- Vectors can also be used to represent functions, and their graphs can be analyzed to determine whether they are one-to-one.
- The Horizontal Line Test is a quick and visual way to determine whether a function is one-to-one by analyzing its graph. If no horizontal line intersects the graph more than once, the function is one-to-one.
- A function can be both one-to-one (injective) and onto (surjective). Such a function is called a bijection, meaning it establishes a one-to-one correspondence between the elements of the domain and codomain.

Examples:

Example 1. Consider the function $f(x) = x^3$. Is this function one-to-one based on its graph?

Solution: The graph of $f(x) = x^3$ is a cubic curve that passes the Horizontal Line Test, as no horizontal line intersects the graph more than once. Therefore, the function is one-to-one.

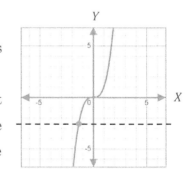

Example 2. Analyze the function $g(x) = x^2$ based on its graph to determine if it is one-to-one.

Solution: The graph of $g(x) = x^2$ is a parabola opening upwards. A horizontal line intersects the graph at two points when drawn above the x-axis, failing the Horizontal Line Test. Therefore, the function is not one-to-one.

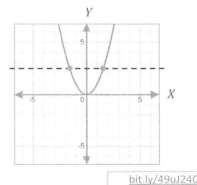

Onto (Surjective) Functions

- In the study of functions, knowing whether a function covers every possible output value in its codomain is vital. Such functions are termed as "onto" or "surjective". This concept can be further refined when considering specific intervals.
- **Definitions**:
  - **Onto (Surjective) Function**: A function $f: A \to B$ is said to be onto (or surjective) if every element y in the codomain B has a pre-image in the domain A, i.e., there exists an x in A such that $f(x) = y$.
  - **Onto on an Interval**: A function is said to be onto on an interval if, for every output value in the codomain, there exists at least one corresponding input value from that specific interval.
- **Note that**:
  - Not every function is onto. For a function to be onto, its range and codomain must be identical.
  - When analyzing whether a function is onto on an interval, it's essential to restrict the domain to that interval and then determine the range.

Examples:

Example 1. Is the function $f(x) = x^2$ from the set of real numbers to the set of real numbers an onto function?

Solution: No, because there's no real number x for which $f(x)$ gives a negative number as the output. Therefore, f doesn't cover all of its codomain and is not surjective.

Example 2. Consider the function $g(x) = x^3$ from real numbers to real numbers. Is it onto?

Solution: Yes, for every real number y, there exists a real number x such that $g(x) = y$. For instance, for $y = 8$, $x = 2$ since $2^3 = 8$.

Example 3. Is the function $f(x) = x^2$ onto on the interval $[-1, 1]$?

Solution: For x in $[-1, 1]$, $f(x)$ will produce values between $(-1)^2 = 1$ and $1^2 = 1$ including 0. Since every value between 0 and 1 (inclusive) has a pre-image in the interval $[-1, 1]$, f is onto on the interval $[-1, 1]$.

Function Inverses

- An inverse function is a function that reverses another function: If the function f applied to an input x gives a result of y, then applying its inverse function g to y gives the result x. $f(x) = y$ if and only if $g(y) = x$.
- The inverse function of $f(x)$ is usually shown by $f^{-1}(x)$.

Examples:

Example 1. Find the inverse of the function: $f(x) = 2x - 1$.

Solution: First, replace $f(x)$ with y:

$y = 2x - 1$.

Then, replace all x's with y and all y's with x:

$x = 2y - 1$.

Now, solve for y:

$x = 2y - 1 \Rightarrow x + 1 = 2y \Rightarrow \frac{1}{2}x + \frac{1}{2} = y$.

Finally replace y with $f^{-1}(x)$:

$f^{-1}(x) = \frac{1}{2}x + \frac{1}{2}$.

Example 2. Find the inverse of the function: $g(x) = \frac{1}{5}x + 3$.

Solution: First, replace $g(x)$ with y:

$g(x) = \frac{1}{5}x + 3 \Rightarrow y = \frac{1}{5}x + 3$,

Then, replace all x's with y and all y's with x: $x = \frac{1}{5}y + 3$,

Now, solve for y:

$x - 3 = \frac{1}{5}y \Rightarrow 5(x - 3) = y \Rightarrow y = 5x - 15 \Rightarrow g^{-1} = 5x - 15$.

Example 3. Find the inverse of the function: $h(x) = \sqrt{x} + 6$.

Solution: $h(x) = \sqrt{x} + 6 \Rightarrow y = \sqrt{x} + 6$, replace all x's with y and all y's with x:

$\Rightarrow x = \sqrt{y} + 6 \Rightarrow x - 6 = \sqrt{y} \Rightarrow (x - 6)^2 = \left(\sqrt{y}\right)^2 \Rightarrow x^2 - 12x + 36 = y$

$\Rightarrow h^{-1}(x) = x^2 - 12x + 36$.

Inverse Function Graph

- When working with functions and their inverses, it is important to be able to identify the inverse of a function from its graph. Graphically, the inverse of a function is represented by reflecting the original graph about the line $y = x$, which swaps the roles of the x and y variables. This means that for every point (a, b) on the graph of f, there is a corresponding point (b, a) on the graph of f^{-1}.
- **Here's how to identify the inverse of a function from its graph:**
  Step 1: Find a few key points on the original graph of the function.
  Step 2: For each point (a, b) on the original graph, plot the point (b, a) on the same coordinate plane.
  Step 3: Draw a curve through the new points to create the graph of the inverse function.
  Step 4: To verify your work, draw the line $y = x$ and ensure that the original graph and its inverse are reflections of each other across this line.
- A function has an inverse if and only if it is one-to-one, meaning it has a unique output for each input. Graphically, this is determined by the Horizontal Line Test: if any horizontal line intersects the graph of the function at more than one point, the function is not one-to-one and does not have an inverse.
- The line $y = x$ serves as the mirror line for the graphs of a function and its inverse. Reflecting the original graph across this line produces the graph of the inverse function, as it swaps the roles of the x and y variables.

Example:

Let's consider the function $f(x) = 2x + 3$. Draw the inverse of function f.

Solution: Plot the original graph of $f(x) = 2x + 3$. Next, plot the points $(3,0)$, $(5,1)$, and $(1,-1)$, which correspond to the inverse function. So, draw a curve through the new points to create the graph of the inverse function. Finally, draw the line $y = x$ to check that the original graph and its inverse are reflections of each other across this line.

Inverse Variation

- Inverse variation is a type of proportion in which one quantity decreases while another increases or vice versa. This means that the amount or absolute value of one quantity decreases if the other quantity increases so that their product always remains the same. This product is also known as the proportionality constant.
- An inverse variation is represented by the equation $xy = k$ or $y = \frac{k}{x}$. That is, if there is some non-zero constant k, y changes inversely so that $xy = k$ or $y = \frac{k}{x}$ where $x \neq 0$, $y \neq 0$.
- If inverse variation includes the points (x_1, y_1) and (x_2, y_2), inverse variation can be represented by the equation $x_1 y_1 = k$ and $x_2 y_2 = k$.

Examples:

Example 1. If y varies inversely as x and $y = 12$ when $x = 5$. What's the value of y when x is 3?

Solution: Use $y = 12$ and $x = 5$ to find the value of k: $xy = k \Rightarrow k = 5 \times 12 \Rightarrow k = 60$. Now that we have found k, we can again use the value of k, which is 60, and the value of x, which is 3, to get the value of y: $k = xy \Rightarrow 60 = 3 \times y \Rightarrow y = 20$.

Example 2. An inverse variation includes points $(4, 9)$ and $(12, m)$. Find m.

Solution: First find the variation's constant. Plug $x_1 = 4$ and $y_1 = 9$ into the equation $x_1 y_1 = k$ and then solve for k: $x_1 y_1 = k \Rightarrow k = 4 \times 9 = 36$. Now use the inverse variation equation $x_2 y_2 = k$ to find m or y_2 when $x_2 = 12$: $x_2 y_2 = k \Rightarrow 12 \times m = 36 \Rightarrow m = \frac{36}{12} = 3 \Rightarrow m = 3$.

Example 3. If y varies inversely as x and $y = 0.5$ when $x = 8$. What's the value of x when y is 2?

Solution: Use $y = 0.5$ and $x = 8$ to find the value of k: $xy = k \Rightarrow k = 8 \times 0.5 \Rightarrow k = 4$. Now that we have found k which is 4, and the value of y which is 2 to get the value of x:
$k = xy \Rightarrow 4 = x \times 2 \Rightarrow x = \frac{4}{2} \Rightarrow x = 2$.

Piecewise-defined Functions

- A piecewise function uses more than one formula to define domain values.
- In general, a piecewise function can be shown as follows:

$$f(x) = \begin{cases} f_1(x), & x \in \text{Domain } f_1(x) \\ f_2(x), & x \in \text{Domain } f_2(x) \\ \vdots & \\ f_n(x), & x \in \text{Domain } f_n(x) \end{cases}$$

Where $n \geq 2$, and the domain of the function is the union of all of the smaller domains.
- Absolute value functions can be shown as piecewise functions.

Examples:

Example 1. Graph: $f(x) = \begin{cases} 2, & x < 0 \\ x + 1, & x \geq 1 \end{cases}$

Solution: Step1: Graph $y = 2$ for $x < 0$. As follows:

Step2: Graph $y = x + 1$ for $x \geq 1$.

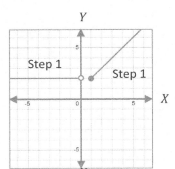

Example 2. Write the piecewise function represented by the graph.

Solution: According to the graph, this function contains three pieces. The domain of the function is the union of three intervals as $(-\infty, -3]$, $[-3, 1)$, and $(1, +\infty)$. Using two points on the graph of each piece, we write the linear function from them.

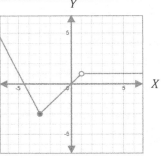

Step1: The interval $(-\infty, -3]$, two points $(-4, -1)$ and $(-3, -3)$ lie on the line $y = -2x - 9$.

Step2: The interval $[-3, 1)$, two points $(-3, -3)$ and $(1, 1)$ lie on the line $y = x$.

Step3: The interval $(1, +\infty)$, the graph is a horizontal function passing through the point $(1, 1)$.

Therefore: $f(x) = \begin{cases} -2x - 9 & x < -3 \\ x & -3 \leq x < 1 \\ 1 & x > 1 \end{cases}$

Chapter 6: Practices

✎ **Solve.**

1) Determine the intervals where the function is increasing and decreasing.

   Submit your solution in interval notation.

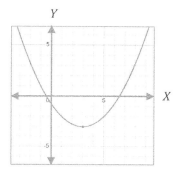

✎ **What is the parent graph of the following function and what transformations have taken place on it?**

2) $y = x^2 - 3$

3) $y = x^3 + 4$

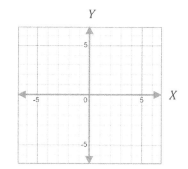
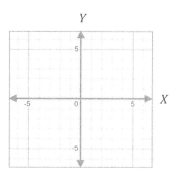

✎ **Identify whether the following functions are even, odd, or neither.**

4) $f(x) = x^2 + 6$

5) $f(x) = x^3 - 4x$

6) $f(x) = 4x^4 + 2$

7) $f(x) = 2x^3 - 2x + 2$

8) $f(x) = x^4 - 4x^2 + 4$

9) $f(x) = 2x^3 + 5x$

✎ **Find the end behavior of the functions.**

10) $f(x) = x^3 - 4x + 2$

11) $f(x) = x^2 - 6x + 12$

12) $f(x) = x^5 - 4x^3 + 4x + 2$

13) $f(x) = -x^2 + 8x$

14) $f(x) = -x^2 + 8x$

15) $f(x) = x^3 + 10x^2 + 22x + 4$

Effortless Math Education

Chapter 6: Functions Operations

✍ **Determine whether the following functions are one-to-one.**

16) $f(x) = x^2 - 4x + 4$

17) $g(x) = e^x$

18) $h(x) = x^5 - 3x^3$

19) $k(x) = x^4 - 2x^2 + 1$

20) $l(x) = 2^x - 3$

21) $m(x) = \sqrt{x}$

✍ **According to the given graphs, check whether the graphs are one-to-one.**

22)

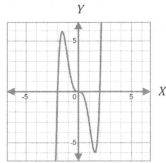

23)

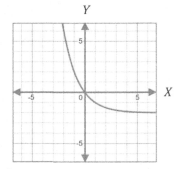

24)

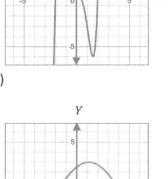

25)

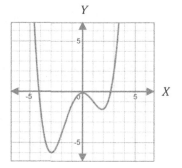

✍ **Find the inverse of each function.**

26) $f(x) = \frac{1}{x} - 6 \Rightarrow f^{-1}(x) =$

27) $g(x) = \frac{7}{-x-3} \Rightarrow g^{-1}(x) =$

28) $h(x) = \frac{x+9}{3} \Rightarrow h^{-1}(x) =$

29) $h(x) = \frac{2x-10}{4} \Rightarrow h^{-1}(x) =$

30) $f(x) = \frac{-15+x}{3} \Rightarrow f^{-1}(x) =$

31) $s(x) = \sqrt{x} - 2 \Rightarrow s^{-1}(x) =$

Effortless Math Education

Draw the inverse of the following graphs.

32)
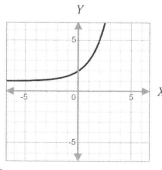

33)
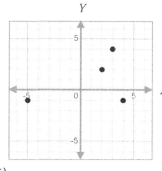

34)
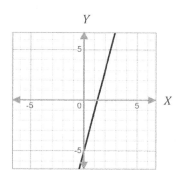

35)
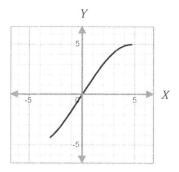

Solve.

36) If y varies inversely as x and $y = 18$ when $x = 6$. What's the value of y when x is 4?

37) If y varies inversely as x and $y = 0.8$ when $x = 6$. What's the value of x when y is 3?

Graph.

38) $f(x) = \begin{cases} 4 - 2, & x < -1 \\ x - 1, & x \geq 0 \end{cases}$

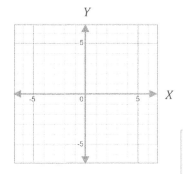

Chapter 6: Answers

1) Increasing intervals: $(3, +\infty)$
   Decreasing intervals: $(-\infty, 3)$
2) Parent: Quadratic
   Transformations: Down 3

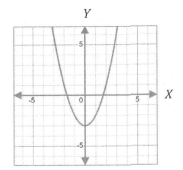

3) Parent: Cubic
   Transformations: Up 4

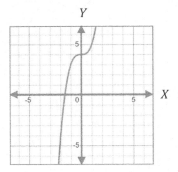

4) Even
5) Odd
6) Even
7) Neither
8) Even
9) Odd
10) $f(x) \to -\infty$, as $x \to -\infty$
    $f(x) \to +\infty$, as $x \to +\infty$
11) $f(x) \to +\infty$, as $x \to -\infty$
    $f(x) \to +\infty$, as $x \to +\infty$
12) $f(x) \to -\infty$, as $x \to -\infty$
    $f(x) \to +\infty$, as $x \to +\infty$

13) $f(x) \to -\infty$, as $x \to -\infty$
    $f(x) \to -\infty$, as $x \to +\infty$
14) $f(x) \to +\infty$, as $x \to -\infty$
    $f(x) \to -\infty$, as $x \to +\infty$
15) $f(x) \to -\infty$, as $x \to -\infty$
    $f(x) \to +\infty$, as $x \to +\infty$
16) No
17) Yes
18) Yes
19) No
20) Yes
21) Yes

22) No

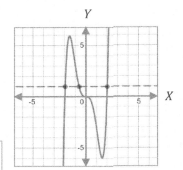

23) Yes

24)
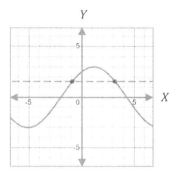

25)
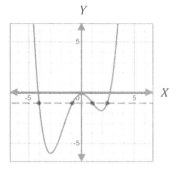

26) $f^{-1}(x) = \frac{1}{x+6}$

27) $g^{-1}(x) = -\frac{7+3x}{x}$

28) $h^{-1}(x) = 3x - 9$

29) $h^{-1}(x) = 2x + 5$

30) $f^{-1}(x) = 3x + 15$

31) $s^{-1}(x) = x^2 + 4x + 4$

32)
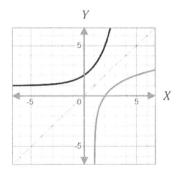

33)
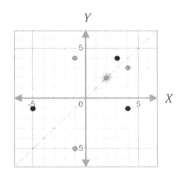

34)
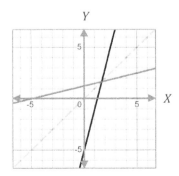

35)
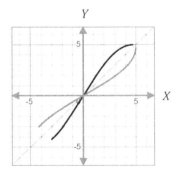

36) $y = 27$

37) $x = 1.6$

38)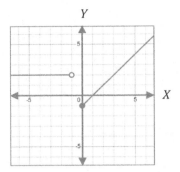

CHAPTER 7: Sequences and Series

Math topics that you'll learn in this chapter:

- ☑ Sequences
- ☑ Recursive Formula
- ☑ Write a Formula for a Recursive Sequence
- ☑ Arithmetic Sequences
- ☑ Geometric Sequences
- ☑ Sigma Notation
- ☑ Arithmetic Series
- ☑ Finite Geometric Series
- ☑ Infinite Geometric Series
- ☑ Convergent and Divergent Series
- ☑ The *n*th Term Test for Divergence
- ☑ Introduction to the Integral Test
- ☑ Comparison, Ratio, and Root Tests
- ☑ Alternating Series and Absolute Convergence
- ☑ Pascal's Triangle
- ☑ The Binomial Theorem

Sequence

- A sequence is an ordered list of numbers.
- Let $a_1, a_2, \cdots, a_i, \cdots$ represent a sequence. Each number in the sequence is called a term. The expression a_i is referred to the general term of the sequence. a_1 is the first term, a_2 is the second term, and so on. The three dots mean to continue forward in the pattern established. The subscript i on the term a_i is called index.
- In order to recognize the terms of the sequence, the general term of the sequence is used. In the sequences whose general term is only dependent on the variable (index value), by plugging the index in the general term, other values of the sequence are obtained.
- **Steps to Evaluate**:
    - Identify the formula representing the sequence.
    - Insert the desired term position n into the formula.
    - Compute to obtain the term's value.

Examples:

Example 1. For the sequence represented by $a_n = 4n + 5$, calculate a_6.
Solution: Insert $n = 6$ into the formula: $a_6 = 4(6) + 5 = 24 + 5 = 29$.

Example 2. For the geometric sequence defined by $a_n = 3(2^n)$, determine a_4.
Solution: Substitute $n = 4$: $a_4 = 3(2^4) = 3(16) = 48$.

Example 3. Evaluate the sequence $a_n = n^2 + 2n + 1$ for a_3.
Solution: Plug $n = 3$ in the formula $a_n = n^2 + 2n + 1$. So, we get:
$$a_3 = 3^2 + 2(3) + 1 = 9 + 6 + 1 = 16$$

Example 4. Find the first three terms of the sequence with the general term $a_n = (-1)^{n-1} n$, where n represents the position of a term in the sequence and $n \geq 1$.

Solution: Since $n \geq 1$, the sequence starts at one. So, to find the first term, plug-in n = 1. Then: $a_1 = (-1)^{1-1} \times 1 = 1$. In a similar way, enter the natural numbers in order to find the other terms of the sequence. Therefore,

Plug in $n = 2$ as $a_2 = (-1)^{2-1} \times 2 = -2$.
Plug in $n = 3$ as $a_3 = (-1)^{3-1} \times 3 = 3$.
The first three terms of the sequence are 1, −2, and 3.

Recursive Formula

- Let $T_1, T_2, \cdots, T_n, \cdots$ is a sequence. T_n denotes the general term of the sequence.
- The sequence whose general term defines each term of a sequence using a previous term or terms is called a recursive sequence. The general formula is as follows:
$$T_{n+1} = f(T_n, T_{n-1}, T_{n-2}, \cdots, T_{n-k})$$
- Where k is the number of preceding terms needed for the formula (as a function of previous terms). The sequence is said to have an order of k.
- To find the terms of a recursive sequence, according to the recursive formula, a number of previous terms of the sequence are required.
- **Steps to Evaluate**:
  - Begin with the given initial term(s).
  - Apply the recursive rule to produce subsequent terms.
  - Repeat the process for the desired number of terms.

Examples:

Example 1. $a_1 = 2$ and $a_n = a_{n-1} + 3$. Find the first five terms.
Solution: We have: $a_1 = 2$, $a_2 = 2 + 3 = 5$, $a_3 = 5 + 3 = 8$, $a_4 = 8 + 3 = 11$ and $a_5 = 11 + 3 = 14$. So, the sequence is: 2, 5, 5, 11, 14.

Example 2. For the sequence $a_1 = 4$ and $a_n = 2 \times a_{n-1}$. Determine a_4.
Solution: We have: $a_1 = 4$, $a_2 = 2 \times 4 = 8$, $a_3 = 2 \times 8 = 16$, and $a_4 = 2 \times 16 = 32$.

Example 3. Write the first five terms of the sequence $T_n = T_{n-1} + T_{n-2}$, where $n \geq 3$, $T_1 = 1$ and $T_2 = 3$.
Solution: Recall that the recursive formula defines each term of a sequence using a previous term or terms, then by looking at the recursive formula $T_n = T_{n-1} + T_{n-2}$, you notice that to generate the terms of the sequence, you need the previous two terms of the sequence. Here you are given the first two terms $T_1 = 1$ and $T_2 = 3$ together with the recursive formula $T_n = T_{n-1} + T_{n-2}$.
To find the third term which is T_3, plug in $n = 3$. So, $T_3 = T_{3-1} + T_{3-2} \Rightarrow T_3 = T_2 + T_1$. Now, substitute the previous terms into the obtained expression. That is $T_3 = 3 + 1 = 4$. Similarly, by substituting $n = 4$ and $n = 5$ into the given recursive formula, you get: $T_4 = T_{4-1} + T_{4-2} \Rightarrow T_4 = T_3 + T_2 \Rightarrow T_4 = 4 + 3 = 7$,
$$T_5 = T_{5-1} + T_{5-2} \Rightarrow T_5 = T_4 + T_3 \Rightarrow T_5 = 7 + 4 = 11.$$
The first five terms of the sequence are 1, 3, 4, 7, and 11.

Write a Formula for a Recursive Sequence

- To find the general formula of a given recursive sequence, follow the steps below:
  - Specify the initial values as a_1 or even a_2.
  - Look for a relationship in the previous terms like a_{n-1} or even a_{n-2} that holds throughout the sequence. Start by evaluating the differences and ratios of consecutive terms.
  - Express the relationship as a function of the previous term or terms.

Examples:

Example 1. Find the recursive formula corresponding to the following sequence.
$$12, 17, 22, 27, 32, \cdots$$
Solution: Let the first term of this sequence $a_1 = 12$. To find the recursive formula, start by looking at the differences and ratios of consecutive terms. By evaluating the difference of terms with the previous term, you notice that the differences between consecutive terms are all the same. That is, $a_n - a_{n-1} = 5$. In this step, rewrite the obtained rule in terms of a_{n-1}. So, $a_n = a_{n-1} + 5$. Since the first term in the sequence is a_1, the term a_{n-1} is not defined for $n \leq 1$.

Example 2. Find the recursive formula for the following sequence.
$$1, 3, 9, 27, 81, \cdots$$
Solution: Here, let the first term of this sequence $a_1 = 1$. Looking at the terms in this sequence, you can see that each term has an equal ratio to the previous term. Thus, the following relationship is obtained: $\frac{a_n}{a_{n-1}} = 3$. Now, rewrite this rule in terms of a_{n-1}. Therefore, $a_n = 3a_{n-1}$. You know that $a_1 = 1$. It means that the terms a_{n-1} define for $n \geq 2$.

Example 3. Find the recursive formula corresponding to the following sequence.
$$1, 3, 2, -1, -3, -2, \cdots$$
Solution: Here, after evaluating the terms in the sequence, since the differences and ratios of consecutive terms are not the same value, therefore, look for another relationship between the previous term or even terms of the sequence. However, by evaluating the difference between the terms of the sequence, you can see that the difference of each term from the previous term makes the following sequence: $2, -1, -3, -4, \cdots$. The term of the last sequence has the formula as $a_n - a_{n-1}$. Therefore, the obtained formula is the recursive formula of the content of question $a_{n+1} = a_n - a_{n-1}$, where $n \geq 2$, $a_1 = 1$, and $a_2 = 3$.

Arithmetic Sequences

- A sequence of numbers such that the difference between the consecutive terms is constant is called an arithmetic sequence. For example, the sequence 6, 8, 10, 12, 14, ⋯ is an arithmetic sequence with common difference of 2.
- To find any term in an arithmetic sequence use this formula:
$$x_n = a + d(n-1)$$
$a =$ the first term, $d =$ the common difference between terms, $n =$ number of items.

Examples:

Example 1. Find the first five terms of the sequence. $a_8 = 38$, $d = 3$

Solution: First, we need to find a_1 or a.

Use the arithmetic sequence formula:

$x_n = a + d(n-1)$.

If $a_8 = 38$, then $n = 8$. Rewrite the formula and put the values provided:

$x_n = a + d(n-1) \Rightarrow 38 = a + 3(8-1) = a + 21$.

Now solve for a:

$38 = a + 21 \Rightarrow a = 38 - 21 = 17$.

First five terms: 17, 20, 23, 26, 29.

Example 2. Given the first term and the common difference of an arithmetic sequence find the first five terms. $a_1 = 18$, $d = 2$.

Solution: Use the arithmetic sequence formula:

$x_n = a + d(n-1)$.

First five terms: 18, 20, 22, 24, 26.

Geometric Sequences

- It is a sequence of numbers where each term after the first is found by multiplying the previous item by the common ratio, a fixed, non-zero number. For example, the sequence 2, 4, 8, 16, 32, ⋯ is a geometric sequence with a common ratio of 2.
- To find any term in a geometric sequence use this formula: $x_n = ar^{(n-1)}$. a = the first term, r = the common ratio, n = number of items.

Examples:

Example 1. Given the first term and the common ratio of a geometric sequence find the first five terms of the sequence. $a_1 = 3$, $r = -2$

Solution: Use geometric sequence formula:

$x_n = ar^{(n-1)} \Rightarrow x_n = 3(-2)^{n-1}$.

If $n = 1$, then: $x_1 = 3(-2)^{1-1} = 3(1) = 3$.

First five terms: 3, −6, 12, −24, 48.

Example 2. Given two terms in a geometric sequence find the 8th term. $a_3 = 10$, and $a_5 = 40$.

Solution: Use geometric sequence formula:

$x_n = ar^{(n-1)} \Rightarrow a_3 = ar^{(3-1)} = ar^2 = 10$.

$x_n = ar^{(n-1)} \Rightarrow a_5 = ar^{(5-1)} = ar^4 = 40$.

Now divide a_5 by a_3. Then: $\frac{a_5}{a_3} = \frac{ar^4}{ar^2} = \frac{40}{10}$.

Now simplifies: $\frac{ar^4}{ar^2} = \frac{40}{10} \Rightarrow r^2 = 4 \Rightarrow r = 2$.

We can find a now: $ar^2 = 10 \Rightarrow a(2^2) = 10 \Rightarrow a = 2.5$.

Use the formula to find the 8th term:

$x_n = ar^{(n-1)} \Rightarrow a_8 = (2.5)(2)^{(8-1)} = 2.5(128) = 320$.

Sigma Notation

- Summation notation is a way to express the sum of terms of a sequence in abbreviated form.
- Let $a_1, a_2, \cdots, a_i, \cdots$ is a sequence with the starting term a_1 and the ith term a_i. The representation of the sum of the kth term to the nth term of this sequence is as follows:

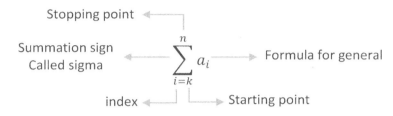

- For sequences a_i and b_i and positive integer n:

  - $\sum_{i=1}^{n} ca_i = c \sum_{i=1}^{n} a_i$

  - $\sum_{i=1}^{n} (a_i + b_i) = \sum_{i=1}^{n} a_i + \sum_{i=1}^{n} b_i$

  - $\sum_{i=1}^{n} c = nc$

  - $\sum_{i=1}^{n} i = \frac{n(n+1)}{2}$

  - $\sum_{i=1}^{n} i^2 = \frac{n(n+1)(2n+1)}{6}$

Example:

Evaluate: $\sum_{k=1}^{10} (k^2 - 1)$.

Solution: Using this property $\sum_{i=1}^{n} (a_i + b_i) = \sum_{i=1}^{n} a_i + \sum_{i=1}^{n} b_i$, we have:

$\sum_{k=1}^{10} (k^2 - 1) = \sum_{k=1}^{10} k^2 - \sum_{k=1}^{10} 1$.

Now, use these formulas $\sum_{i=1}^{n} i^2 = \frac{n(n+1)(2n+1)}{6}$ and $\sum_{i=1}^{n} c = nc$, so, $\sum_{k=1}^{10} 1 = 10$, and $\sum_{k=1}^{10} k^2 = \frac{10(10+1)(2\times 10+1)}{6} = 385$. Therefore: $\sum_{k=1}^{10} (k^2 - 1) = 385 - 10 = 375$.

Arithmetic Series

- An arithmetic series is the sum of sequence in which each term is computed from the previous one by adding (or subtracting) a constant value d.
- The sum of the sequence of the first n terms is given by:
$$S_n = \sum_{k=1}^{n} a_k = \sum_{k=1}^{n}[a_1 + (k-1)d] = na_1 + d\sum_{k=1}^{n}(k-1)$$
- Using the sum identify $\sum_{k=1}^{n} \frac{1}{2}n(n+1)$, then gives:
$$S_n = na_1 + \frac{1}{2}dn(n-1) = \frac{1}{2}n[2a_1 + d(n-1)]$$
- Note that: $a_1 + a_n = a_1 + [a_1 + d(n-1)] = 2a_1 + d(n-1)$, so:
$$S_n = \frac{1}{2}n(a_1 + a_n)$$

Examples:

Example 1. In the arithmetic series 4, 11, 18, ⋯ find the sum of the first 10 terms.

Solution: $a_1 = 4$, $d = 11 - 4 = 7$, $n = 10$.

Use the arithmetic series formula to find the sum:
$S_n = \frac{1}{2}n[2a_1 + d(n-1)]$.
Therefore: $S_{10} = \frac{10}{2}[2(4) + 7(10-1)] \Rightarrow S_{10} = 5(8 + 63) \Rightarrow S_{10} = 355$.

Example 2. Find the sum of the first four terms of the sequence. $a_{10} = 46$, $d = 4$.

Solution: First, we need to find a_1 or a. Use the arithmetic sequence formula:
$a_n = a + d(n-1)$.

If $a_{10} = 46$, then $n = 10$. Rewrite the formula and put the values provided: $a_n = a + d(n-1) \Rightarrow 46 = a + 4(10-1) = a + 36$, now solve for a.

$46 = a + 36 \Rightarrow a = 46 - 36 = 10$.

First four terms: 10, 14, 18, 22. Therefore:

$S_n = \frac{1}{2}n[2a_1 + d(n-1)] = \frac{1}{2}(4)[2(10) + 4(4-1)] = 64$.

Finite Geometric Series

- The sum of a geometric series is finite when the absolute value of the ratio is less than 1.
- Finite Geometric Series Formula: $S_n = \sum_{i=1}^{n} a_1 r^{i-1} = a_1 \left(\frac{1-r^n}{1-r}\right)$.

Examples:

Evaluate each geometric series described.

Example 1. $\sum_{n=1}^{4} 3^{n-1}$.

Solution: Use this formula:
$S_n = \sum_{i=1}^{n} a_1 r^{i-1} = a_1 \left(\frac{1-r^n}{1-r}\right) \Rightarrow \sum_{n=1}^{4} 3^{n-1} = (1)\left(\frac{1-3^4}{1-3}\right)$.
Then: $(1)\left(\frac{1-3^4}{1-3}\right) = 1\left(\frac{1-81}{1-3}\right) = \left(\frac{-80}{-2}\right)1 = 40$.

Example 2. $\sum_{n=1}^{5} -2^{n-1}$.

Solution: Use this formula:
$S_n = \sum_{i=1}^{n} a_1 r^{i-1} = a_1 \left(\frac{1-r^n}{1-r}\right) \Rightarrow \sum_{n=1}^{5} -2^{n-1} = (-1)\left(\frac{1-2^5}{1-2}\right)$.
Then: $(-1)\left(\frac{1-32}{1-2}\right) = (-1)\left(\frac{-31}{-1}\right) = -31$.

Example 3. $\sum_{n=1}^{7} \left(-\frac{1}{2}\right)^{n-1}$.

Solution: Use this formula:
$S_n = \sum_{i=1}^{n} a_1 r^{i-1} = a_1 \left(\frac{1-r^n}{1-r}\right) \Rightarrow \sum_{n=1}^{7} \left(-\frac{1}{2}\right)^{n-1} = (1)\left(\frac{1-\left(-\frac{1}{2}\right)^7}{1-\left(-\frac{1}{2}\right)}\right)$.
Then: $(1)\left(\frac{1+\frac{1}{128}}{1+\frac{1}{2}}\right) = \left(\frac{\frac{129}{128}}{\frac{3}{2}}\right) = \frac{129}{192} = \frac{43}{64}$.

Infinite Geometric Series

- Infinite Geometric Series: The sum of a geometric series is infinite when the absolute value of the ratio is more than 1.
- Infinite Geometric Series Formula: $S = \sum_{i=0}^{\infty} a_i r^i = \frac{a_1}{1-r}$.

Examples:

Example 1. Evaluate the infinite geometric series described. $\sum_{i=1}^{\infty} (-\frac{2}{3})^{i-1}$

Solution: Since the absolute value of the ratio is $\frac{2}{3}$ and less than 1, the sum of a geometric series is finite.
Therefore, by using this formula:

$\sum_{i=0}^{\infty} a_i r^i = \frac{a_1}{1-r} \Rightarrow \sum_{i=1}^{\infty} (-\frac{2}{3})^{i-1} = \frac{1}{1-(-\frac{2}{3})} = \frac{1}{\frac{5}{3}} = \frac{3}{5}$.

Example 2. Evaluate the infinite geometric series described. $\sum_{i=1}^{\infty} (\frac{1}{3})^{i-1}$

Solution: The absolute value of the ratio is $\frac{1}{3}$. Use this formula:

$\sum_{i=0}^{\infty} a_i r^i = \frac{a_1}{1-r} \Rightarrow \sum_{i=1}^{\infty} (\frac{1}{3})^{i-1} = \frac{1}{1-\frac{1}{3}} = \frac{1}{\frac{2}{3}} = \frac{3}{2}$.

Example 3. Evaluate the infinite geometric series described. $\sum_{k=1}^{\infty} -2(\frac{1}{4})^{k-1}$

Solution: The absolute value of the ratio is $\frac{1}{4}$. Use this formula:

$\sum_{i=0}^{\infty} a_i r^i = \frac{a_1}{1-r}$. Put $a_1 = -2$ and $r = \frac{1}{4}$. Therefore:

$\sum_{i=0}^{\infty} a_i r^i = \frac{a_1}{1-r} \Rightarrow \sum_{k=1}^{\infty} -2(\frac{1}{4})^{k-1} = \frac{-2}{1-\frac{1}{4}} = \frac{-2}{\frac{3}{4}} = \frac{-8}{3}$.

Example 4. Evaluate the infinite geometric series described. $\sum_{k=1}^{\infty} (\frac{1}{4})7^{k-1}$

Solution: Since the absolute value of the ratio is 7 and more than 1, the sum of a geometric series is infinite.

Convergent and Divergent Series

- In mathematics, a series is the sum of the terms of a sequence. Series can be used to represent a wide range of mathematical objects and are particularly important in calculus and analysis. One of the key questions about a series is whether it converges or diverges. Understanding the convergence or divergence of a series is crucial in determining its behavior and its applicability in various contexts.
- A series is said to be **convergent** if the sum of its terms approaches a finite value as the number of terms increases indefinitely. Conversely, a series is said to be **divergent** if the sum of its terms does not approach a finite value as the number of terms increases indefinitely; instead, it may tend toward infinity, oscillate, or not approach any value at all.

Examples:

Example 1. Check the convergence of the Harmonic Series.
Solution: The harmonic series is the sum of the terms of the harmonic sequence. It takes the form:
$$S = \sum_{i=1}^{\infty} \frac{1}{i} = 1 + \frac{1}{2} + \frac{1}{3} + \frac{1}{4} + \cdots$$
The harmonic series diverges, meaning that its sum does not approach a finite value as the number of terms increases indefinitely.

Example 2. Check the convergence of the Alternating Harmonic Series.
Solution: An alternating series is a series whose terms alternate in sign. The alternating harmonic series is an example of an alternating series:
$$R = \sum_{i=1}^{\infty} \frac{(-1)^{i+1}}{i} = 1 - \frac{1}{2} + \frac{1}{3} - \frac{1}{4} + \cdots$$
The alternating harmonic series converges by the Alternating Series Test, which states that if the absolute values of the terms of an alternating series decrease to zero, then the series converges.
In this case, the absolute values of the terms are $\frac{1}{n}$, which decrease to zero as n approaches infinity, so the series converges.

The nth Term Test for Divergence

- The nth term test for divergence is a fundamental concept in calculus. It is a simple rule that provides a quick way to determine whether an infinite series converges or diverges. This test states that if the terms of a series do not approach zero as the index approaches infinity, then the series must diverge. Conversely, if the terms of a series do approach zero as the index approaches infinity, then the series might converge or might not - the test is inconclusive. However, it is important to note that the nth term test can only be used to prove divergence and not convergence.
- Note that the nth term test for divergence provides a quick way to determine whether an infinite series diverges or not. If the terms of a series do not approach zero as the index approaches infinity, then the series must diverge. However, if the terms do approach zero, the test is inconclusive and additional tests are needed to determine convergence or divergence.

Examples:

Example 1. Consider the series: $1 + \frac{1}{2} + \frac{1}{3} + \frac{1}{4} + \cdots$.
Solution: Here, the nth term of the series is given by $a_n = \frac{1}{n}$. As n gets larger and larger, a_n gets smaller and smaller and approaches 0. However, the nth term test is inconclusive in this case, and we cannot determine whether the series converges or diverges using the nth term test alone. (In fact, this series, known as the harmonic series, actually diverges.)

Example 2. Consider the series: $1 + 2 + 3 + 4 + 5 + \cdots$.
Solution: Here, the nth term of the series is given by $a_n = n$. As n gets larger and larger, a_n gets larger and larger and does not approach 0. Therefore, by the nth term test for divergence, the series must diverge.

Example 3. Consider the series: $1 - 1 + 1 - 1 + 1 - 1 + \cdots$.
Solution: Here, the nth term of the series is given by $a_n = (-1)^n$. As n gets larger and larger, a_n does not approach 0. It alternates between -1 and 1. Therefore, by the nth term test for divergence, the series must diverge.

Introduction to the Integral Test

- The integral test is a method used to determine the convergence or divergence of an infinite series. It works by comparing the series to a related improper integral. This test is particularly useful for series whose terms come from a function that is continuous, positive, and decreasing on the interval $[1, \infty)$. The basic idea is to check the behavior of the improper integral and use it to infer the behavior of the series.
- The integral test allows us to determine the convergence or divergence of a series by comparing it to an improper integral. If the integral has a finite value, the series converges. If the integral goes to infinity, the series diverges. This method can be applied to series whose terms come from a function that is continuous, positive, and decreasing on the interval $[1, \infty)$.

To apply the integral test:
1. Identify a function $f(x)$ such that $f(n) = a_n$ for all positive integers n, where a_n are the terms of the series.
2. Ensure that $f(x)$ is continuous, positive, and decreasing on the interval $[1, \infty)$.
3. Integrate $f(x)$ from 1 to infinity.
4. If the integral has a finite value, then the series converges. If the integral goes to infinity, then the series diverges.

Examples:

Example 1. Consider the series $\sum_{n=1}^{\infty} \frac{1}{n^2}$.

Solution: We associate this series with the function $f(x) = \frac{1}{x^2}$, which is continuous, positive, and decreasing on the interval $[1, \infty)$.
The improper integral of $f(x)$ from 1 to infinity is equal to $\int_1^{\infty} \frac{1}{x^2} dx$, which is equal to 1 (you can verify this by finding the antiderivative of $\frac{1}{x^2}$, which is $-\frac{1}{x}$, and evaluating it from 1 to infinity).
Since the integral has a finite value, the series $\sum_{n=1}^{\infty} \frac{1}{n^2}$ converges.

Example 2. Consider the series $\sum_{n=1}^{\infty} \frac{1}{n}$ (the harmonic series).

Solution: We associate this series with the function $f(x) = \frac{1}{x}$, which is continuous, positive, and decreasing on the interval $[1, \infty)$.
The improper integral of $f(x)$ from 1 to infinity is equal to $\int_1^{\infty} \frac{1}{x} dx$, which goes to infinity (the antiderivative of $\frac{1}{x}$ is $ln|x|$, and as x goes to infinity, $ln|x|$ also goes to infinity). Since the integral goes to infinity, the series $\sum_{n=1}^{\infty} \frac{1}{n}$ diverges.

Comparison, Ratio, and Root Tests

The Comparison Test, Ratio Test, and Root Test are powerful tools for analyzing the convergence or divergence of infinite series. They work by comparing the series in question with another series or by examining the behavior of the series' terms.

- **Comparison Test**: This test compares the series in question with a known series. If a series is smaller term-by-term than a convergent series, it also converges. Conversely, if it's larger than a divergent series, it diverges.
- **Ratio Test**: This test examines the ratio of consecutive terms in a series. If this ratio approaches a number smaller than 1, the series converges; if it approaches a number greater than 1, it diverges; if it approaches 1, the test is inconclusive.
- **Root Test**: This test examines the nth root of the nth term of a series. If this root approaches a number smaller than 1, the series converges; if it approaches a number greater than 1, it diverges; if it approaches 1, the test is inconclusive.

Examples:

Example 1. Check the convergence of the series $\sum_{n=1}^{\infty} \frac{1}{2n^2}$ by Comparison Test.

Solution: We know that $\sum_{n=1}^{\infty} \frac{1}{2n^2}$ converges (it's a p-series with $p = 2$). Since $\frac{1}{2n^2} \leq \frac{1}{n^2}$ for all n, the series $\sum_{n=1}^{\infty} \frac{1}{2n^2}$ also converges.

Example 2. Check the convergence of the series $\sum_{n=1}^{\infty} \frac{1}{2n^2}$ by Ratio Test.

Solution: Using the Ratio Test, we consider the ratio of consecutive terms:

$$\frac{a_{n+1}}{a_n} = \frac{\frac{(n+1)!}{(n+1)^{n+1}}}{\frac{n!}{n^n}} = \frac{(n+1)! n^n}{n!(n+1)^{n+1}} = \frac{n+1}{(n+1)^{n+1}} \cdot n^n = \frac{n^n}{(n+1)^n} \to 0$$

Since the ratio approaches 0, which is less than 1, the series converges.

Example 3. Check the convergence of the series $\sum_{n=1}^{\infty} \frac{2^n}{n^3}$ by Root Test.

Solution: Using the Root Test, we consider the nth root of the nth term:

$$\sqrt[n]{a_n} = \sqrt[n]{\frac{2^n}{n^3}} = \frac{2}{n^{\frac{3}{n}}}$$

As n becomes large, $n^{\frac{3}{n}} \to 1$, so $\sqrt[n]{a_n} \to 2$.

Since the root approaches 2, which is greater than 1, the series diverges.

Alternating Series and Absolute Convergence

- The general form of an alternating series is as follows:
$$\sum_{i=1}^{\infty}(-1)^k a_k.$$

Where $a_n \geq 0$ and the first index is arbitrary. It means that the starting term for an alternating series can have any sign.

- An alternating series $\{a_k\}_{k=1}^{\infty}$ is called convergent if:
  - $0 \leq a_{k+1} \leq a_k$, for all $k \geq 1$.
  - $a_k \to 0$, as $k \to +\infty$.

Examples:

Example 1. Determine whether the following series converge or diverge:
$$\sum_{i=1}^{\infty}(-1)^i \frac{2}{i+5}$$

Solution: Let $a_i = \frac{2}{i+5}$. Then:

$\frac{2}{i+5} \to 0$ as $i \to +\infty$.

In addition, $0 \leq a_{k+1} \leq a_k$:

$\frac{2}{(i+1)+5} \leq \frac{2}{i+5} \Rightarrow \frac{2}{i+6} \leq \frac{2}{i+5} \Rightarrow i+6 \geq i+5 \Rightarrow 6 \geq 5$.

This is true. Therefore, the alternating series of the problem is convergent.

Example 2. Determine whether the following series converge or diverge:
$$\sum_{k=1}^{\infty} \frac{(-1)^k k}{2k+1}.$$

Solution: Let $a_k = \frac{k}{2k+1}$. Then:

$\frac{k}{2k+1} \to \frac{1}{2} \neq 0$ as $i \to +\infty$.

Therefore, the alternating series of the problem is divergent.

Pascal's Triangle

- Pascal's triangle is shown below:

$$_0C_0$$
$$_1C_0 \quad _1C_1$$
$$_2C_0 \quad _2C_1 \quad _2C_2$$
$$_3C_0 \quad _3C_1 \quad _3C_2 \quad _3C_3$$
$$\ddots \quad \vdots \quad \ddots$$
$$_nC_0 \quad _nC_1 \quad _nC_2 \quad \cdots \quad _nC_{n-2} \quad _nC_{n-1} \quad _nC_n$$
$$_{n+1}C_0 \quad _{n+1}C_1 \quad _{n+1}C_2 \quad \cdots \quad _{n+1}C_{n-1} \quad _{n+1}C_n \quad _{n+1}C_{n+1}$$

- The nth row of Pascal's triangle contains $n+1$ components.
- In the nth row of Pascal's triangle, the kth component is equal to $_nC_{k-1}$.
- For all entries in Pascal's triangle in row n: $\sum_{k=0}^{n} {_nC_k} = 2^n$.
- $_nC_{k-1} + {_nC_k} = {_{n+1}C_k}$, where $0 < k \leq n$.

Examples:

Example 1. Find the 5th entry in row 7 of Pascal's triangle.

Solution: The kth entry in row n of Pascal's triangle is $_nC_{k-1}$.
(5th entry in row 7) = $_7C_{5-1} = {_7C_4} = \frac{7!}{3!4!} = 35$.

Example 2. Find the 8th entry in row 10 of Pascal's triangle.

Solution: The kth entry in row n of Pascal's triangle is $_nC_{k-1}$.
(8th entry in row 10) = $_{10}C_{8-1} = {_{10}C_7} = \frac{10!}{7!3!} = 120$.

Example 3. Find the location of $_{10}C_2$ entry in Pascal's triangle. Then give its value of it.

Solution: We know that the kth entry in row n of Pascal's triangle is $_nC_{k-1}$. Then the value of n and k for $_{10}C_2$ is $n = 10$ and $k - 1 = 2 \Rightarrow k = 3$. So $_{10}C_2$ is the 3rd entry in row 10 of Pascal's triangle. Now, $_{10}C_2 = \frac{10!}{2!8!} = 45$.

The Binomial Theorem

- The formula of the binomial theorem for positive integer n is as follows:

$$(x + y)^n = \sum_{k=0}^{n} \binom{n}{k} x^{n-k} y^k$$
$$= \binom{n}{0} x^n y^0 + \binom{n}{1} x^{n-1} y^1 + \cdots + \binom{n}{n-1} x^1 y^{n-1} + \binom{n}{n} x^0 y^n$$

Where $\binom{n}{k} = \frac{n!}{k!(n-k)!}$, and $0 \leq k \leq n$.

- In the expansion of $(x + y)^n$, there are $n + 1$ terms and the kth term is equal to:

$$\binom{n}{k-1} x^{n-k+1} y^{k-1}$$

Examples:

Example 1. Write the expansion $(x + y)^4$.

Solution: $(x + y)^4 = \sum_{k=0}^{4} \binom{4}{k} x^{4-k} y^k$
$$= \binom{4}{0} x^4 + \binom{4}{1} x^3 y + \binom{4}{2} x^2 y^2 + \binom{4}{3} xy^3 + \binom{4}{4} y^4$$
$$= x^4 + 4x^3 y + 6x^2 y^2 + 4xy^3 + y^4$$

Example 2. Write the 3rd term of the expansion of $(a - 1)^5$.

Solution: Use this formula: The 3th term $= \binom{n}{k-1} x^{n-k+1} y^{k-1}$

The 3th term $= \binom{5}{3-1} (a)^{5-3+1} (-1)^{3-1}$
$$= \binom{5}{2} (a)^3 (-1)^2 = 10a^3$$

Example 3. Write the expansion $(2b + 2)^3$.

Solution: $(2b + 2)^3 = \sum_{k=0}^{3} \binom{3}{k} (2b)^{3-k} (2)^k$
$$= \binom{3}{0} (2b)^3 + \binom{3}{1} (2b)^2 (2) + \binom{3}{2} (2b)(2)^2 + \binom{3}{3} (2)^3$$
$$= 8b^3 + 24b^2 + 24b + 8$$

Chapter 7: Practices

↘ Solve.

1) Find the first four terms of the sequence with general term $T_{n+1} = T_n + 5$, where $n \geq 1$ and $T_1 = -12$.

2) Find a_3, where the first term is $a_1 = 1$, and the general term is $a_n = 6a_{n-1}$.

3) Find a_6, where the first term is $a_1 = 3$, and the general term is $a_n = a_{n-1} + 8$.

4) Find the first four terms of the sequence with the general term $x_n = 2(3)^n$, where n represents the position of a term in the sequence and starts with $n = 1$.

5) Find the first three terms of the sequence with the general term $a_n = -7n - 2$, where n represents the position of a term in the sequence and starts with $n = 1$.

6) A sequence is defined by the formula $u_n = 3n + 1$, calculate the first 4 terms of this sequence.

↘ Write the recursive formula for the following sequence.

7) $-2.5, -10, -40, -160, \cdots$

8) $1, 6, 11, 16, \cdots$

9) $4, 11, 25, \cdots$

10) $-1, -4, -16, -64, \cdots$

↘ Find the next three terms of each arithmetic sequence.

11) $15, 11, 7, 3, -1, \ldots$

12) $-21, -14, -7, 0, \ldots$

13) $3, 6, 9, 12, 15, \ldots$

14) $4, 8, 12, 16, 20, \ldots$

Given the first term and the common difference of an arithmetic sequence find the first five terms and the explicit formula.

15) $a_1 = 24, d = 2$

16) $a_1 = -15, d = -5$

17) $a_1 = 18, d = 10$

18) $a_1 = -38, d = -10$

Find the first five terms of the sequence.

19) $a_1 = -120, d = -100$

20) $a_1 = 55, d = 23$

21) $a_1 = 12.5, d = 4.2$

Determine if the sequence is geometric. If it is, find the common ratio.

22) $1, -5, 25, -125, \ldots$

23) $-2, -4, -8, -16, \ldots$

24) $4, 16, 36, 64, \ldots$

25) $-3, -15, -75, -375, \ldots$

Given the first term and the common ratio of a geometric sequence find the first four terms and the explicit formula.

26) $a_1 = 0.8, r = -5$

27) $a_1 = 1, r = 2$

Evaluate each geometric series described.

28) $1, +2, +4, +8, \ldots, n = 6$

29) $1, -4, +16, -64, \ldots, n = 9$

30) $-2, -6, -18, -54, \ldots, n = 9$

31) $2, -10, +50, -250, \ldots, n = 8$

32) $1, -5, +25, -125, \ldots, n = 7$

33) $-3, -6, -12, -24, \ldots, n = 9$

Determine if each geometric series converges or diverges.

34) $a_1 = -1, r = 3$

35) $a_1 = 3.2, r = 0.2$

36) $a_1 = 5, r = 2$

37) $-1, 3, -9, 27, ...$

38) $2, -1, \frac{1}{2}, -\frac{1}{4}, \frac{1}{8}, ...$

39) $81, +27, +9, +3, ...$

Solve.

40) Find the 6th entry in row 8 of Pascal's triangle.

41) Find the 5th entry in row 9 of Pascal's triangle.

Solve.

42) Write the 5th term of the expansion of $(1 - 4b^2)^4$.

43) Write the expansion $(2x^2 - 5)^3$.

Write the terms of the series.

44) $\sum_{j=1}^{6} 4(j-2)^2$

45) $\sum_{b=1}^{5} (b^2 - 4)^2$

46) $\sum_{k=3}^{10} 2(k+3)$

47) $\sum_{x=1}^{8} (3x^2 + 2)$.

Determine whether the following series converge or diverge.

48) $\sum_{n=1}^{\infty} \frac{(-1)^n}{n^2}$

49) $\sum_{i=1}^{\infty} (3)^i \frac{1}{i-2}$

50) $\sum_{n=1}^{\infty} \frac{n^2+1}{n^3+1}$

51) $\sum_{i=1}^{\infty} \frac{(-1)^{i+3}}{i^2+4i+2}$

Chapter 7: Answers

1) $-12, -7, -2, 3$
2) 36
3) 43
4) $6, 18, 54, 162$
5) $-9, -16, -23$
6) $4, 7, 10, 13$
7) $a_n = -2.5(4^{n-1})$
8) $a_n = a_{n-1} + 5, n \geq 2$
9) $a_n = 2a_{n-1} + 3, n \geq 2$
10) $a_n = 4a_{n-1}, n \geq 2$
11) $-5, -9, -13$
12) $7, 14, 21$
13) $18, 21, 24$
14) $24, 28, 32$
15) First Five Terms: $24, 26, 28, 30, 32$, Explicit: $a_n = 2n + 22$
16) First Five Terms: $-15, -20, -25, -30, -35$, Explicit: $a_n = -5n - 10$
17) First Five Terms: $18, 28, 38, 48, 58$, Explicit: $a_n = 10n + 8$
18) First Five Terms: $-38, -48, -58, -68, -78$, Explicit: $a_n = -10n - 28$
19) $-120, -220, -320, -420, -520$
20) $55, 78, 101, 124, 147$
21) $12.5, 16.7, 20.9, 25.1, 29.3$
22) $r = -5$
23) $r = 2$
24) Not geometric
25) $r = 5$
26) First Four Terms: $0.8, -4, 20, -100$
    Explicit: $a_n = 0.8(-5)^{n-1}$
27) First Four Terms: $1, 2, 4, 8$
    Explicit: $a_n = 2^{n-1}$
28) 63
29) $52,429$
30) $-19,682$
31) $-130,208$
32) $13,021$
33) $-1,533$
34) Diverge
35) Converge
36) Diverge
37) Diverge
38) Converge
39) Converge
40) 56
41) 126
42) $256b^8$
43) $8x^6 - 60x^4 + 150x^2 - 125$
44) 124
45) 619
46) 152
47) 628
48) Converge
49) Diverge
50) Diverge
51) Converge

Effortless Math Education

3 Trigonometric and Polar Functions

CHAPTER 8 Trigonometry

Math topics that you'll learn in this chapter:

- ☑ Degrees, Radians and Angle Conversions
- ☑ Coterminal and Reference Angles
- ☑ Angles of Rotation and Unit Circle
- ☑ Arc length and Sector Area
- ☑ Sine, Cosine, and Tangent
- ☑ Reciprocal Functions: Cosecant, Secant, and Cotangent
- ☑ Domain and Range of Trigonometric Functions
- ☑ Arcsine, Arccosine, and Arctangent
- ☑ Applications of Inverse Trigonometric Function
- ☑ Fundamental Trigonometric Identities
- ☑ Pythagorean Trigonometric Identities
- ☑ Co-Function, Even-Odd, and Periodicity Identities
- ☑ Double Angle and Half-Angle Formulas
- ☑ Sum and Difference Formulas
- ☑ Product-to-Sum and Sum-to-Product Formulas

Degrees, Radians and Angle Conversions

- Degrees and radians are two systems for measuring angles.
  - **Degrees**: The degree system is based on dividing a circle into 360 equal parts, with each part representing one degree (1°). Degrees are a widely used unit of angle measurement, and they can be further divided into minutes (') and seconds (") for more precise measurements. There are 60 minutes in a degree and 60 seconds in a minute.

  For example, an angle of 45° represents 45 parts out of the 360 parts of a circle, and an angle of 90° corresponds to a quarter of a circle.

  - **Radians**: The radian system is based on the radius of a circle. An angle of one radian is formed when the length of the arc between the two radii is equal to the length of the radius. In terms of a circle, there are 2π radians in a full circle, where π (pi) is the mathematical constant approximately equal to 3.14159.

  For example, an angle of $\frac{\pi}{4}$ radians correspond to $\frac{1}{8}$ of a circle, and an angle of $\frac{\pi}{2}$ radians corresponds to $\frac{1}{4}$ of a circle.

- To convert degrees to radians, use this formula: $Radian = Degrees \times \frac{\pi}{180}$.
- To convert radians to degrees, use this formula: $Degrees = Radian \times \frac{180}{\pi}$.

Examples:

Example 1. Convert 120 degrees to radians.
Solution: Use this formula: $Radian = Degrees \times \frac{\pi}{180}$.
Therefore: $Radian = 120 \times \frac{\pi}{180} = \frac{120\pi}{180} = \frac{2\pi}{3}$.

Example 2. Convert $\frac{\pi}{3}$ to degrees.
Solution: Use this formula: $Degrees = Radians \times \frac{180}{\pi}$.
Then: $Degrees = \frac{\pi}{3} \times \frac{180}{\pi} = \frac{180\pi}{3\pi} = 60$.

Example 3. Convert $\frac{2\pi}{5}$ to degrees.
Solution: Use this formula: $Degrees = Radians \times \frac{180}{\pi}$.
Therefore: $Degrees = \frac{2\pi}{5} \times \frac{180}{\pi} = \frac{360\pi}{5\pi} = 72$.

Coterminal and Reference Angles

- Angle addition and subtraction are important concepts in trigonometry and geometry that deal with the operations of combining and separating angles.
  - **Degree**: To add or subtract angles in degrees, simply perform the arithmetic operation between the degree values.

  For example, if angle $A = 30°$ and angle $B = 45°$:

  Angle addition: $A + B = 30° + 45° = 75°$

  Angle subtraction: $A - B = 30° - 45° = -15°$ (a negative result indicates the angle is measured in the opposite direction)
  - **Radian**: To add or subtract angles in radians, perform the arithmetic operation between the radian values.

  For example, if angle $C = \frac{\pi}{66}$ radians and angle $D = \frac{\pi}{4}$ radians:

  Angle addition: $C + D = \frac{\pi}{6} + \frac{\pi}{4} = \frac{2\pi + 3\pi}{12} = \frac{5\pi}{12}$ radians

  Angle subtraction: $C - D = \frac{\pi}{6} - \frac{\pi}{4} = \frac{2\pi - 3\pi}{12} = -\frac{\pi}{12}$ radians

- **Coterminal** angles are equal angles.
- To find a coterminal of an angle, add or subtract 360 degrees (Or 2π for radians) from the given angle.
- The **reference** angle is the smallest angle that you can make from the terminal side of an angle with the x-axis.

Examples:

Example 1. Find a positive and a negative coterminal angle to angle $65°$.

Solution: By definition, we have:

$65° - 360° = -295°$,

$65° + 360° = 425°$.

$-295°$ and a $425°$ are coterminal with a $65°$.

Example 2. Find positive and negative coterminal angle to angle $\frac{\pi}{2}$.

Solution: According to the definition, we have:

$\frac{\pi}{2} + 2\pi = \frac{5\pi}{2}$,

$\frac{\pi}{2} - 2\pi = -\frac{3\pi}{2}$.

This means that $\frac{5\pi}{2}$ and a $-\frac{3\pi}{2}$ are coterminal with a $\frac{\pi}{2}$.

Angles of Rotation and Unit Circle

- In trigonometry, an angle is defined by a ray that revolves around its endpoint. Each position of the rotated ray, relative to its starting position, creates an angle of rotation. The letter θ is used to name the angle of rotation.
- The initial position of the ray is called the initial side of the angle, and the final position is called the terminal side of the angle.
- An angle is said to be in standard position when the initial side is along the positive x-axis and its endpoint is at the origin.
- The unit circle is a circle with a center at the origin and a radius of 1 and has the equation $x^2 + y^2 = 1$
- If $\angle POQ$ is an angle in standard position and P is the point that the terminal side of the angle intersects the unit circle and $m\angle POQ = \theta$. Then:
  - The sine function is a set of ordered pairs $(\theta, \sin\theta)$ that $\sin\theta$ is the y coordinate of P.
  - The cosine function is the set of ordered pairs $(\theta, \cos\theta)$ that $\cos\theta$ is the x-coordinate of P.

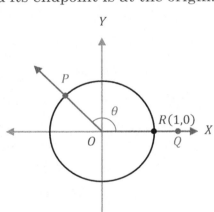

Examples:

Example 1. If $P\left(\frac{\sqrt{3}}{2}, -\frac{1}{2}\right)$ is a point on the unit circle and the terminal side of an angle in a standard position whose size is θ. Find $\sin\theta$ and $\cos\theta$.
Solution: $\sin\theta = y$-coordinate of $P = -\frac{1}{2}$, and $\cos\theta = x$-coordinate of $P = \frac{\sqrt{3}}{2}$.

Example 2. Does point $P\left(\frac{1}{4}, \frac{1}{4}\right)$ lie on the unit circle?
Solution: The equation of a unit circle is: $x^2 + y^2 = 1$. Now substitute $x = \frac{1}{4}$ and $y = \frac{1}{4}$: $\left(\frac{1}{4}\right)^2 + \left(\frac{1}{4}\right)^2 = \frac{1}{8} \neq 1$. Since, $x^2 + y^2 \neq 1$, the point $P\left(\frac{1}{4}, \frac{1}{4}\right)$ does not lie on the unit circle.

bit.ly/3IFZYKO

Arc Length and Sector Area

- To find a sector of a circle, use this formula:
$$\text{Area of a sector} = \pi r^2 \left(\frac{\theta}{360}\right)$$
Where r is the radius of the circle and θ is the central angle of the sector.
- To find the arc of a sector of a circle, use this formula:
$$\text{Arc of a sector} = \left(\frac{\theta}{180}\right)\pi r$$

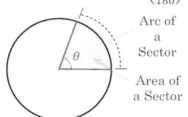

Examples:

Example 1. Find the length of the arc. Round your answers to the nearest tenth.
$$(\pi = 3.14), r = 24\ cm, \theta = 60°$$
Solution: Use this formula: Length of a sector $= \left(\frac{\theta}{180}\right)\pi r$.

Therefore:
Length of a sector $= \left(\frac{60}{180}\right)\pi(24) = \left(\frac{1}{3}\right)\pi(24) = 8 \times 3.14 \cong 25.1\ cm$.

Example 2. Find the area of the sector. $r = 6\ ft, \theta = 90°, (\pi = 3.14)$
Solution: Use this formula: Area of a sector $= \pi r^2 \left(\frac{\theta}{360}\right)$.

Therefore:
Area of a sector $= (3.14)(6^2)\left(\frac{90}{360}\right) = (3.14)(36)\left(\frac{1}{4}\right) = 28.26\ ft^2$.

Example 3. If the length of the arc is $18,84\ cm$, where $r = 4\ cm$. Find the area of the sector. $(\pi = 3.14)$
Solution: Use this formula: Arc of a sector $= \left(\frac{\theta}{180}\right)\pi r$.

Then:
$18.84 = (3.14)(4)\left(\frac{\theta}{180}\right) \Rightarrow 18.84 = 12.56\left(\frac{\theta}{180}\right) \Rightarrow \theta = 270°$,
Now, use this formula: Area of a sector $= \pi r^2 \left(\frac{\theta}{360}\right)$.
Therefore: Area of a sector $= \left(\frac{270}{360}\right)(3.14)(4)^2 = 37.68\ cm^2$.

Sine, Cosine, and Tangent

- Sine, cosine, and tangent are fundamental trigonometric functions used in mathematics to relate the angles of a right triangle to the lengths of its sides. These functions are essential for understanding various mathematical concepts, including geometry, calculus, and physics.
  - **Sine** (**sin**): The sine function relates the ratio of the length of the side opposite to an angle in a right triangle to the length of the hypotenuse (the longest side). It is defined as $sin(\theta) = \frac{opposite}{hypotenuse}$, where θ is the angle.
  - **Cosine** (**cos**): The cosine function relates the ratio of the length of the side adjacent to an angle in a right triangle to the length of the hypotenuse. It is defined as $cos(\theta) = \frac{adjacent}{hypotenuse}$, where θ is the angle.
  - **Tangent** (**tan**): The tangent function relates the ratio of the sine function to the cosine function or the ratio of the length of the side opposite to an angle in a right triangle to the length of the side adjacent to the angle. It is defined as $tan(\theta) = \frac{sin(\theta)}{cos(\theta)}$ or $\frac{opposite}{adjacent}$, where θ is the angle.
- These functions are widely used in various applications, including solving problems involving right triangles, graphing periodic functions, and analyzing real-world phenomena like waves, vibrations, and oscillations.

Example:

Find the value of Sine, Cosine, and Tangent of the angle $\widehat{BAC}$ in the figure below.

Solution: According to the size of the sides of the triangle and using the Sine, Cosine, and Tangent formulas, we will have:

$$sin(\theta) = \frac{opposite}{hypotenuse} = \frac{6.81}{10.5} \cong 0.65$$

$$cos(\theta) = \frac{adjacent}{hypotenuse} = \frac{8}{10.5} \cong 0.76$$

$$tan(\theta) = \frac{opposite}{adjacent} = \frac{6.81}{8} \cong 0.85$$

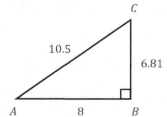

Reciprocal Functions: Cosecant, Secant, and Cotangent

- The trigonometric functions that can be defined in terms of $\sin \theta$, $\cos \theta$, and $\tan \theta$ are called the reciprocal functions.
- The secant function is the set of ordered pairs $(\theta, \sec \theta)$ for all θ for which $\cos \theta \neq 0$, $\sec \theta = \frac{1}{\cos \theta}$.
- The set of secant function values is the set of real numbers that is $\{x : x \geq 1 \text{ or } x \leq -1\}$.
- The cosecant function is the set of ordered pairs $(\theta, \csc \theta)$ for all θ for which $\sin \theta \neq 0$, $\csc \theta = \frac{1}{\sin \theta}$.
- The set of cosecant function values is the set of real numbers that is $\{x : x \geq 1 \text{ or } x \leq -1\}$.
- The cotangent function is the set of ordered pairs $(\theta, \cot \theta)$ that for all θ for which $\tan \theta$ is defined and not equal to 0, $\cot \theta = \frac{1}{\tan \theta}$, and for all θ for which $\tan \theta$ is not defined, $\cot \theta = 0$.
- The set of cotangent function values is the set of real numbers.

Examples:

Example 1. Find the value of $\sec \theta$ if $\cos \theta = \frac{2}{7}$ using the reciprocal identity.

Solution: The reciprocal identity of $\sec$ is: $\sec \theta = \frac{1}{\cos \theta}$. If $\cos \theta = \frac{2}{7}$, then $\sec \theta = \frac{1}{\frac{2}{7}} = \frac{7}{2}$.

Example 2. Simplify the function $\tan(\theta) \cot(\theta) \sin(\theta)$.

Solution: The reciprocal identity of $\cot \theta$: $\cot \theta = \frac{1}{\tan(\theta)}$.
$\tan(\theta) \cot(\theta) \sin(\theta) = \tan(\theta) \times \frac{1}{\tan(\theta)} \times \sin(\theta) = \sin \theta$

Domain and Range of Trigonometric Functions

- The domain of the sine function and cosine function is the set of real numbers.
- The range of the sine function and cosine function is the set of real numbers $[-1,1]$.
- The domain of the tangent function is the set of real numbers except for $\frac{\pi}{2} + n\pi$ for all integral values of n.
- The range of the tangent function is the set of all real numbers.
- The domain of the cotangent function is the set of real numbers except for $n\pi$ for all integral values of n.
- The range of the cotangent function is the set of all real numbers.
- The domain of the secant function is the set of real numbers except for $\frac{\pi}{2} + n\pi$ for all integral values of n.
- The range of the secant function is the set of real numbers $(-\infty, -1] \cup [1, +\infty)$.
- The domain of the cosecant function is the set of real numbers except for $n\pi$ for all integral values of n.
- The range of the cosecant function is the set of real numbers $(-\infty, -1] \cup [1, +\infty)$.

Examples:

Example 1. Find the range of $y = 4 \tan x$.

Solution: The range of $y = 4 \tan x$ is $(-\infty, +\infty)$.

Example 2. Find the domain and range of $y = \sin x - 4$.

Solution: The range of $\sin x$ is $[-1,1]$.

$-1 \leq \sin x \leq 1 \Rightarrow -1 - 4 \leq \sin x - 4 \leq 1 - 4 \Rightarrow -5 \leq y \leq -3$

The domain is $(-\infty, +\infty)$.

Example 3. Find the domain of $y = 3 \cos x + 4$.

Solution: The domain of $y = 3 \cos x + 4$ is $(-\infty, +\infty)$.

Arcsine, Arccosine, and Arctangent

- *Arcsine*, *arccosine*, and *arctangent* are inverse trigonometric functions, also known as inverse circular functions or simply as arc functions. These functions reverse the action of their respective trigonometric counterparts: sine, cosine, and tangent. In mathematics, they are used to determine the angle of a right-angled triangle when the lengths of two sides are known. They are denoted as $sin^{-1}(x)$, $cos^{-1}(x)$, and $tan^{-1}(x)$ or as $arcsin(x)$, $arccos(x)$, and $arctan(x)$, respectively.

- **Arcsine ($sin^{-1}(x)$ or $arcsin(x)$)**: This function is the inverse of the sine function, and it returns the angle (in radians) whose sine value is x. The domain of the arcsine function is $-1 \leq x \leq 1$, and the range is $-\frac{\pi}{2} \leq sin^{-1}(x) \leq \frac{\pi}{2}$.

- **Arccosine ($cos^{-1}(x)$ or $arccos(x)$)**: This function is the inverse of the cosine function, and it returns the angle (in radians) whose cosine value is x. The domain of the arccosine function is $-1 \leq x \leq 1$, and the range is $0 \leq cos^{-1}(x) \leq \pi$.

- **Arctangent ($tan^{-1}(x)$ or $arctan(x)$)**: This function is the inverse of the tangent function, and it returns the angle (in radians) whose tangent value is x. The domain of the arctangent function is $-\infty < x < +\infty$, and the range is $-\frac{\pi}{2} < tan^{-1}(x) < \frac{\pi}{2}$.

Examples:

Example 1. Determine the value of $cos^{-1}\left(cos\frac{13\pi}{6}\right)$.
Solution: $cos^{-1}\left(cos\frac{13\pi}{6}\right) = cos^{-1}\left[cos\left(2\pi + \frac{\pi}{6}\right)\right] = cos^{-1}\left[cos\frac{\pi}{6}\right] = \frac{\pi}{6}$

Example 2. Find the value of $tan^{-1}(sin 90°)$.
Solution: $tan^{-1}(sin 90°) = tan^{-1}(1) = 45°$ or $\frac{\pi}{4}$

Example 3. What is the value of $cos^{-1}\left(sin\frac{7\pi}{6}\right)$?
Solution: $cos^{-1}\left(sin\frac{7\pi}{6}\right) = cos^{-1}\left[sin\left(\pi + \frac{\pi}{6}\right)\right] = cos^{-1}\left[-sin\frac{\pi}{6}\right] = cos^{-1}\left(-\frac{1}{2}\right) = \frac{\pi}{3}$

Applications of Inverse Trigonometric Function

- Inverse trigonometric functions, also known as arc functions or cyclometric functions, are the inverses of the basic trigonometric functions like sine, cosine, and tangent. They are used to determine the angles of a triangle when the lengths or ratios of sides are known. Applications of inverse trigonometric functions are widespread in various fields, including engineering, physics, and mathematics. Key applications include:

- **Geometry:** Inverse trigonometric functions help solve triangles and calculate angles in various geometric problems.

- **Trigonometric Identities:** They are used to derive and prove various trigonometric identities and relationships.

- **Calculus:** In calculus, inverse trigonometric functions are essential for solving integrals and derivatives involving trigonometric functions.

- **Engineering:** Inverse trigonometric functions are used in various engineering fields, such as electronics, mechanics, and civil engineering, to solve problems related to waveforms, oscillations, and structural analysis.

- **Physics:** They play a crucial role in understanding wave mechanics, analyzing oscillatory systems, and studying kinematics and dynamics.

- **Navigation:** Inverse trigonometric functions are used in determining distances, bearings, and angles in navigation and cartography.

- **Computer Graphics:** They help in rendering and transforming 2D and 3D models, as well as in image processing and computational geometry.

Fundamental Trigonometric Identities

- The following equations are important trigonometric identities:
  - $\tan \theta = \frac{\sin \theta}{\cos \theta}$
  - $\cot \theta = \frac{\cos \theta}{\sin \theta}$
  - $\csc \theta = \frac{1}{\sin \theta}$
  - $\sec \theta = \frac{1}{\cos \theta}$
  - $\cot \theta = \frac{1}{\tan \theta}$
  - $\cos^2 \theta + \sin^2 \theta = 1$
  - $\sin^2 \theta = 1 - \cos^2 \theta$
  - $\cos^2 \theta = 1 - \sin^2 \theta$
  - $\tan^2 \theta + 1 = \sec^2 \theta$
  - $1 + \cot^2 \theta = \csc^2 \theta$

- You can use fundamental identities to rewrite trigonometric expressions in terms of a single trigonometric function.

Examples:

Example 1. Confirm the identity $\cos \theta + \sin \theta \tan \theta = \sec \theta$.

Solution: You can use fundamental trigonometric identities to solve this problem:
$(\cos \theta) + (\sin \theta)\left(\frac{\sin \theta}{\cos \theta}\right) = \sec \theta$
$\frac{\cos^2 \theta + \sin^2 \theta}{\cos \theta} = \sec \theta$
$\frac{1}{\cos \theta} = \sec \theta$
$\sec \theta = \sec \theta$.

Example 2. Find the value of $\tan \theta$ using $\cot \theta = \frac{3}{5}$.

Solution: Use fundamental trigonometric identities to solve this problem:
$\cot \theta = \frac{1}{\tan \theta}$, and $\frac{3}{5} = \frac{1}{\tan \theta} \Rightarrow \tan \theta = \frac{1}{\frac{3}{5}} = \frac{5}{3}$.

Pythagorean Trigonometric Identities

- An identity is an equation that is true for all variable values for which the variable expressions are defined.
- Since the identity $sin^2\theta + cos^2\theta = 1$ is based on the Pythagorean theorem, we refer to it as the Pythagorean identity.
- Two related Pythagorean identities can be written by dividing both sides of the equation by the same expression:
  - $1 + tan^2\theta = sec^2\theta$
  - $cot^2\theta + 1 = csc^2\theta$

Examples:

Example 1. Verify that $sin^2\frac{\pi}{4} + cos^2\frac{\pi}{4} = 1$.

Solution: $cos\frac{\pi}{4} = \frac{\sqrt{2}}{2}$ and $sin\frac{\pi}{4} = \frac{\sqrt{2}}{2}$:

$sin^2\frac{\pi}{4} + cos^2\frac{\pi}{4} = \left(\frac{\sqrt{2}}{2}\right)^2 + \left(\frac{\sqrt{2}}{2}\right)^2 = \frac{1}{2} + \frac{1}{2} = 1$

Example 2. If $cos\, x = \frac{3}{5}$ and x is in the 1st quadrant, find $sin\, x$.

Solution: Use Pythagorean identity:

$sin^2 x = 1 - cos^2 x$

$sin(x) = \pm\sqrt{1 - cos^2(x)} = \pm\sqrt{1 - \left(\frac{3}{5}\right)^2} = \pm\frac{4}{5}$

Since x is in the first quadrant, $sin\, x$ is positive. So $sin\, x = \frac{4}{5}$.

Example 3. Use a Pythagorean identity to simplify the $14 + 5\,cos^2(x) + 5\,sin^2(x)$.

Solution: The Pythagorean identity is $sin^2\theta + cos^2\theta = 1$.

$14 + 5\,cos^2(x) + 5\,sin^2(x) = 14 + 5\bigl(cos^2(x) + sin^2(x)\bigr)$

$= 14 + 5(1) = 19.$

Co-Function, Even-Odd, and Periodicity Identities

- **Co-Function Identities:** Co-Function identities describe the relationship between sine, cosine, and other trigonometric functions. They are derived from complementary angles (two angles whose sum equals 90 degrees). The Co-Function Identities are as follows:

    $sin(90° - x) = cos(x)$ $cot(90° - x) = tan(x)$
    $cos(90° - x) = sin(x)$ $sec(90° - x) = csc(x)$
    $tan(90° - x) = cot(x)$ $csc(90° - x) = sec(x)$

- **Even-Odd Identities:** Even-Odd identities describe the behavior of trigonometric functions with respect to the input sign. A function is even if $f(x) = f(-x)$, and it's odd if $f(x) = -f(-x)$. The Even-Odd Identities are as follows:

    $sin(-x) = -sin(x)$ (*sine* is an odd function)
    $cos(-x) = cos(x)$ (*cosine* is an even function)
    $tan(-x) = -tan(x)$ (*tangent* is an odd function)
    $cot(-x) = -cot(x)$ (*cotangent* is an odd function)
    $sec(-x) = sec(x)$ (*secant* is an even function)
    $csc(-x) = -csc(x)$ (*cosecant* is an odd function)

- **Periodicity Identities:** Periodicity identities describe the behavior of trigonometric functions when their input is incremented by a specific value called the period. A function is periodic if $f(x + P) = f(x)$ for all x, where P is the period. The Periodicity Identities are as follows:

    $sin(x + 2\pi n) = sin(x)$ for all integers n (*sine* has a period of 2π)
    $cos(x + 2\pi n) = cos(x)$ for all integers n (*cosine* has a period of 2π)
    $tan(x + \pi n) = tan(x)$ for all integers n (*tangent* has a period of π)
    $cot(x + \pi n) = cot(x)$ for all integers n (*cotangent* has a period of π)
    $sec(x + 2\pi n) = sec(x)$ for all integers n (*secant* has a period of 2π)
    $csc(x + 2\pi n) = csc(x)$ for all integers n (*cosecant* has a period of 2π)

Examples:

Example 1. Find the value of $tan\ 120°$ using cofunction identities.
Solution: Use cofunction identity, $cot(90° - x) = tan(x)$.
$tan\ 120° = cot(90° - 120°) = cot(-30°) = -cot\ 30° = -\sqrt{3}$.

Example 2. Use the concept of periodicity to solve this problem: Find the exact value of $cos\left(\frac{15\pi}{6}\right)$ using the periodicity identity of the cosine function.
Solution: Using the periodicity of the cosine function, we can simplify $\frac{15\pi}{6}$ to $\frac{\pi}{2}$, ($\frac{15\pi}{6} - 2\pi = \frac{\pi}{2}$). Thus, $cos\left(\frac{15\pi}{6}\right) = cos\left(\frac{\pi}{2}\right) = 0$.

Double Angle and Half-Angle Formulas

- Double-angle formulas are used for trigonometric ratios of double angles in terms of trigonometric ratios of single angles.
- The double-angle formulas are as follows:
  - $\sin 2\theta = 2 \sin \theta \cos \theta$
  - $\sin 2\theta = \dfrac{2 \tan \theta}{1 + \tan^2 \theta}$
  - $\cos 2\theta = \cos^2 \theta - \sin^2 \theta$
  - $\cos 2\theta = 1 - 2 \sin^2 \theta$
  - $\cos 2\theta = 2 \cos^2 \theta - 1$
  - $\cos 2\theta = \dfrac{1 - \tan^2 \theta}{1 + \tan^2 \theta}$
  - $\tan 2\theta = \dfrac{2 \tan \theta}{1 - \tan^2 \theta}$
- The half-angle formulas are as follows:
  - $\sin \dfrac{\theta}{2} = \pm \sqrt{\dfrac{1 - \cos \theta}{2}}$
  - $\cos \dfrac{\theta}{2} = \pm \sqrt{\dfrac{1 + \cos \theta}{2}}$
  - $\tan \dfrac{\theta}{2} = \pm \sqrt{\dfrac{1 - \cos \theta}{1 + \cos \theta}} = \dfrac{\sin \theta}{1 + \cos \theta} = \dfrac{1 - \cos \theta}{\sin \theta}$

Examples:

Example 1. If $\tan \theta = \dfrac{4}{3}$, find the values of $\cos 2\theta$.

Solution: Use the double-angle formulas:

$$\cos 2\theta = \frac{1 - \tan^2 \theta}{1 + \tan^2 \theta} = \frac{1 - \left(\frac{4}{3}\right)^2}{1 + \left(\frac{4}{3}\right)^2} = \frac{1 - \frac{16}{9}}{1 + \frac{16}{9}} = \frac{-\frac{7}{9}}{\frac{25}{9}} = -\frac{7}{25}$$

Example 2. If $\cos \theta = \dfrac{1}{2}$, find the values of $\sin \dfrac{\theta}{2}$.

Solution: Use the half-angle formulas:

$$\sin \frac{\theta}{2} = \pm \sqrt{\frac{1 - \cos \theta}{2}} = \pm \sqrt{\frac{1 - \frac{1}{2}}{2}} = \pm \sqrt{\frac{\frac{1}{2}}{2}} = \pm \sqrt{\frac{1}{4}} = \pm \frac{1}{2}$$

Sum and Difference Formulas

- The sum and difference formulas in trigonometry are used to find the value of trigonometric functions at certain angles.
- These formulas help us evaluate the value of trigonometric functions at angles that can be expressed as the sum or difference of certain angles 0°, 30°, 45°, 60°, 90°, and 180°.
- The sum and difference formulas are as follows:
  - $sin(A + B) = \sin A \cos B + \cos A \sin B$
  - $sin(A - B) = \sin A \cos B - \cos A \sin B$
  - $cos(A + B) = \cos A \cos B - \sin A \sin B$
  - $cos(A - B) = \cos A \cos B + \sin A \sin B$
  - $tan(A + B) = \frac{\tan(A) + \tan(B)}{1 - \tan(A)\tan(B)}$
  - $tan(A - B) = \frac{\tan(A) - \tan(B)}{1 - \tan(A)\tan(B)}$

Examples:

Example 1. Find the value of $sin(120° + 45°)$.

Solution: Use the sum and difference formula:

$$sin(120° + 45°) = sin(120°)\cos(45°) + \cos(120°)\sin(45°)$$
$$= \left(\frac{\sqrt{3}}{2}\right)\left(\frac{\sqrt{2}}{2}\right) + \left(-\frac{1}{2}\right)\left(\frac{\sqrt{2}}{2}\right)$$
$$= \frac{\sqrt{6}}{4} - \frac{\sqrt{2}}{4} = \frac{\sqrt{6} - \sqrt{2}}{4}.$$

Example 2. Find the value of $\cos 105°$.

Solution: Use the sum and difference formula:

$$\cos 105° = \cos(60° + 45°) = \cos 60° \cos 45° - \sin 60° \sin 45°$$
$$= \left(\frac{1}{2}\right)\left(\frac{\sqrt{2}}{2}\right) - \left(\frac{\sqrt{3}}{2}\right)\left(\frac{\sqrt{2}}{2}\right) = \frac{\sqrt{2} - \sqrt{6}}{4}.$$

Product-to-Sum and Sum-to-Product Formulas

- The Product-to-Sum and Sum-to-Product formulas are trigonometric identities that help convert products of sine and cosine functions into sums or differences of these functions, and vice versa. These identities are particularly useful for simplifying trigonometric expressions, solving trigonometric equations, and in areas such as Fourier analysis, signal processing, and calculus.

1) **Product-to-Sum Formulas:** These formulas help convert products of sines and cosines into sums or differences of sines and cosines. The formulas are as follows:
   - $sin(A) sin(B) = \frac{1}{2}[cos(A - B) - cos(A + B)]$
   - $cos(A) cos(B) = \frac{1}{2}[cos(A - B) + cos(A + B)]$
   - $sin(A) cos(B) = \frac{1}{2}[sin(A + B) + sin(A - B)]$

2) **Sum-to-Product Formulas:** These formulas help convert sums or differences of sines and cosines into products of sines and cosines. The formulas are as follows:
   - $sin(A) + sin(B) = 2 \, sin\left(\frac{A+B}{2}\right) cos\left(\frac{A-B}{2}\right)$
   - $sin(A) - sin(B) = 2 \, cos\left(\frac{A+B}{2}\right) sin\left(\frac{A-B}{2}\right)$
   - $cos(A) + cos(B) = 2 \, cos\left(\frac{A+B}{2}\right) cos\left(\frac{A-B}{2}\right)$
   - $cos(A) - cos(B) = -2 \, sin\left(\frac{A+B}{2}\right) sin\left(\frac{A-B}{2}\right)$

Example:

How can the product-to-sum formula be applied to express $sin(2x)cos(3x)$ as a sum?

Solution: To express $sin(2x)cos(3x)$ as a sum using the product-to-sum formula, we can use the following identity: $sin(A) cos(B) = \frac{1}{2}[sin(A + B) + sin(A - B)]$

Substituting $2x$ for A and $3x$ for B, we get:
$$sin(2x) cos(3x) = \left(\frac{1}{2}\right)[sin(5x) + sin(-x)]$$

Since $sin(-x) = -sin(x)$, we can simplify the above equation as:
$$sin(2x) cos(3x) = \left(\frac{1}{2}\right)[sin(5x) - sin(x)]$$

Therefore, $sin(2x) cos(3x)$ can be expressed as the difference between two sine functions, which are $\left(\frac{1}{2}\right)sin(5x)$ and $-\left(\frac{1}{2}\right)sin(x)$.

Chapter 8: Practices

✍ Convert degrees to radians and radians to degrees.

1) 445°

2) 130°

3) 432°

4) 1,140°

5) 1,000°

6) 7π

7) $\frac{3\pi}{18}$

8) $\frac{10\pi}{9}$

9) $\frac{9\pi}{5}$

10) $\frac{15\pi}{6}$

✍ Calculate.

11) 137° + 16° =

12) 76° − 109° =

13) 24° + (−55°) =

14) 177° − 22° =

15) 68° − 9° =

16) $\frac{4\pi}{5} + \frac{7\pi}{15} =$

17) $\frac{6\pi}{9} - \frac{\pi}{27} =$

18) $\frac{2\pi}{8} + \frac{2\pi}{11} =$

19) $\frac{\pi}{2} - \frac{14\pi}{5} =$

20) $\frac{5\pi}{24} + \frac{13\pi}{8} =$

✍ Find.

21) Find the reference angle of 130°.

22) Find the reference angle of 150°.

23) Find the reference angle of 115°.

24) Find the reference angle of 95°.

✍ Solve.

25) Find two positive values of 55° that are less than 360°.

26) Find two positive values of 83° that are less than 360°.

Effortless
Math
Education

Chapter 8: Trigonometry

🌐 Find a coterminal angle between 0° and 360° for each angle provided.

27) $-310° =$

28) $-325° =$

29) $-440° =$

30) $-640° =$

🌐 Find a coterminal angle between 0 and 2π for each given angle.

31) $\frac{14\pi}{5} =$

32) $-\frac{16\pi}{9} =$

33) $\frac{41\pi}{18} =$

34) $\frac{29\pi}{12} =$

35) $-\frac{14\pi}{9} =$

36) $\frac{22\pi}{7} =$

🌐 Solve.

37) If $P\left(-\frac{\sqrt{3}}{2}, \frac{1}{2}\right)$ is a point on the unit circle and the terminal side of an angle in a standard position whose size is θ. Find $\sin\theta$ and $\cos\theta$.

38) If $P\left(\frac{\sqrt{2}}{2}, -\frac{\sqrt{2}}{2}\right)$ is a point on the unit circle and the terminal side of an angle in a standard position whose size is θ. Find $\sin\theta$ and $\cos\theta$.

🌐 Find the length of each arc. Round your answers to the nearest tenth.

39) $r = 14 \, ft, \, \theta = 45°$

40) $r = 18 \, m, \, \theta = 60°$

41) $r = 26 \, m, \, \theta = 90°$

42) $r = 20 \, m, \, \theta = 120°$

🌐 Find the area of the sector. Round your answers to the nearest tenth.

43) $r = 4 \, m, \, \theta = 20°$

44) $r = 2 \, m, \, \theta = 45°$

45) $r = 8 \, m, \, \theta = 90°$

46) $r = 4 \, m, \, \theta = 135°$

Effortless Math Education

Find the value of Sine, Cosine, and Tangent of the angle γ in the following figures.

47)
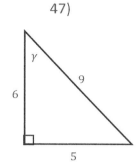

48)
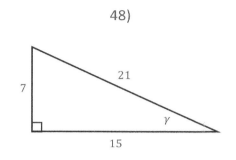

49)
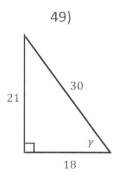

Solve.

50) Find the value of $sec\ x$ if $cos\ x = \frac{3}{5}$ using the reciprocal identity.

51) Find the value of $csc\ x$ if $sin\ x = \frac{2}{3}$ using the reciprocal identity.

Find the domain and range of functions.

52) $y = cos\ x - 4$

   Domain:

   Range:

53) $y = sin\ x - 3$

   Domain:

   Range:

54) $y = \frac{1}{2 - sin\ 2x}$

   Domain:

   Range:

55) $y = 2\ cos\ x + 6$

   Domain:

   Range:

Solve.

56) Consider the equation $y = arccos(x)$. Determine the domain and range of values for x and y based on the definition of the inverse cosine function. Suppose the range of values for y is $-\frac{\pi}{2} \leq y \leq \frac{\pi}{2}$. Solve for x using the inverse cosine function when $y = \frac{\pi}{4}$.

57) Consider the equation $y = arctan(x)$. Determine the domain and range of values for x and y based on the definition of the inverse tangent function. Suppose the domain of values for x is $-\infty < x < \infty$. Solve for y using the inverse tangent function when $x = \sqrt{3}$.

🕮 Find the value of each expression.

58) $\cos^{-1}\left(\cos\frac{2\pi}{3}\right)$

59) $\tan^{-1}\left(\tan\frac{3\pi}{4}\right)$

60) $\tan^{-1}(\sec \pi)$

61) $\sin^{-1}\left(\sin\frac{11\pi}{6}\right)$

62) $\sec(\cos^{-1} x)$

63) $\csc\left(\sec^{-1}\frac{\sqrt{6}}{2}\right)$

64) $\sin^{-1}(\sec 0)$

65) $\sin^{-1}\left(\cot\frac{\pi}{4}\right)$

🕮 Simplify each expression using fundamental trigonometric identities.

66) $\cot x \sec x \sin x =$ _____

67) $\sin x \cos^2 x - \sin x =$ _____

68) $\tan^3 x \csc^3 x =$ _____

69) $\frac{\tan x}{\sec x} =$ _____

🕮 Simplify each trigonometric expression using Pythagorean identities.

70) $(\sin x + \cos x)^2 =$

71) $(1 + \cot^2 x) \sin^2 x =$

72) $\csc^2 x - \cot^2 x =$

73) $2\sin^2 x + \cos^2 x =$

🕮 Solve using cofunction identities.

74) $\sin x = \cos 35°$

75) $\cot x = \tan 80°$

76) $\csc 68° = \sec x$

77) $\sec(3x) = \csc(x + 22°)$

🔖 Solve using periodicity identities.

78) $\sin \frac{22\pi}{3}$

79) $\tan \frac{17\pi}{2}$

80) $\cos \frac{25\pi}{4}$

81) $\sin \frac{14\pi}{3}$

🔖 Solve.

82) If $\sin(\theta) = \frac{2}{5}$ and θ is in the second quadrant, find exact values for $\cos(2\theta)$.

83) If $\cos(\theta) = \frac{4}{5}$ and θ is in the fourth quadrant, find exact values for $\sin(2\theta)$.

84) Use a half-angle identity to find the exact value of each expression.

$\cos 30° =$

$\cos 105° =$

🔖 Find the value of angles.

85) $\cos 75°$

86) $\sin 30°$

87) $\sin(30° + 45°)$

88) $\cos(-15°)$

89) $\tan 75°$

90) $\sin(-75°)$

🔖 Simplify the expressions.

91) $\cos\left(\frac{\pi}{4}\right) \times \cos\left(\frac{3\pi}{4}\right)$

92) $2\sin^2(2\theta) + \cos(4\theta)$

93) $\sin(7x) - \sin(3x)$

94) $\cos(5x) + \cos(x)$

Chapter 8: Answers

1) $\frac{89\pi}{36}$

2) $\frac{13\pi}{18}$

3) $\frac{12\pi}{5}$

4) $\frac{19\pi}{3}$

5) $\frac{50\pi}{9}$

6) $1,260°$

7) $30°$

8) $200°$

9) $324°$

10) $450°$

11) $153°$

12) $-33°$

13) $-31°$

14) $155°$

15) $59°$

16) $\frac{19\pi}{15}$

17) $\frac{17\pi}{27}$

18) $\frac{19\pi}{44}$

19) $-\frac{23\pi}{10}$

20) $\frac{11\pi}{6}$

21) $50°$

22) $30°$

23) $65°$

24) $85°$

25) $\theta = 235°$
    $\theta = 305°$

26) $\theta = 263°$
    $\theta = 277°$

27) $50°$

28) $35°$

29) $280°$

30) $280°$

31) $\frac{4\pi}{5}$

32) $\frac{2\pi}{9}$

33) $\frac{5\pi}{18}$

34) $\frac{5\pi}{12}$

35) $\frac{4\pi}{9}$

36) $\frac{8\pi}{7}$

37) $\sin\theta = y$ −coordinate of $P = \frac{1}{2}$
    $\cos\theta = x$ −coordinate of $P = -\frac{\sqrt{3}}{2}$

38) $\sin\theta = y$ −coordinate of $P = -\frac{\sqrt{2}}{2}$
    $\cos\theta = x$ −coordinate of $P = \frac{\sqrt{2}}{2}$

39) 11.0

40) 18.8

41) 40.8

42) 41.9

43) 2.8

44) 1.6

45) 50.2

46) 18.8

47) $\sin\gamma = \frac{5}{9}, \cos\gamma = \frac{2}{3}, \tan\frac{5}{6}$

48) $\sin\gamma = \frac{1}{3}, \cos\gamma = \frac{5}{7}, \tan\frac{7}{15}$

49) $\sin\gamma = \frac{7}{10}, \cos\gamma = \frac{6}{10}, \tan\frac{7}{6}$

50) $\frac{5}{3}$

51) $\frac{3}{2}$

52) Domain: $(-\infty, +\infty)$
    Range: $[-5, -3]$

53) Domain: $(-\infty, +\infty)$
    Range: $[-4, -2]$

54) Domain: $(-\infty, +\infty)$
    Range: $[\frac{1}{3}, 1]$

55) Domain: $(-\infty, +\infty)$
    Range: $[4, 8]$

56) The domain: $-1 \le x \le 1$
    The range: $0 \le f(x) \le \pi$
    $x = \frac{\sqrt{2}}{2}$

57) The domain: $-\infty < x < +\infty$
    The range: $-\frac{\pi}{2} < f(x) < \frac{\pi}{2}$
    $y = \frac{\pi}{3}$

58) $\frac{2\pi}{3}$

59) $-\frac{\pi}{4}$

60) $-\frac{\pi}{4}$

61) $-\frac{\pi}{6}$

62) $\frac{1}{x}$

63) $\sqrt{3}$

64) $\frac{\pi}{2}$

65) $\frac{\pi}{2}$

66) 1

67) $-\sin^3 x$

68) $\sec^3 x$

69) $\sin x$

70) $1 + \sin(2x)$

71) 1

72) 1

73) $1 + \sin^2 x$

74) $55°$

75) $10°$

76) $22°$

77) $17°$

78) $-\frac{\sqrt{3}}{2}$

79) Undefined

80) $\frac{\sqrt{2}}{2}$

81) $\frac{\sqrt{3}}{2}$

82) $\frac{17}{25}$

83) $-\frac{24}{25}$

84) $a = \frac{\sqrt{3}}{2}, b = \frac{\sqrt{2}-\sqrt{6}}{4}$

85) $\frac{\sqrt{6}-\sqrt{2}}{4}$

86) $\frac{1}{2}$

87) $\frac{\sqrt{6}+\sqrt{2}}{4}$

88) $\frac{\sqrt{6}+\sqrt{2}}{4}$

89) $2 + \sqrt{3}$

90) $\frac{-\sqrt{6}--\sqrt{2}}{4}$

91) $-\frac{1}{2}$

92) 0

93) $2\sin(2x)\cos(5x)$

94) $2\cos(3x)\cos(2x)$

Effortless
Math
Education

CHAPTER 9
Trigonometric Functions and Graphs

Math topics that you'll learn in this chapter:

- ☑ Graph of the Sine Function
- ☑ Graph of the Cosine Function
- ☑ Amplitude, Period, and Phase Shift
- ☑ Writing the Equation of a Sine Graph
- ☑ Writing the Equation of a Cosine Graph
- ☑ Graph of the Tangent Function
- ☑ Graph of the Cosecant Function
- ☑ Graph of the Secant Function
- ☑ Graph of the Cotangent Function
- ☑ Graph of Inverse of the Sine Function
- ☑ Graph of Inverse of the Cosine Function
- ☑ Graph of Inverse of the Tangent Function
- ☑ Sketching Trigonometric Graphs

Graph of the Sine Function

- The sine function is a set of ordered pairs of real numbers. Each ordered pair can be shown as a point on the coordinate plane.
- To graph the sine function, we plot a portion of the graph using a subset of the real numbers in the interval $0 \leq x \leq 2\pi$.
- We can see how x and y change by using the graph:
  - By increasing x from 0 to $\frac{\pi}{2}$, y increases from 0 to 1.
  - By increasing x from $\frac{\pi}{2}$ to π, y decreases from 1 to 0.
  - By increasing x from π to $\frac{3\pi}{2}$, y continues to decrease from 0 to -1.
  - By increasing x from $\frac{3\pi}{2}$ to 2π, y increases from -1 to 0.

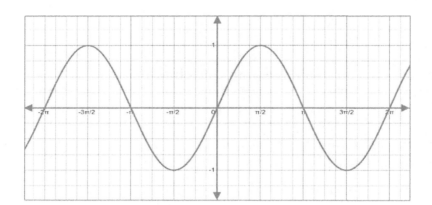

Example:

In the interval $-2\pi \leq x \leq 0$, for what values of x do $y = \sin x$ increase?

Solution: From the graph, we can see $y = \sin x$ increases in the interval $-2\pi \leq x \leq -\frac{3\pi}{2}$ and $-\frac{\pi}{2} \leq x \leq 0$.

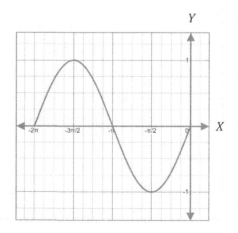

Graph of the Cosine Function

- The cosine function is a set of ordered pairs of real numbers.
- To graph the cosine function, we plot a portion of the graph using a subset of the real numbers in the interval $0 \leq x \leq 2\pi$.
- From the graph, we can know how x and y change:
  - By increasing x from 0 to $\frac{\pi}{2}$, y decreases from 1 to 0.
  - By increasing x from $\frac{\pi}{2}$ to π, y decreases from 0 to -1.
  - By increasing x from π to $\frac{3\pi}{2}$, y increases from -1 to 0.
  - By increasing x from $\frac{3\pi}{2}$ to 2π, y increases from 0 to 1.

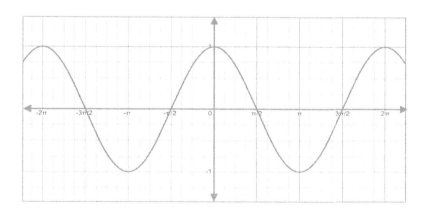

Example:

For what values of x in the interval $0 \leq x \leq 2\pi$, does $y = \cos x$ have a maximum value?

Solution: From the graph, we can see $y = \cos x$ at $x = 0$, and $x = 2\pi$ has a maximum value of 1.

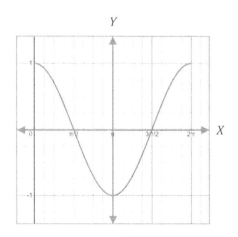

Amplitude, Period, and Phase Shift

- For the function $y = a \sin x$, the maximum value of the function is $|a|$, and the minimum value of the function is $-|a|$.
- For the function $y = a \cos x$, the maximum value of the function is $|a|$, and the minimum value of the function is $-|a|$.
- The amplitude of a periodic function is the absolute value of half the difference between the maximum and minimum value of y.
- The difference between the x −coordinates of the endpoints of the interval for one graph cycle is the graph period.
- The period of $y = \cos bx$ and $y = \sin bx$ is $\left|\frac{2\pi}{b}\right|$.
- The phase shift is a horizontal translation of a trigonometric function.
- For the $y = a \sin b(x + c)$ and $y = a \cos b(x + c)$, the phase shift is $-c$.

Examples:

Example 1. Determine the amplitude, the period, and the phase shift of $y = -9 \cos(8x + \pi) - 8$.

Solution: Amplitude = 9

Period = $\frac{\pi}{4}$

Phase shift = $-\frac{\pi}{8}$

Example 2. Determine the amplitude, the period, and the phase shift of $y = \sin(3x - 4) + 5$.

Solution: Amplitude = 1

Period = $\frac{2\pi}{3}$

Phase shift = $\frac{4}{3}$

Writing the Equation of a Sine Graph

- Using these steps, we can write an equation for the sine graph:
  - Find a by identifying the maximum and minimum values of y for the function. $a = \frac{maximum - minimum}{2}$
  - Define a basic cycle of the sine graph that starts at $y = 0$, increases to a maximum value, decreases to 0, continues to decrease to the minimum value, and then increases to 0. Find the x-coordinates of the endpoints of this cycle. Write the domain of a cycle in interval notation, $x_0 \leq x \leq x_1$ or $[x_0, x_1]$.
  - The period of one cycle is $\frac{2\pi}{b} = x_1 - x_0$. Use this formula to find b.
  - The c value is the opposite of the lower endpoint of the interval of the basic cycle: $c = -x_0$.

Example:

Determine the equation of the graph below in the form $y = a \sin bx$.

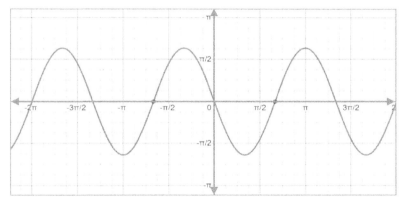

Solution: The max and min values of y are 2 and -2. So, $a = \frac{2-(-2)}{2} = 2$.
The cycle of the curve is in the interval $-\frac{2\pi}{3} \leq x \leq \frac{2\pi}{3}$. The period is $\frac{2\pi}{3} - \left(-\frac{2\pi}{3}\right)$ or $\frac{4\pi}{3}$. So $\frac{2\pi}{b} = \frac{4\pi}{3} \Rightarrow b = \frac{3}{2}$.
The c value is $-\left(-\frac{2\pi}{3}\right)$, therefore the phase shift is $\frac{2\pi}{3}$.
$y = 2 \sin\left(\frac{3}{2}x + \frac{2\pi}{3}\right)$

Writing the Equation of a Cosine Graph

- Using these steps, we can write an equation for the cosine graph:
  - Find a by identifying the maximum and minimum values of y for the function. $a = \frac{maximum - minimum}{2}$.
  - Define one basic cycle of the graph that starts at the maximum value, decreases to 0, continues to decrease to the minimum value, increases to 0, and then increases to the maximum value. Find the x-coordina-tes of the endpoints of this cycle. Write the domain of a cycle in interval notation, $x_0 \leq x \leq x_1$ or $[x_0, x_1]$.
  - The period of one cycle is $\frac{2\pi}{b} = x_1 - x_0$. Use this formula to find b.
  - The c value is the opposite of the lower endpoint of the interval of the basic cycle: $c = -x_0$.

Example:

Determine the equation of the graph below in the form $y = a \cos bx$.

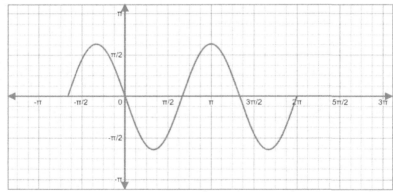

Solution: The max and min values of y are 2 and -2. So, $a = \frac{2-(-2)}{2} = 2$.
The cycle of the curve is in the interval $-\frac{\pi}{3} \leq x \leq \pi$. The period is $\pi - \left(-\frac{\pi}{3}\right)$ or $\frac{4\pi}{3}$.
So, $\frac{2\pi}{b} = \frac{4\pi}{3} \Rightarrow b = \frac{3}{2}$.
The c value is $-\left(-\frac{\pi}{3}\right)$, therefore the phase shift is $\frac{\pi}{3}$.
The equation of the graph is $y = 2 \cos \frac{3}{2}\left(x + \frac{\pi}{3}\right)$.

Graph of the Tangent Function

- The tangent graph is a curve that increases through negative values of $\tan x$ to 0 and then continues to increase through positive values.
- The graph is discontinuous at odd multiples of $\frac{\pi}{2}$ and then repeats the same pattern.
- The $\tan$ graph displays a vertical line at $x = \frac{\pi}{2}$ and at every value of x that is an odd multiple of $\frac{\pi}{2}$. These lines are vertical asymptotes.
- The one complete cycle of the curve is in the interval from $x = -\frac{\pi}{2}$ to $x = \frac{\pi}{2}$ and the period of the curve is π.

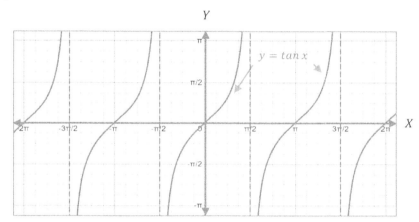

Example:

Draw the graph of $y = \tan\left(x - \frac{\pi}{4}\right)$ in the interval of $-\frac{\pi}{4} < x < \frac{3\pi}{4}$.

Solution: The graph of $y = \tan\left(x - \frac{\pi}{4}\right)$ is the graph of $y = \tan x$ but the phase shift is $\frac{\pi}{4}$.

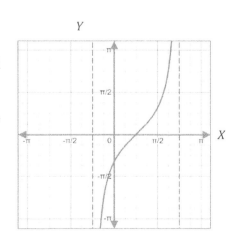

Graph of the Cosecant Function

- The cosecant function is identified in terms of the sine function: $\csc x = \frac{1}{\sin x}$.

- To draw the cosecant function graph, use the reciprocals of the sine function values.

- There are reciprocals of the sine function for $-1 \leq \sin x < 0$, and for $0 < \sin x < 1$. So, $-\infty < \csc x \leq -1$, $1 \leq \csc x < \infty$.

- For values of x that are multiples of π, $\sin x = 0$, and $\csc x$ is not defined.

- For integral values of n, the vertical lines on the graph are asymptote at $x = n\pi$.

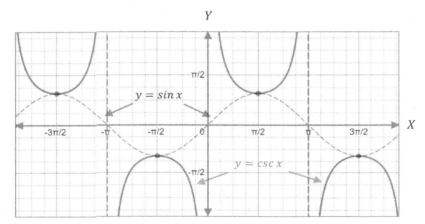

Example:

Draw one period of $y = -3\csc(4x)$.

Solution: Draw a graph of the function $y = -3\sin(4x)$. Sketch vertical asymptotes and fill in the cosecant curve in between the asymptotes.

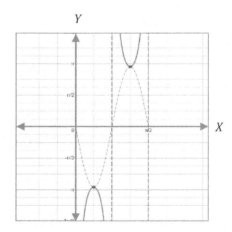

Graph of the Secant Function

- The secant function is identified in terms of the cosine function: $\sec x = \frac{1}{\cos x}$.
- To draw the secant function, use reciprocals of the cosine function values.
- There are reciprocals of the cosine function for $-1 \leq \cos x < 0$, and for $0 < \cos x \leq 1$. So, $-\infty < \sec x \leq -1$, $1 \leq \sec x < \infty$.
- For x values that are odd multiples of $\frac{\pi}{2}$, $\cos x = 0$, and $\sec x$ is not defined.
- For integral values of n, the vertical lines on the graph are asymptote at $x = \frac{\pi}{2} + n\pi$.

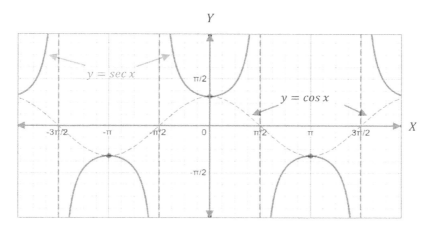

Example:

Draw one period of $y = \sec\left(2x - \frac{\pi}{2}\right) + 3$.

Solution: Draw a graph of the function.
$$y = \cos\left(2x - \frac{\pi}{2}\right) + 3$$

Sketch vertical asymptotes and fill in the secant curve in between the asymptotes.

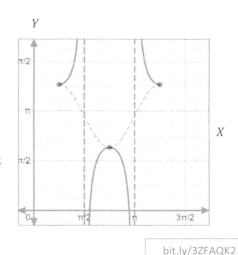

Graph of the Cotangent Function

- The cotangent function is identified in terms of the tangent function:
$$\cot x = \frac{1}{\tan x}$$
- To draw the cotangent function, use the reciprocals of the tangent function values.
- For values of x that are multiples of π, $\tan x = 0$, and $\cot x$ is not defined.
- For values of x that $\tan x$ is not defined, $\cot x = 0$.
- For integral values of n, the vertical lines on the graph are asymptote at $x = n\pi$.

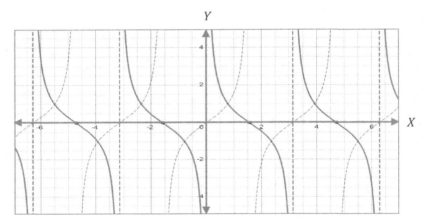

Example:

Draw one period of $y = \cot\left(x + \frac{\pi}{2}\right)$.

Solution: Draw a graph of the function.
$$y = \tan\left(x + \frac{\pi}{2}\right)$$
Sketch vertical asymptotes and fill in the cotangent curve in between the asymptotes.

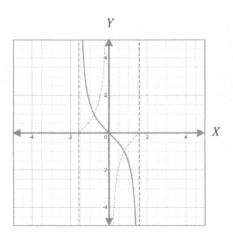

Graph of Inverse of the Sine Function

- If we limit the domain of the sine function to $-\frac{\pi}{2} \leq x \leq \frac{\pi}{2}$, that subset of the sine function is a one-to-one function and has an inverse function.
- When we reflect that subset on the line $y = x$, the image of the function is $y = \arcsin x$ or $y = \sin^{-1} x$.

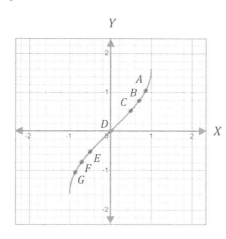

$A: \left(\frac{\sqrt{3}}{2}, \frac{\pi}{3}\right)$

$B: \left(\frac{\sqrt{2}}{2}, \frac{\pi}{4}\right)$

$C: \left(\frac{1}{2}, \frac{\pi}{6}\right)$

$D: (0,0)$

$E: \left(-\frac{1}{2}, -\frac{\pi}{6}\right)$

$F: \left(-\frac{\sqrt{2}}{2}, -\frac{\pi}{4}\right)$

$G: \left(-\frac{\sqrt{3}}{2}, -\frac{\pi}{3}\right)$

Example:

Draw the function $y = 3\sin^{-1}(x+1)$.

Solution: The graph of $y = 3\sin^{-1}(x+1)$ is the graph of $y = \sin^{-1} x$ but the phase shift is -1.

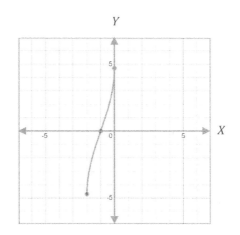

Graph of Inverse of the Cosine Function

- If we limit the domain of the cosine function to $0 \leq x \leq \pi$, that subset of the cosine function is a one-to-one function and has an inverse function.

- When we reflect that subset on the line $y = x$, the image of the function is $y = \arccos x$ or $y = \cos^{-1} x$.

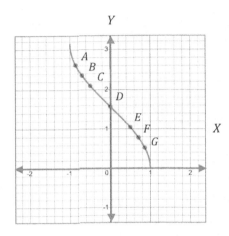

A: $\left(\frac{\sqrt{3}}{2}, \frac{\pi}{6}\right)$

B: $\left(\frac{\sqrt{2}}{2}, \frac{\pi}{4}\right)$

C: $\left(\frac{1}{2}, \frac{\pi}{3}\right)$

D: $\left(0, \frac{\pi}{2}\right)$

E: $\left(-\frac{1}{2}, \frac{2\pi}{3}\right)$

F: $\left(-\frac{\sqrt{2}}{2}, \frac{3\pi}{4}\right)$

G: $\left(-\frac{\sqrt{3}}{2}, \frac{5\pi}{6}\right)$

Example:

Draw the function $y = 2\cos^{-1}(x - 1)$.

Solution: The graph of $y = 2\cos^{-1}(x - 1)$ is the graph of $y = \cos^{-1} x$ but the phase shift is 1.

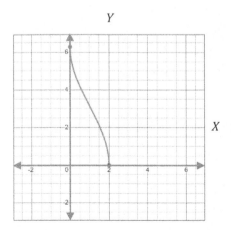

Graph of Inverse of the Tangent Function

- If we limit the domain of the tangent function to $-\frac{\pi}{2} < x < \frac{\pi}{2}$, that subset of the tangent function is a one-to-one function and has an inverse function.
- When we reflect that subset on the line $y = x$, the image of the function is $y = \arctan x$ or $y = \tan^{-1} x$.

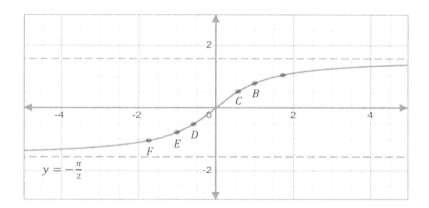

A: $\left(\sqrt{3}, \frac{\pi}{3}\right)$
B: $\left(1, \frac{\pi}{4}\right)$
C: $\left(\frac{\sqrt{3}}{3}, \frac{\pi}{6}\right)$
D: $\left(-\frac{\sqrt{3}}{3}, -\frac{\pi}{6}\right)$
E: $\left(-1, -\frac{\pi}{4}\right)$
F: $\left(-\sqrt{3}, -\frac{\pi}{3}\right)$

Example:

Draw the function $y = -2\tan^{-1}(x - 1)$.

Solution: The graph of $y = -2\tan^{-1}(x - 1)$ is the graph of $y = \tan^{-1} x$ but the phase shift is 1.

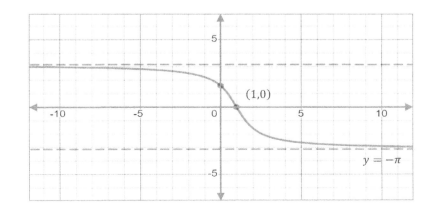

Sketching Trigonometric Graphs

- For $y = a \cos b(x + c)$ and $y = a \sin b(x + c)$:
  - amplitude = $|a|$
  - number of cycles in a 2π interval = $|b|$
  - period of the graph = $\frac{2\pi}{|b|}$
  - phase shift = $-c$
- The values of a, b, and c change the curves of sine and cosine without changing the fundamental shape of a cycle of the graph.

Example:

Draw two cycles of the graph of $y = 2 \sin\left(x - \frac{\pi}{4}\right)$.

Solution: For $y = 2 \sin\left(x - \frac{\pi}{4}\right)$, $a = 2$, $b = 1$, $c = \frac{\pi}{4}$. So, one cycle starts at $x = \frac{\pi}{4}$. There is a complete cycle in the interval 2π, which is from $\frac{\pi}{4}$ to $\frac{9\pi}{4}$. Divide this interval into four equal intervals and draw one cycle of the sine curve with a maximum of 2 and a minimum of -2.

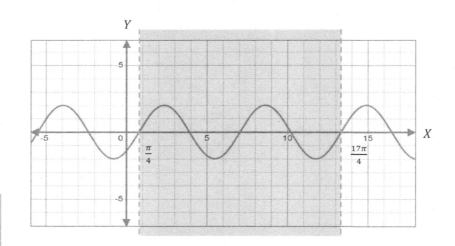

Chapter 9: Practices

✎ **Graph the following functions.**

1) $y = 2 \sin 2x$

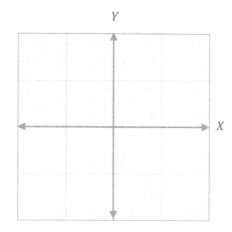

2) $y = -3 \sin x$

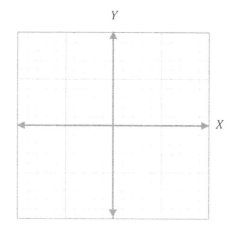

✎ **Graph the following functions.**

3) $y = -2 \cos x$

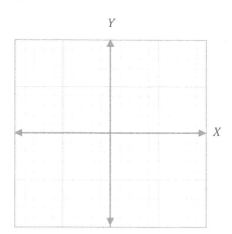

4) $y = 3 \cos 2x - 2$

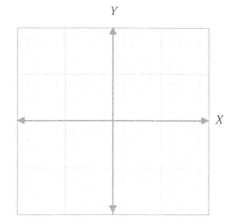

Chapter 9: Trigonometric Functions and Graphs

✍ **Determine the amplitude, the period, and the phase shift of:**

5) $y = \sin\left(x - \frac{\pi}{4}\right) - 2$

   Amplitude: ___

   Period: ___

   Phase shift: ___

6) $y = 3\cos\left(2x - \frac{\pi}{6}\right)$

   Amplitude: ___

   Period: ___

   Phase shift: ___

7) $y = -2\sin\left(\frac{2}{3}x - \frac{\pi}{3}\right)$

   Amplitude: ___

   Period: ___

   Phase shift: ___

8) $y = \frac{2}{3}\cos\left(2x + \frac{\pi}{3}\right) - 2$

   Amplitude: ___

   Period: ___

   Phase shift: ___

✍ **Determine the equation of the graph below.**

9) _____

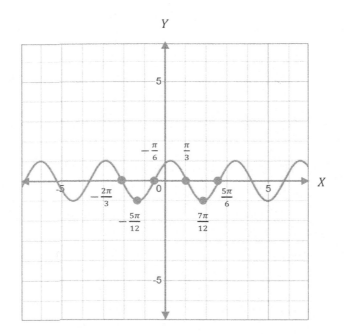

Effortless Math Education

EffortlessMath.com

Determine the equation of the graph below.

10) _____

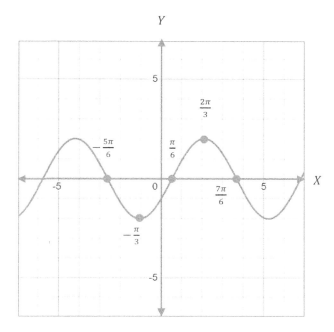

Draw the graph of equations.

11) $y = \tan\left(x - \frac{\pi}{4}\right)$

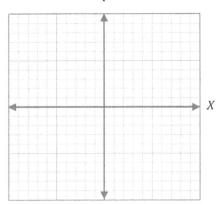

12) $y = 2\csc(3x)$

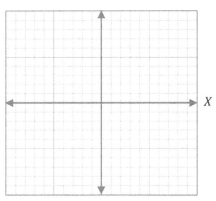

13) $y = 4\sin^{-1}(x + 4)$

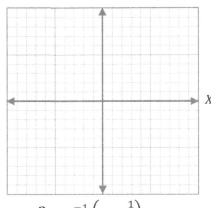

14) $y = 2\cos^{-1}\left(x - \frac{1}{2}\right)$

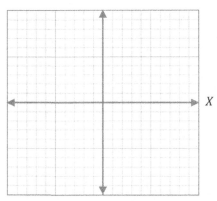

Draw two cycles of the graph.

15) $y = 3\cos\left(x - \frac{\pi}{2}\right)$

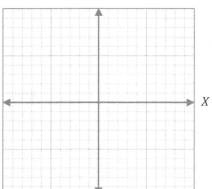

Chapter 9: Answers

1)
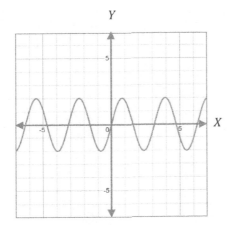

2)
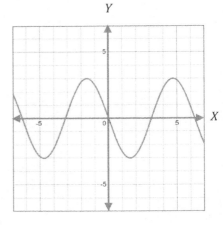

3)
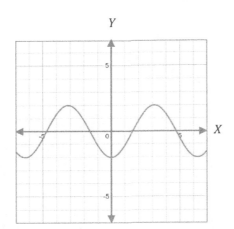

4)
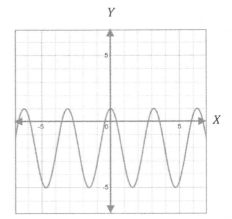

5) Amplitude: 1

   Period: 2π

   Phase shift: $\frac{\pi}{4}$

6) Amplitude: 3

   Period: π

   Phase shift: $\frac{\pi}{12}$

7) Amplitude: 2

   Period: 3π

   Phase shift: $\frac{\pi}{2}$

8) Amplitude: $\frac{2}{3}$

   Period: π

   Phase shift: $-\frac{\pi}{6}$

Effortless Math Education

9) $y = sin\left(2x + \frac{\pi}{3}\right)$

10) $y = 2\,cos\left(x - \frac{2\pi}{3}\right)$

11)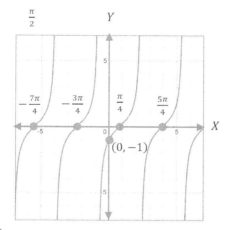

12)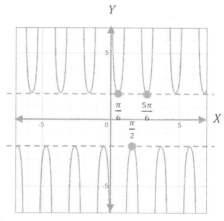

13)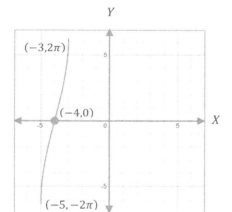

14)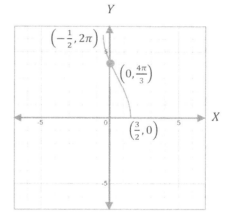

15)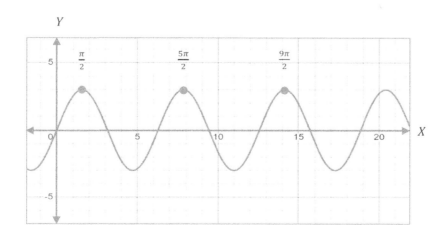

CHAPTER 10: Trigonometric Equations

Math topics that you'll learn in this chapter:

- ☑ Basic Techniques for Solving Trigonometric Equations
- ☑ Factoring and Simplifying Trigonometric Expressions
- ☑ Solving Equations with Multiple Angles

Basic Techniques for Solving Trigonometric Equations

- Basic Techniques for Solving Trigonometric Equations involve the application of fundamental trigonometric identities and algebraic methods to find the values of the unknown variable(s) in equations that involve trigonometric functions. Key techniques include:
  - **Simplification:** Reduce the equation to its simplest form by applying trigonometric identities such as reciprocal, quotient, Pythagorean, co-function, and double-angle identities.
  - **Factoring:** Factor trigonometric expressions to simplify complex equations, which may allow them to be solved more easily.
  - **Isolating the variable:** Rearrange the equation so that the trigonometric function containing the variable is isolated on one side, making it easier to solve for the variable.
  - **Using inverse trigonometric functions:** Apply inverse trigonometric functions ($sin^{-1}, cos^{-1}, tan^{-1}$) to both sides of the equation to cancel out the trigonometric functions and obtain the value of the variable.
  - **Solving for multiple angles:** In some cases, an equation may have multiple solutions within a given range. Use the periodicity and symmetries of trigonometric functions to find all possible solutions.
  - **Graphing:** Graph the trigonometric function to visualize its behavior and obtain approximate solutions, particularly when algebraic methods prove difficult.
- By employing these techniques in combination, you can effectively solve a wide range of trigonometric equations.

Example:

Solve the trigonometric equation: $3 \sin(x) = 2 \cos^2(x)$, for x between 0 and 2π.
Solution: To solve this trigonometric equation, we can use the identity $cos^2(x) + sin^2(x) = 1$ to rewrite the equation in terms of $sin(x)$:
$3 \sin(x) = 2(1 - \sin^2(x)) \Rightarrow 3 \sin(x) = 2 - 2 \sin^2(x)$
Rearranging and factoring, we obtain: $2 \sin^2(x) + 3 \sin(x) - 2 = 0$. This is a quadratic equation in $sin(x)$, so we can solve it using the quadratic formula:
$sin(x) = \frac{-3 \pm \sqrt{3^2 - 4(2)(-2)}}{2(2)} \Rightarrow sin(x) = \frac{-3 \pm \sqrt{25}}{4} \Rightarrow sin(x) = \frac{1}{2}$, or $sin(x) = -2$.
The second solution is not possible since the range of $sin(x)$ is between -1 and 1, so we only consider the solution $sin(x) = \frac{1}{2}$. To find the values of x that satisfy $sin(x) = \frac{1}{2}$, so the solutions for x between 0 and 2π are: $x = \frac{\pi}{6}$ or $x = \frac{5\pi}{6}$.

Factoring and Simplifying Trigonometric Expressions

- Factoring and Simplifying Trigonometric Expressions are essential techniques in trigonometry, used to break down complex expressions and equations into simpler forms. This makes it easier to analyze, understand, and solve trigonometric problems. Key methods include:
  - **Basic Factoring:** Identify common factors in the terms of an expression and use the distributive property to factor them out.
  - **Trigonometric Identities:** Apply fundamental trigonometric identities like reciprocal, quotient, Pythagorean, co-function, and double-angle identities to simplify expressions or rewrite them in equivalent forms.
  - **Trig Functions as Algebraic Expressions:** Use substitutions to represent trigonometric functions as algebraic expressions (e.g., using $sin^2 x + cos^2 x = 1$), which can then be factored and simplified using standard algebraic techniques.
  - **Factoring Techniques:** Apply algebraic factoring techniques such as factoring by grouping, the difference of squares, and the sum/difference of cubes to simplify trigonometric expressions.
  - **Rationalizing Denominators:** Simplify expressions with trigonometric functions in the denominator by multiplying the numerator and denominator by the conjugate of the denominator, which helps eliminate complex trigonometric terms.
- By using these techniques, trigonometric expressions can be simplified, making it easier to solve related equations and understand the underlying mathematical relationships.

Example:

Factor the following trigonometric expression: $sin^2 x - sin x - 6$.

Solution: To factor the expression $sin^2 x - sin x - 6$, we can first look for two numbers that multiply to -6 and add to -1 (the coefficient of $sin x$). These numbers are -3 and 2, since $-3 \times 2 = -6$ and $-3 + 2 = -1$.

Now we can express the expression as $sin^2 x - 3 sin x + 2 sin x - 6$, and group the terms as follows: $(sin^2 x - 3 sin x) + (2 sin x - 6)$.

Next, we can factor out $sin x$ from the first group and factor out 2 from the second group: $sin x (sin x - 3) + 2(sin x - 3)$.

Notice that we now have a common factor of $(sin x - 3)$, so we can simplify the expression as: $(sin x - 3)(sin x + 2)$.

Therefore, the factored form of $sin^2 x - sin x - 6$ is: $(sin x - 3)(sin x + 2)$.

Solving Equations with Multiple Angles

- Solving Equations with Multiple Angles involves finding the values of the unknown variable(s) in trigonometric equations that contain multiple angles, like $2x$ or $3x$, instead of a single angle. Key techniques include:
    - **Simplification:** Use trigonometric identities, such as double-angle, half-angle, or triple-angle identities, to rewrite expressions involving multiple angles in simpler terms, making it easier to solve the equation.
    - **Substitution:** Temporarily replace the multiple-angle expression (e.g., $2x$) with a new variable (e.g., $y = 2x$) to convert the equation into a single-angle equation. Solve for the new variable, and then replace it with the original expression to find the solution(s) for the initial variable.
    - **Solve for one angle first:** If the equation contains more than one trigonometric function with different multiples of the angle (e.g., $sin(2x)$ and $cos(x)$), try to express all trigonometric functions in terms of a single angle using identities.
    - **Consider the periodicity of trigonometric functions:** Since trigonometric functions are periodic, multiple-angle equations may have multiple solutions within a given range.
- By employing these techniques, you can efficiently solve trigonometric equations involving multiple angles and find all possible solutions.

Example:

Solve the following equation for values of x between 0 and 360 degrees:
$$2\sin(2x) + \cos(x) = 0$$
Solution: We can use double-angle and sum-to-product identities to simplify the equation. First, let's rewrite the double-angle identity for sine:
$$2\sin(2x) = 2(2\sin(x)\cos(x))$$
Now, let's substitute this into the equation: $2(2\sin(x)\cos(x)) + \cos(x) = 0$.
Expanding and rearranging the terms:
$$4\sin(x)\cos(x) + \cos(x) = 0 \Rightarrow \cos(x)(4\sin(x) + 1) = 0$$
Now, we have two possible cases:
$$\cos(x) = 0$$
$$4\sin(x) + 1 = 0$$
For the first case, $\cos(x) = 0$, we know that $\cos(x) = 0$ when $x = 90$ degrees and $x = 270$ degrees. For the second case, $4\sin(x) + 1 = 0$, we can solve for $\sin(x)$:
$$4\sin(x) = -1 \Rightarrow \sin(x) = -\frac{1}{4}$$
Using the inverse sine function, we find two solutions:
$x = \arcsin\left(-\frac{1}{4}\right) \approx -14.48$ degrees and $x = 180 - \arcsin\left(-\frac{1}{4}\right) \approx 194.48$ degrees.

Chapter 10: Practices

🖎 Solve.

1) $3\sin(2x) - 2\cos(x) = 0$ for x between 0 and 2π

2) $2\tan(2x) + 1 = 0$ in the interval $[0, 360°)$

3) $\sin(x) + 2\cos(2x) = 1$ in the interval $[0, 360°)$

🖎 Factor the expression.

4) $4\cos^2\theta - 4\cos\theta + 1$

5) $\sin^2\theta + \sin\theta - 2$

6) $\cos^3\theta - 8\cos\theta - 3\cos^2\theta + 24$

7) $3\sin^3 x - 3\sin^2 x - 5\sin x + 5$

🖎 Solve.

8) $5\sin(\theta) + 3\cos(2\theta) = 4$

9) $2\sin(2x) - 3\cos(x) = 0$

10) $\sqrt{\cos x} = 2\cos x - 1$

11) $2\tan^4 x - \tan^2 x - 15 = 0$

12) $3\sin(\theta) + 2\sin^2(\theta) = -1$

Chapter 10: Answers

1) $\frac{\pi}{2}, \frac{3\pi}{2}, 0.34, \pi - 0.34$

2) 67.72°, 166.72°, 256.72°

3) 39.82°, 140.18°, 202.97°, 337.02°

4) $(2\cos\theta - 1)^2$

5) $(\sin\theta - 1)(\sin\theta + 2)$

6) $(\cos\theta - 3)(\cos^2\theta - 8)$

7) $(\sin x - 1)(3 - 5)$

8) 30°, 19.47°, 160.52°, 150°

9) 90°, 270°, 48.59°, 131.41°

10) 0°

11) 60°, 120°

12) 210°, 330°, 270°

Chapter 11: Trigonometric Applications

Math topics that you'll learn in this chapter:

- ☑ Law of Sines: Definition and Applications
- ☑ Law of Cosines: Definition and Applications
- ☑ Area of a Triangle Using Trigonometry

Law of Sines: Definition and Applications

- When you know the measures of 2 factors in a triangle as well as one of the sides, as in the case of ASA or AAS, you can use the law of sines to determine the measures of the other two angles and the other side.
- For $\triangle ABC$, the Law of Sines states the following:
$$\frac{a}{\sin A} = \frac{b}{\sin B} = \frac{c}{\sin C}$$

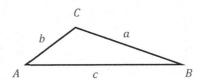

Examples:

Example 1. For a triangle, it is given $a = 12\ cm$, $c = 14.5\ cm$ and angle $C = 54°$. Find the angle A of the triangle.

Solution: Use the Law of Sines to find the angle A.

$$\frac{a}{\sin A} = \frac{c}{\sin C}$$

$$\frac{12}{\sin A} = \frac{14.5}{\sin 54°} \Rightarrow \sin A = \frac{12 \times \sin 54°}{14.5}$$

$$\sin A = \frac{12 \times 0.8}{14.5} = \frac{9.6}{14.5} = 0.66 \Rightarrow A = 42.03°$$

Example 2. In the ABC triangle, find side a.

Solution: Use the Law of Sines to find side a.

$$\frac{a}{\sin 30°} = \frac{54}{\sin 20°} \Rightarrow a = \frac{54 \times \sin 30°}{\sin 20°}$$

$$a = \frac{54 \times 0.5}{0.34} = \frac{27}{0.34} = 79.41$$

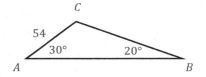

Example 3. For a triangle, it is given $A = 62°$, $B = 55°$ and $c = 5\ cm$. Find side b of the triangle.

Solution: Use the Law of Sines to find side b.

$62° + 55° + C = 180° \Rightarrow C = 63°$

$$\frac{b}{\sin B} = \frac{c}{\sin C} \Rightarrow \frac{b}{\sin 55°} = \frac{5}{\sin 63°} \Rightarrow b = \frac{\sin 55° \times 5}{\sin 63°} \Rightarrow b = 4.59\ cm$$

Law of Cosines: Definition and Applications

- The Law of Cosines states: $c^2 = a^2 + b^2 - 2ab \times cos(C)$
  Where: a, b, and c are the lengths of the sides of a triangle.
  C is the angle opposite side c.
- Here's a derivation of the Law of Cosines using the dot product concept from vector algebra:
  - Consider a non-right triangle with sides a, b, and c, with C being the angle between sides a and b. To derive the law of cosines, first, draw a line from the angle C perpendicular to side c, forming two right triangles. This line divides side c into two segments: one with length x and the other with length $(c - x)$.
  - By the Pythagorean theorem, the length of the line drawn (h) can be determined in terms of a, b, and x: $h^2 = b^2 - x^2$ and $h^2 = a^2 - (c - x)^2$.

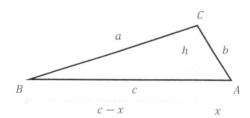

  - By equating and simplifying these equations, we get:
    $a^2 - (c - x)^2 = b^2 - x^2 \Rightarrow a^2 - (c^2 - 2cx + x^2) = b^2 - x^2$
  - This simplifies to: $a^2 - b^2 = c^2 - 2cx$.
  - We know that $cos(A) = \frac{x}{b}$ from one of the right triangles. Solving for x gives us $x = b \times cos(A)$. Substitute this into the previous equation:
    $a^2 - b^2 = c^2 - 2c \times b \times cos(A)$
  - Rearranging terms, we get the law of cosines:
    $a^2 = b^2 + c^2 - 2b \times c \times cos(A)$

Example:

Find angle B in the ABC triangle.
Solution: Use the Law of Cosines to find angle B. $cos B = \frac{a^2+c^2-b^2}{2ac}$
$cos B = \frac{8^2+10^2-14^2}{2\times 8\times 10} = \frac{64+100-196}{160} = -0.2 \Rightarrow B = 101.54°$

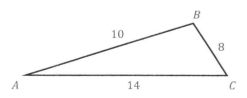

Area of a Triangle Using Trigonometry

- The area of a triangle can be found using trigonometry, especially when dealing with vectors in two dimensions. Trigonometry allows us to calculate the area when given information about the triangle's angles and side lengths. One common formula for finding the area of a triangle using trigonometry is derived from the sine of one of its angles.

- Given a triangle with sides a, b, and c, and an angle C opposite side c, the area A of the triangle can be calculated as follows:
$$A = \frac{1}{2} a \cdot b \cdot \sin C$$

Where:
- a and b are the lengths of two sides of the triangle.
- $\sin C$ is the sine of the angle C opposite side c.

- This formula is particularly useful when dealing with vectors, as we can apply it to find the area of triangles formed by vectors in two-dimensional space. Moreover, this approach can be generalized to calculate areas of other shapes, such as parallelograms and polygons, by decomposing them into triangles.

Example:

Consider a triangle with sides $a = 5$ and $b = 7$, and an angle $C = 60°$. Evaluate the area of the triangle.

Solution: The area A of the triangle can be calculated as follows:
$$A = \frac{1}{2} \times 5 \times 7 \times \sin 60° = \frac{1}{2} \times 5 \times 7 \times \frac{\sqrt{3}}{2} = \frac{35\sqrt{3}}{4} \approx 15.3$$

In this example, we used trigonometry to calculate the area of the triangle by taking half of the product of the two given sides and the sine of the given angle.

Chapter 11: Practices

✎ **Solve.**

1) Triangle ABC is a non-right triangle with side lengths $AB = 10\ cm$, $BC = 12\ cm$, and $CA = 8\ cm$. Angle BAC measures 60 degrees. Calculate the measures of angles ABC.

2) In a non-right triangle ABC, where angle A is acute and angle B is obtuse, the lengths of the sides are given as follows: side $AB = 8\ cm$, side $BC = 10\ cm$, and side $AC = 12\ cm$. Find the measures of angles A.

✎ **Find each measurement indicated. Round your answers to the nearest tenth.**

3) _____

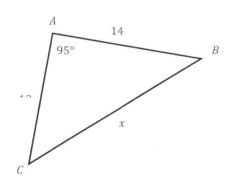

4) _____

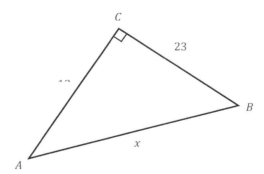

5) In $\triangle ABC$, $a = 15\ cm$,
   $b = 10\ cm$, $c = 7\ cm$

   _____

6) In $\triangle ABC$, $a = 18\ cm$,
   $b = 15\ cm$, $c = 11\ cm$

   _____

7) In $\triangle ABC$, $a = 12\ cm$,
   $b = 8\ cm$, $c = 10\ cm$

   _____

8) In $\triangle ABC$, $a = 12\ cm$,
   $m\angle B = 42°$, $c = 15\ cm$

   _____

Effortless Math Education

✎ Evaluate.

9) Given a triangle with sides $a = 4$ units, $b = 5$ units, and an included angle $C = 60°$, find the area of the triangle.

10) If the sides of a triangle are $6\ cm$, $8\ cm$, and the angle between them is $45°$, what is its area?

11) Determine the area of a triangle given two sides of lengths $9\ cm$ and $10\ cm$, with an angle of $120°$ between them.

12) Calculate the area of a triangle given sides of $10\ cm$ and $18\ cm$, and the included angle is 45.

13) A triangle has sides $15\ cm$ and $16\ cm$ with the angle between them being $\frac{\pi}{3}$. Find its area.

14) Given sides $9\ cm$ and $7\ cm$ of a triangle, and the angle between them is $150°$, find its area.

Chapter 11: Answers

1) 41.41°

2) 55.77°

3) $x = 19.2$

4) $x = 25.9$

5) $m\angle A = 122.9°, m\angle B = 34°, m\angle C = 23.1°$

6) $m\angle A = 86.1°, m\angle B = 56.3°, m\angle C = 37.6°$

7) $m\angle A = 82.8°, m\angle B = 41.4°, m\angle C = 55.8°$

8) $m\angle A = 52.9°, m\angle C = 85.1°, b = 10\ cm$

9) $10\sqrt{3}$

10) $24\sqrt{2}\ cm^2$

11) $45\sqrt{3}\ cm^2$

12) $52\ cm^2$

13) $120\sqrt{3}\ cm^2$

14) $38.25\ cm^2$

CHAPTER

12 Complex Numbers

Math topics that you'll learn in this chapter:

☑ Polar Coordinate System
☑ Converting Between Polar and Rectangular Coordinates
☑ Introduction to Complex Numbers
☑ Adding and Subtracting Complex Numbers
☑ Multiplying and Dividing Complex Numbers
☑ Rationalizing Imaginary Denominators
☑ Polar Form of Complex Numbers
☑ Multiplying and Dividing in Polar Form
☑ Powers and Roots in Polar Form
☑ Graphs of Polar Equations

Polar Coordinate System

- Polar coordinates are a two-dimensional coordinate system, just like the Cartesian (or rectangular) coordinate system. However, instead of using horizontal and vertical displacements (x and y) to locate points, polar coordinates locate points in the plane using a distance and an angle.
- The polar coordinate system is particularly useful in situations where the problem has rotational symmetry, for example in the study of circular and elliptical paths in physics and engineering.
- Here's a breakdown of polar coordinates:
  - **Radius (r):** The first element of a polar coordinate is 'r', which represents the direct distance from the origin (O) to the point in the plane. The value of 'r' can be any non-negative real number.
  - **Theta (θ):** The second element of a polar coordinate is 'θ', an angle measured counterclockwise from the positive x-axis to the line segment that joins the point to the origin.
- For example, the polar coordinates $(r, \theta) = \left(3, \frac{\pi}{2}\right)$ represent the point that is 3 units away from the origin, in the direction $\frac{\pi}{2}$ radians (or 90 degrees) counterclockwise from the positive x-axis. This point would be at (0,3) in Cartesian coordinates.

Example:

Find the angle, in degrees, between the positive x-axis and the line segment connecting the origin to the point (3,4) in the polar coordinate system.

Solution: To find the angle between the positive x-axis and the line segment connecting the origin to the point (3,4) in the polar coordinate system, we can use the angular coordinate (θ) of the point.

The angular coordinate (θ) represents the angle measured counterclockwise from the positive x-axis to the line segment connecting the origin to the point. In this case, θ can be found using the tangent function:

$$\theta = arctan\left(\frac{y}{x}\right) = arctan\left(\frac{4}{3}\right)$$

Using a calculator, we can find that $arctan\left(\frac{4}{3}\right)$ is approximately 53.13°.

Therefore, the angle between the positive x-axis and the line segment connecting the origin to the point (3,4) is approximately 53.13°.

Converting Between Polar and Rectangular Coordinates

Rectangular to Polar Conversion:
- Given a point in rectangular coordinates (x, y), we can find the polar coordinates (r, θ) using the following equations:
  - The radial coordinate 'r' is found using the Pythagorean theorem:
  $$r = \sqrt{(x^2 + y^2)}$$
  - The angular coordinate 'θ' can be found using trigonometric functions. The tangent of 'θ' is $\frac{y}{x}$, so $\theta = arctan\left(\frac{y}{x}\right)$. However, the value of 'θ' must be adjusted based on the quadrant of the point:
    - Quadrant I: $\theta = arctan\left(\frac{y}{x}\right)$
    - Quadrant II: $\theta = \pi + arctan\left(\frac{y}{x}\right)$
    - Quadrant III: $\theta = \pi + arctan\left(\frac{y}{x}\right)$
    - Quadrant IV: $\theta = 2\pi + arctan\left(\frac{y}{x}\right)$

Polar to Rectangular Conversion:
- Given a point in polar coordinates (r, θ), we can find the rectangular coordinates (x, y) using the following equations:
  - The x-coordinate can be found using the formula: $x = r \times cos(\theta)$.
  - The y-coordinate can be found using the formula: $y = r \times sin(\theta)$.
- Note: Make sure that the angle θ is in the correct form (usually radians) for the trigonometric functions.
- Remember, these conversion methods are applicable in a $2D$ plane. If you are working with $3D$ space, you would use cylindrical or spherical coordinates instead of polar.

Example:

Sarah is located at coordinates $(1, \sqrt{3})$ in the rectangular coordinate system. Convert Sarah's coordinates to polar coordinates.

Solution: To convert Sarah's coordinates $(1, \sqrt{3})$ from rectangular to polar coordinates, we can use the following formulas: $r = \sqrt{(x^2 + y^2)}$, $\theta = arctan\left(\frac{y}{x}\right)$.

Plugging in the values for Sarah's coordinates, we have:

$r = \sqrt{1^2 + \left(\sqrt{3}\right)^2} = \sqrt{1 + 3} = \sqrt{4} = 2$, and $\theta = arctan\left(\frac{\sqrt{3}}{1}\right) = arctan(\sqrt{3}) = \frac{\pi}{3}$.

Therefore, Sarah's coordinates in the polar form are approximately $\left(2, \frac{\pi}{3}\right)$.

Introduction to Complex Numbers

Complex numbers are a type of number that consists of two parts: a real part and an imaginary part. The imaginary part is a multiple of the imaginary unit, i, where i is defined as the square root of -1.

Complex numbers can be represented in the form $a + bi$, where a and b are real numbers. They play a fundamental role in various areas of mathematics and engineering, especially in the study of waves, oscillations, and quantum mechanics.

Introduction to the Complex Coordinate Plane:

The complex coordinate plane (also known as the Argand plane) is a graphical representation of complex numbers. It is similar to the Cartesian plane used to plot real numbers, but instead of having an x-axis and a y-axis, it has a real axis and an imaginary axis. The real part of a complex number corresponds to the horizontal axis, while the imaginary part corresponds to the vertical axis. Every point in the complex plane corresponds to a unique complex number.

Finding the magnitude of a complex number:

The magnitude (or absolute value) $|Z|$ of a complex number $Z = a + bi$ is given by
$$|Z| = \sqrt{a^2 + b^2}$$

Examples:

Example 1. Determine which of the following numbers are complex or real: $3 - 4i$, $-2 + 7i$, and 5.

Solution: We have:

$3 - 4i$: In this complex number, the real part is 3 and the imaginary part is -4.

$-2 + 7i$: In this complex number, the real part is -2 and the imaginary part is 7.

5: This is a real number, which is a special case of a complex number where the imaginary part is zero $5 + 0i$.

Example 2. Plot point $Z = -4 + i$ on the complex coordinate plane.

Solution: To plot the complex number, move 4 units to the left on the real axis and 1 units up on the imaginary axis. The point $(-4, 1)$ on the complex plane corresponds to the complex number $Z = -4 + i$.

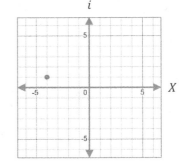

Example 3. Find the magnitude of the complex number $A = 3 + 4i$.

Solution: The magnitude of $A = 3 + 4i$ is $|A| = \sqrt{3^2 + 4^2} = \sqrt{9 + 16} = \sqrt{25} = 5$.

Adding and Subtracting Complex Numbers

- A complex number is expressed in the form $a + bi$, where a and b are real numbers, and i, which is called an imaginary number, is a solution of the equation $i^2 = -1$.

- For adding complex numbers:
$$(a + bi) + (c + di) = (a + c) + (b + d)i$$

- For subtracting complex numbers:
$$(a + bi) - (c + di) = (a - c) + (b - d)i$$

Examples:

Example 1. Solve: $(8 + 4i) + (6 - 2i)$.

Solution: Remove parentheses:

$(8 + 4i) + (6 - 2i) = 8 + 4i + 6 - 2i$.

Combine like terms:

$8 + 4i + 6 - 2i = 14 + 2i$.

Example 2. Solve: $(10 + 8i) + (8 - 3i)$.

Solution: Remove parentheses:

$(10 + 8i) + (8 - 3i) = 10 + 8i + 8 - 3i$.

Group like terms:

$10 + 8i + 8 - 3i = 18 + 5i$.

Example 3. Solve: $(-5 - 3i) - (2 + 4i)$.

Solution: Remove parentheses by multiplying -1 to the second parentheses:

$(-5 - 3i) - (2 + 4i) = -5 - 3i - 2 - 4i$.

Combine like terms:

$-5 - 3i - 2 - 4i = -7 - 7i$.

Multiplying and Dividing Complex Numbers

- You can use FOIL (First-Out-In-Last) method or the following rule to multiply imaginary numbers. Remember that: $i^2 = -1$.

$$(a + bi) \cdot (c + di) = (ac - bd) + (ad + bc)i$$

- To divide complex numbers, you need to find the conjugate of the denominator. the conjugate of $(a + bi)$ is $(a - bi)$.
- Dividing complex numbers: $\frac{a+bi}{c+di} = \frac{a+bi}{c+di} \times \frac{c-di}{c-di} = \frac{ac+bd}{c^2+d^2} + \frac{bc-ad}{c^2+d^2}i$.

Examples:

Example 1. Solve: $\frac{6-2i}{2+i}$.

Solution: The conjugate of $(2 + i)$ is $(2 - i)$. Use the rule for dividing complex numbers:

$\frac{a+bi}{c+di} = \frac{a+bi}{c+di} \times \frac{c-di}{c-di} = \frac{ac+bd}{c^2+d^2} + \frac{bc-ad}{c^2+d^2}i$.

Therefore:

$\frac{6-2i}{2+i} \times \frac{2-i}{2-i} = \frac{6 \times (2)+(-2)(1)}{2^2+(1)^2} + \frac{-2 \times 2-(6)(1)}{2^2+(1)^2}i = \frac{10}{5} + \frac{-10}{5}i = 2 - 2i$.

Example 2. Solve: $(2 - 3i)(6 - 3i)$.

Solution: Use the multiplication of imaginary numbers rule:

$(a + bi) \cdot (c + di) = (ac - bd) + (ad + bc)i.$

Therefore:

$(2 \times 6 - (-3)(-3)) + (2(-3) + (-3) \times 6)i = 3 - 24i.$

Example 3. Solve: $\frac{3-2i}{4+i}$.

Solution: Use the rule for dividing complex numbers:

$\frac{a+bi}{c+di} = \frac{a+bi}{c+di} \times \frac{c-di}{c-di} = \frac{ac+bd}{c^2+d^2} + \frac{bc-ad}{c^2+d^2}i$

Therefore: $\frac{3-2i}{4+i} \times \frac{4-i}{4-i} = \frac{(3 \times 4+(-2i) \times (-i))+(-2 \times 4-3 \times 1)i}{4^2-i^2} = \frac{10-11i}{17} = \frac{10}{17} - \frac{11}{17}i$.

Rationalizing Imaginary Denominators

- **Step 1:** Find the conjugate. (It's the denominator with different sign between the two terms.)
- **Step 2:** Multiply the numerator and denominator by the conjugate.
- **Step 3:** Simplify if needed.

Examples:

Example 1. Solve: $\frac{4-3i}{6i}$.

Solution: Multiply both numerator and denominator by $\frac{i}{i}$:

$\frac{4-3i}{6i} = \frac{4-3i}{6i} \times \frac{i}{i}$.

Therefore:

$\frac{4-3i}{6i} = \frac{(4-3i)(i)}{6i(i)} = \frac{(4)(i)-(3i)(i)}{6(i^2)} = \frac{4i-3i^2}{6(-1)} = \frac{4i-3(-1)}{-6} = \frac{4i}{-6} + \frac{3}{-6} = -\frac{1}{2} - \frac{2}{3}i$.

Example 2. Solve: $\frac{6i}{2-i}$.

Solution: Multiply both numerator and denominator by the conjugate $\frac{2+i}{2+i}$:

$\frac{6i}{2-i} = \frac{6i(2+i)}{(2-i)(2+i)}$.

Apply complex arithmetic rule: $(a+bi)(a-bi) = a^2 + b^2$.

Therefore: $2^2 + (-1)^2 = 5$, then:

$\frac{6i(2+i)}{(2-i)(2+i)} = \frac{-6+12i}{5} = -\frac{6}{5} + \frac{12}{5}i$.

Example 3. Solve: $\frac{8-2i}{2i}$.

Solution: Factor 2 from both sides: $\frac{8-2i}{2i} = \frac{2(4-i)}{2i}$, divide both sides by 2:

$$\frac{2(4-i)}{2i} = \frac{(4-i)}{i}$$

Multiply both numerator and denominator by $\frac{i}{i}$:

$$\frac{(4-i)}{i} = \frac{(4-i)}{i} \times \frac{i}{i} = \frac{(4i-i^2)}{i^2} = \frac{1+4i}{-1} = -1 - 4i$$

Polar Form of Complex Numbers

- Complex numbers in trigonometric form, also known as polar form, is a way to represent complex numbers using the magnitude (r) and the angle (θ) instead of the traditional Cartesian form, which uses real and imaginary components ($a + bi$). This representation is particularly useful in solving problems involving multiplication, division, and powers of complex numbers, as it simplifies the calculations.
- A complex number in trigonometric form is represented as:
$$z = r(\cos(\theta) + i \times \sin(\theta))$$
- where z is the complex number, r is the magnitude (also called the modulus) of the complex number, θ is the angle (also called the argument or phase) measured in radians, and i is the imaginary unit ($i^2 = -1$).
- To convert a complex number from Cartesian form to trigonometric form, the following formulas are used:
$$r = \sqrt{(a^2 + b^2)}, \theta = \arctan\frac{b}{a}$$
- Conversely, to convert a complex number from trigonometric form to Cartesian form, use:
$$a = r\cos(\theta), b = r\sin(\theta)$$
- The trigonometric form is particularly useful when performing operations like multiplication and division of complex numbers, as well as when calculating powers and roots, as these operations become much simpler when dealing with magnitudes and angles.

Example:

Find the trigonometric form of the complex number $8 + 6i$, where $0 < \theta < \pi$.
Solution: We need to determine its magnitude (r) and argument (θ).
The magnitude (r) of a complex number $z = x + yi$ is given by the formula:
$$r = \sqrt{x^2 + y^2}$$
In this case, $x = 8$ and $y = 6$, so we have: $r = \sqrt{6^2 + 8^2} = 10$.
The argument (θ) of a complex number can be determined using the *arctan* function: $\theta = \arctan\frac{y}{x} \Rightarrow \theta = \arctan\left(\frac{6}{8}\right) = \arctan(0.75) \approx 0.6435$ in radians
Since the given condition is $0 < \theta < \pi$, the calculated argument is already within the desired range.
$$z = 10(\cos(0.6435) + i\sin(0.6435))$$

Multiplying and Dividing in Polar Form

- Multiplication and division of complex numbers in trigonometric form is a streamlined process that involves manipulating the magnitudes and angles of the numbers involved. This representation simplifies these operations compared to using the Cartesian form.
- Given two complex numbers in the trigonometric form:
$$z_1 = r_1(cos(\theta_1) + i\,sin(\theta_1))$$
$$z_2 = r_2(cos(\theta_2) + i\,sin(\theta_2))$$

1) **Multiplication:**
   - To multiply z_1 and z_2, multiply their magnitudes and add their angles:
   $$z_1 \times z_2 = (r_1 \times r_2)(cos(\theta_1 + \theta_2) + i \times sin(\theta_1 + \theta_2))$$

2) **Division:**
   - To divide z_1 by z_2, divide their magnitudes and subtract their angles:
   $$\frac{z_1}{z_2} = \left(\frac{r_1}{r_2}\right)(cos(\theta_1 - \theta_2) + i \times sin(\theta_1 - \theta_2))$$

- These formulas make multiplication and division of complex numbers in a trigonometric form much simpler than in Cartesian form, as they require fewer calculations and avoid dealing with the imaginary unit (i) directly.

Example:

Given the complex numbers z_1 and z_2 in trigonometric form, find the product and quotient of the two numbers. Let $z_1 = 4(cos(30°) + i\,sin(30°))$ and $z_2 = 5(cos(150°) + i\,sin(150°))$. Find: $z_1 \times z_2, \frac{z_1}{z_2}$.

Solution: To find the product and quotient of two complex numbers in trigonometric form, we follow these steps:

Multiply (or divide) their magnitudes. Add (or subtract) their angles.

Given $z_1 = 4(cos(30°) + i\,sin(30°))$ and $z_2 = 5(cos(150°) + i\,sin(150°))$:

Product: $z_1 \times z_2$. Magnitude: $4 \times 5 = 20$. Angle: $30° + 150° = 180°$.
$$z_1 \times z_2 = 20(cos(180°) + i \times sin(180°))$$
Quotient: $\frac{z_1}{z_2}$. Magnitude: $\frac{4}{5} = 0.8$. Angle: $30° - 150° = -120°$.
Finally, $\frac{z_1}{z_2} = 0.8(cos(-120°) + i \times sin(-120°))$, then:
$$\frac{z_1}{z_2} = 0.8(cos(240°) + i \times sin(240°))$$

Powers and Roots in Polar Form

- **Powers of Complex Numbers:** De Moivre's theorem is typically used to find the power of a complex number in trigonometric form. The theorem states that for any integer n:
$$[r(\cos\theta + i\sin\theta)]^n = r^n(\cos(n\theta) + i\sin(n\theta))$$
- So, to find the nth power of a complex number, you raise r to the nth power and multiply the angle θ by n.
- **Roots of Complex Numbers:** The nth root of a complex number in trigonometric form can be found by taking the nth root of r and dividing the angle θ by n. However, there's a catch: because of the periodic nature of trigonometric functions, there are n different complex numbers that are nth roots of a given complex number. These roots are evenly spaced around the unit circle in the complex plane.
- If $z = r(\cos\theta + i\sin\theta)$, the nth roots of z are given by:
$$z_k = r^{\frac{1}{n}}\left[\cos\left(\frac{\theta + 2\pi k}{n}\right) + i\sin\left(\frac{\theta + 2\pi k}{n}\right)\right], \text{ for } k = 0, 1, \cdots, n-1.$$
- This formula gives n roots, including z itself.
- In summary, the trigonometric form of complex numbers simplifies the process of finding powers and roots of complex numbers, thanks to De Moivre's theorem and the cyclical properties of trigonometric functions.

Example:

Find the fourth power of the complex number $z = 3\left(\cos\frac{\pi}{6} + i\sin\frac{\pi}{6}\right)$ in trigonometric form.

Solution: In this case, we have $z = 3\left(\cos\frac{\pi}{6} + i\sin\frac{\pi}{6}\right)$, so the magnitude r is 3, and the angle θ is $\frac{\pi}{6}$. We want to find z^4. Using De Moivre's theorem, we have:
$$z^4 = \left[3\left(\cos\frac{\pi}{6} + i\sin\frac{\pi}{6}\right)\right]^4$$

First, let's raise the magnitude to the power of 4: $r^4 = 3^4 = 81$.

Next, we multiply the angle by 4: $\theta \times 4 = \left(\frac{\pi}{6}\right) \times 4 = \frac{\pi}{6} + \frac{\pi}{6} + \frac{\pi}{6} + \frac{\pi}{6} = \frac{4\pi}{6} = \frac{2\pi}{3}$.

Now, we have the magnitude and the angle for z^4: $z^4 = 81\left(\cos\left(\frac{2\pi}{3}\right) + i\sin\left(\frac{2\pi}{3}\right)\right)$.

Graphs of Polar Equations

- Graphing polar equations involves plotting points that satisfy the equation on a polar coordinate plane, which uses radial and angular coordinates instead of the conventional Cartesian coordinates.
- Here's a brief step-by-step process:
    - **Understand the Polar Coordinate System:** This system is defined by a distance (r) from a central point (the origin) and an angle (θ) from the positive x-axis.
    - **Identify the Polar Equation:** Polar equations can take various forms, such as circles, spirals, or roses.
    - **Create a Table of Values:** Substitute various values of θ into the equation and solve for r to understand what points satisfy the equation.
    - **Plot Points:** Plot these (r, θ) values on your polar graph. The angle θ is counterclockwise from the x-axis, and r is the distance from the origin.
    - **Connect the Dots:** Draw a smooth curve that connects these plotted points to form the graph of the polar equation.
    - **Analyze the Graph:** Identify the graph's properties, such as symmetry or intercepts, and determine the maximum and minimum values.

Example:

Consider the polar equation $r = 4 + 2\cos(\theta)$. Sketch the graph of the polar equation on the coordinate plane.

Solution: To sketch the graph, we can plot points for different values of θ and corresponding values of r:

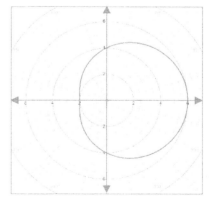

When $\theta = 0°$, $r = 6$. Plot a point at $(6, 0)$.
When $\theta = 45°$,
$r = 4 + 2\cos(45°) = 4 + 2\left(\frac{\sqrt{2}}{2}\right) = 4 + \sqrt{2} \approx 5.41$.
Plot a point at $(5.41, 45°)$.
When $\theta = 90°$, $r = 4$. Plot a point at $(4, 90°)$.
When $\theta = 135°$, $r = 4 + 2\cos(135°) = 4 + 2\left(-\frac{\sqrt{2}}{2}\right) = 4 - \sqrt{2} \approx 2.59$. Plot a point at $(2.59, 135°)$.
When $\theta = 180°$, $r = 2$. Plot a point at $(2, 180°)$.
Continue this process until you complete the full $360°$ rotation.
Once all the points are plotted, connect them smoothly to form the graph of the polar equation $r = 4 + 2\cos(\theta)$.

Rate of Change in Polar Functions

- Understanding the Rate of Change in Polar Functions involves recognizing how the distance from the origin changes as the angle changes.

Definition and Conditions:

- Rate of change in a polar function $R(\theta)$ refers to how fast the radius R changes with respect to the angle θ.
- Calculated as the difference in radii over the difference in angles $\frac{\Delta R}{\Delta \theta} = \frac{R_2 - R_1}{\theta_2 - \theta_1}$.

Examples:

Example 1. For the polar function $R(\theta) = 3 + 2\sin\theta$, determine the rate of change between $\theta = 0$ and $\theta = \frac{\pi}{2}$.

Solution: Let $\theta_1 = 0$ and $\theta_2 = \frac{\pi}{2}$. So, we get:

$R(\theta_1) = 3 + 2\sin\theta_1 \Rightarrow R(0) = 3 + 2\sin 0 = 3$

$R(\theta_2) = 3 + 2\sin\theta_2 \Rightarrow R\left(\frac{\pi}{2}\right) = 3 + 2\sin\frac{\pi}{2} = 5$

Therefore, we have:
Rate of change $= \frac{R(\theta_2) - R(\theta_1)}{\theta_2 - \theta_1} = \frac{5-3}{\frac{\pi}{2} - 0} = \frac{2}{\frac{\pi}{2}} = \frac{4}{\pi}$.

Example 2. Find the rate of change between $\theta = \frac{\pi}{6}$ and $\theta = \frac{\pi}{4}$ for function $R^2(\theta) = 4\cos(2\theta)$.

Solution: First evaluate $R(\theta)$ for $\frac{\pi}{4}$ and $\frac{\pi}{2}$. So, we have:

$\theta_1 = \frac{\pi}{6} \Rightarrow R^2\left(\frac{\pi}{6}\right) = 4\cos\left(2 \times \frac{\pi}{6}\right) = 4\cos\left(\frac{\pi}{3}\right) = 2 \Rightarrow R\left(\frac{\pi}{6}\right) = \sqrt{2}$

$\theta_2 = \frac{\pi}{4} \Rightarrow R^2\left(\frac{\pi}{4}\right) = 4\cos\left(2 \times \frac{\pi}{4}\right) = 4\cos\left(\frac{\pi}{2}\right) \Rightarrow R\left(\frac{\pi}{4}\right) = 0$

Therefore, we get:
Rate of change $= \frac{R(\theta_2) - R(\theta_1)}{\theta_2 - \theta_1} = \frac{0 - \sqrt{2}}{\frac{\pi}{4} - \frac{\pi}{6}} = \frac{\sqrt{2}}{\frac{\pi}{12}} = \frac{12\sqrt{2}}{\pi}$.

Chapter 12: Practices

Solve.

1) Find the distance between the origin and the point $\left(5, \frac{\pi}{3}\right)$ in the polar coordinate system.

2) A satellite is orbiting the Earth in a polar orbit with a radius of 1,000 kilometers. Determine the polar coordinates of the satellite's position after it completes a full orbit around the Earth.

3) A radar station is tracking an aircraft that is flying at a distance of 500 meters from the origin at an angle of 30 degrees counterclockwise from the positive x-axis. Determine the polar coordinates of the aircraft's position.

4) A target is positioned at a distance of 10 units from the origin at an angle of 60 degrees counterclockwise from the positive x-axis. What are the polar coordinates of the target's position?

Determine the rectangular coordinates of points.

5) $(6, 45°)$

6) $(8, 30°)$

7) $\left(12, \frac{2\pi}{3}\right)$

8) $\left(1, \frac{\pi}{2}\right)$

9) $(5, 60°)$

10) $\left(8, \frac{\pi}{4}\right)$

Plot the following points on the complex coordinate plane and find the magnitude.

11) $A = 4 + 2i$

12) $B = 4i$

13) $C = 1 - i$

14) $D = -3$

15) $E = 5$

16) $F = -6 - 5i$

17) $G = -4 + 4i$

18) $H = -i$

Effortless Math Education

Solve.

19) $(-4i) - (7 - 2i) =$

20) $(-3 - 2i) - (2i) =$

21) $(8 - 6i) + (-5i) =$

22) $(-3 + 6i) - (-9 - i) =$

23) $(-5 + 15i) - (-3 + 3i) =$

24) $(-14 + i) - (-12 - 11i) =$

25) $(-18 - 3i) + (11 + 5i) =$

26) $(-11 - 9i) - (-9 - 3i) =$

27) $-8 + (2i) + (-8 + 6i) =$

Evaluate.

28) $(-2 - i)(4 + i) =$

29) $(2 - 2i)^2 =$

30) $(4 - 3i)(6 - 6i) =$

31) $(5 + 4i)^2 =$

32) $(4i)(-i)(2 - 5i) =$

33) $(2 - 8i)(3 - 5i) =$

34) $9i \div (3 - i) =$

35) $(2 + 4i) \div (14 + 4i) =$

36) $(5 + 6i) \div (-1 + 8i) =$

37) $(-8 - i) \div (-4 - 6i) =$

Simplify.

38) $\frac{-1+5i}{-8-7i} =$

39) $\frac{-2-9i}{-2+7i} =$

40) $\frac{-8}{-5i} =$

41) $\frac{-5}{-i} =$

42) $\frac{3}{5i} =$

43) $\frac{6}{-4i} =$

44) $\frac{-6-i}{-1+6i} =$

45) $\frac{-9-3i}{-3+3i} =$

46) $\frac{4i+1}{-1+3i} =$

47) $\frac{6-3i}{2-i} =$

48) $\frac{-5+2i}{2-3i} =$

Find the trigonometric form of the following complex number.

49) $5 - 12i$

50) $24 - 7i$

51) $3 + 4i$

52) $21 + 20i$

✍ Solve.

53) Given the complex numbers z_1 and z_2 in trigonometric form, determine the product and quotient of the two numbers. Let $z_1 = 3(cos(45°) + i\, sin(45°))$ and $z_2 = 2(cos(120°) + i\, sin(120°))$.

Calculate: $z_1 \times z_2$ and $z_1 \div z_2$.

54) Given the complex numbers z_1 and z_2 in trigonometric form, determine the product and quotient of the two numbers. Let $z_1 = 2(cos(60°) + i\, sin(60°))$ and $z_2 = 3(cos(210°) + i\, sin(210°))$.

Calculate: $z_1 \times z_2$ and $z_1 \div z_2$.

55) Given the complex numbers z_1 and z_2 in trigonometric form, determine the product and quotient of the two numbers. Let $z_1 = 8(cos(200°) + i\, sin(200°))$ and $z_2 = 2(cos(110°) + i\, sin(110°))$.

Calculate: $z_1 \times z_2$ and $z_1 \div z_2$.

56) Given the complex numbers z_1 and z_2 in trigonometric form, determine the product and quotient of the two numbers. Let $z_1 = 9(cos(90°) + i\, sin(90°))$ and $z_2 = 5(cos(40°) + i\, sin(40°))$.

Calculate: $z_1 \times z_2$ and $z_1 \div z_2$.

✍ Write the answer in the trigonometric form of the complex number.

57) $z = 2\left(cos\left(\frac{\pi}{3}\right) + i\, sin\left(\frac{\pi}{3}\right)\right) \Rightarrow z^6 =$

58) $z = 5\left(cos\left(\frac{4\pi}{5}\right) + i\, sin\left(\frac{4\pi}{5}\right)\right) \Rightarrow z^3 =$

59) $z = 512\left(cos\left(\frac{\pi}{4}\right) + i\, sin\left(\frac{\pi}{4}\right)\right) \Rightarrow \sqrt[3]{z} =$

60) $z = 81\left(cos\left(\frac{\pi}{3}\right) + i\, sin\left(\frac{\pi}{3}\right)\right) \Rightarrow \sqrt[4]{z} =$

✍ Sketch the graph of the polar equations on the coordinate plane.

61) $r = 6 - 6\, cos(\theta)$

62) $r = 9 + 5\, cos(\theta)$

Determine the average rate of change of the following.

63) $R^2(\theta) = 9 \sin 3\theta$

From $\theta = \frac{\pi}{6}$ to $\theta = \frac{\pi}{3}$

64) $R(\theta) = 2\theta$

From $\theta = \frac{\pi}{4}$ to $\theta = \frac{\pi}{3}$

65) $R(\theta) = 3 \cos \theta$

From $\theta = 0$ to $\theta = \frac{\pi}{3}$

66) $R(\theta) = 2 \sin 2\theta - 1$

From $\theta = \frac{\pi}{4}$ to $\theta = \pi$

Chapter 12: Answers

1) 5 unit
2) $(1,000, 0°)$
3) $(500, 30°)$
4) $(10, 60°)$
5) $(4.24, 4.24)$
6) $(6.93, 4)$
7) $(-6, 10.39)$
8) $(0, 1)$
9) $(2.5, 4.33)$
10) $(5.66, 5.66)$
11) $|A| = 2\sqrt{5}$
12) $|B| = 4$
13) $|C| = \sqrt{2}$
14) $|D| = 3$
15) $|E| = 5$
16) $|F| = \sqrt{61}$
17) $|G| = 4\sqrt{2}$
18) $|H| = 1$

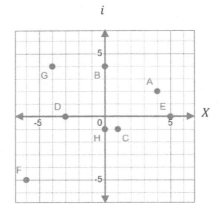

19) $-7 - 2i$
20) $-3 - 4i$
21) $8 - 11i$
22) $6 + 7i$
23) $-2 + 12i$
24) $-2 + 12i$
25) $-7 + 2i$
26) $-2 - 6i$
27) $-16 + 8i$
28) $-7 - 6i$
29) $-8i$
30) $6 - 42i$
31) $9 + 40i$
32) $8 - 20i$
33) $-34 - 34i$
34) $-\frac{9}{10} + \frac{27}{10}i$
35) $\frac{11}{53} + \frac{12}{53}i$
36) $\frac{43}{65} - \frac{46}{65}i$
37) $\frac{19}{26} - \frac{11}{13}i$
38) $-\frac{27}{113} - \frac{47}{113}i$

39) $-\frac{59}{53} + \frac{32}{53}i$

40) $\frac{-8}{5}i$

41) $-5i$

42) $-\frac{3}{5}i$

43) $\frac{3}{2}i$

44) i

45) $1 + 2i$

46) $\frac{11}{10} - \frac{7}{10}i$

47) 3

48) $-\frac{16}{13} - \frac{11}{13}i$

49) $13(cos(2\pi - 1.18) + i\,sin(2\pi - 1.18))$

50) $25(cos(2\pi - 0.28) + i\,sin(2\pi - 0.28))$

51) $5(cos(0.93) + i\,sin(0.93))$

52) $29(cos(0.76) + i\,sin(0.76))$

53) $z_1 \times z_1 = 6[cos(165°) + i\,sin(165°)]$

$z_1 \div z_1 = \left(\frac{3}{2}\right)[cos(-75°) + i\,sin(-75°)]$

54) $z_1 \times z_1 = 6[cos(270°) + i\,sin(270°)] = -6i$

$z_1 \div z_1 = \left(\frac{2}{3}\right)[cos(-150°) + i\,sin(-150°)] = -\frac{1}{3}(\sqrt{3} + i)$

55) $z_1 \times z_1 = 16[cos(310°) + i\,sin(310°)]$

$z_1 \div z_1 = 4[cos(90°) + i\,sin(90°)] = 4i$

56) $z_1 \times z_1 = 45[cos(130°) + i\,sin(130°)]$

$z_1 \div z_1 = \left(\frac{9}{5}\right)[cos(50°) + i\,sin(50°)]$

57) 64

58) $125\left(cos\left(\frac{2\pi}{5}\right) + i\,sin\left(\frac{2\pi}{5}\right)\right)$

59) $8\left(cos\left(\frac{\pi}{12}\right) + i\,sin\left(\frac{\pi}{12}\right)\right)$

60) $3\left(cos\left(\frac{\pi}{12}\right) + i\,sin\left(\frac{\pi}{12}\right)\right)$

Effortless Math Education

61)
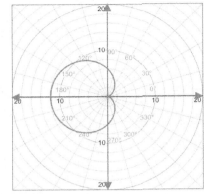

62)
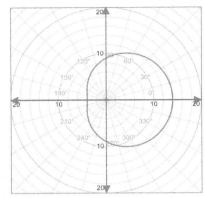

63) $-\frac{18}{\pi}$

65) $-\frac{3}{2\pi}$

64) 2

66) $-\frac{8}{3\pi}$

4 Functions Involving Parameters, Vectors, and Matrices

CHAPTER 13 Real Numbers and Relation

Math topics that you'll learn in this chapter:

- ☑ Real Numbers
- ☑ Real Numbers Line
- ☑ Coordinate Plane
- ☑ Relations
- ☑ Showing the Relation in the Coordinate Plane
- ☑ Domain and Range of Relation
- ☑ Functions
- ☑ Identifying the Function from the Graph

Real Numbers

- Real numbers are the set of all numbers that can be located on the number line, and they encompass a wide range of numbers that are used in mathematics and everyday life. The real numbers can be divided into various categories:

1. Rational Numbers: These are numbers that can be expressed in the form $\frac{p}{q}$, where p and q are integers and $q \neq 0$. Rational numbers can further be classified into:
   - Integers: These are whole numbers, both positive and negative, including zero.
   - Fractions: Numbers that are not whole but can be represented as a quotient of two integers, such as $\frac{1}{2}, \frac{3}{4}$, and so on.

2. Irrational Numbers: These are numbers that cannot be expressed as a quotient of two integers. Their decimal expansions are non-repeating and non-terminating. Some examples are:
   - Transcendental Numbers: These are numbers that are not the solution to any non-zero polynomial equation with rational coefficients. The most well-known examples are e (the base of natural logarithms) and π (the ratio of the circumference of a circle to its diameter).
   - Algebraic Irrationals: These are numbers that are solutions to polynomial equations with rational coefficients but are not themselves rational. The square root of any prime number, like $\sqrt{2}$, is an example.

Examples:

Example 1. Is 0 a real number?

Solution: Yes, 0 is a real number and is also considered a rational number since it can be expressed as the fraction $\frac{0}{1}$.

Example 2. Is the number 1.41421356 a rational or irrational number?

Solution: This number is a rational number because it has a finite decimal expansion. However, it is an approximation of the irrational number $\sqrt{2}$, which has a non-terminating, non-repeating decimal expansion.

EffortlessMath.com

Real Numbers Line

- The real number line is a graphical representation of all real numbers, which include both rational and irrational numbers. It is a straight line on which every point corresponds to a unique real number and vice versa. The number line is divided into two halves by the origin (0), with positive numbers to the right and negative numbers to the left. The distance between any two points on the number line represents the absolute difference between the corresponding real numbers.

Examples:

Example 1. Plotting rational numbers: Locate $\frac{2}{3}$ on the number line.
Solution: First, find the point corresponding to 1 (since $\frac{2}{3}$ is between 0 and 1), then divide the interval between 0 and 1 into three equal parts, and mark the point that is two-thirds of the way from 0 to 1.

Example 2. Plotting irrational numbers: Locate $\sqrt{2}$ on the number line.
Solution: To plot $\sqrt{2}$ (approximately 1.414) on the number line, find the point corresponding to 1, and then move slightly to the right, past the 1.4 mark.

Example 3. Can we represent every real number on the number line?
Solution: Yes, every real number, whether rational or irrational, can be represented by a unique point on the number line.

Example 4. Is there a largest or smallest number on the number line?
Solution: No, the real number line extends infinitely in both directions. There is no largest or smallest real number.

Coordinate Plane

- The coordinate plane, also known as the Cartesian plane, is a two-dimensional plane formed by the intersection of two perpendicular lines, called axes. The horizontal axis is called the x-axis, and the vertical axis is called the y-axis. The point where the axes intersect is called the origin, represented by the coordinates (0,0). Every point in the coordinate plane can be represented by a pair of numbers, (x, y), called the coordinates of the point. The x-coordinate represents the horizontal position, while the y-coordinate represents the vertical position.

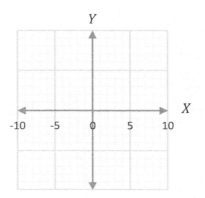

Examples:

Example 1. Draw point (3,2).

Solution: To plot the point (3,2) on the coordinate plane, start at the origin, move three units to the right along the x-axis, and then move two units up along the y-axis. Mark the point where these two positions intersect.

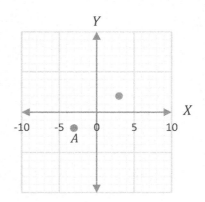

Example 2. Find the coordinates of point A.

Solution: Given a point on the coordinate plane, find its coordinates by determining its horizontal and vertical positions relative to the origin. The point A located three units to the left and two units down from the origin has the coordinates $(-3, -2)$.

Relation

- In mathematics, a relation is a set of ordered pairs, often used to describe a relationship between two sets of elements. A relation from set A to set B consists of pairs (a, b) where "a" belongs to set A, and "b" belongs to set B. Relations are often represented as graphs, matrices, or equations.

Examples:

Example 1. Given the sets of ordered pairs,
$$\{(1, a), (5, x), (3, b)\}$$
$$\{(5, b), (3, b), (1, a)\}$$
are the same representation of relation R from $A = \{1,3,5\}$ and $B = \{a, b, c\}$. Find the value of x.

Solution: To determine the value of x, we should note that if two sets of ordered pairs represent the same relation, then they should contain the same pairs.

We can see that the ordered pairs $(1, a)$ and $(3, b)$ are present in both sets. However, the pair $(5, x)$ in the first set corresponds to the pair $(5, b)$ in the second set. Thus, to make the two sets equivalent in terms of the relation they represent, x must be equal to b. That is, $x = b$.

Example 2. Is the set of ordered pairs of $R = \{(1, -1), (3, -1), (2, 0), (3, 4), (2, -1)\}$ a relation from the set $A = \{-1, 0, 4\}$ and $B = \{1, 2, 3, 5\}$?

Solution: To determine whether the set of ordered pairs R is a relation from set A to set B, every first element in the ordered pairs of R should be in set B, and every second element in the ordered pairs of R should be in set A.

From the pairs in R:

  $(1, -1)$: The element 1 is in set B and -1 is in set A.

  $(3, -1)$: The element 3 is in set B and -1 is in set A.

  $(2, 0)$: The element 2 is in set B and 0 is in set A.

  $(3, 4)$: The element 3 is in set B and 4 is in set A.

  $(2, -1)$: The element 2 is in set B and -1 is in set A.

All the first elements of the ordered pairs in R are found in set B, and all the second elements are found in set A. Therefore, R is a relation from set B to set A.

Showing the Relation in the Coordinate Plane

- In mathematics, a relation can be represented graphically on the coordinate plane by plotting the ordered pairs that constitute the relation as points on the plane.
- The horizontal axis (x-axis) represents the first element of each ordered pair (domain), while the vertical axis (y-axis) represents the second element (range). Each ordered pair (a, b) corresponds to a unique point on the coordinate plane.

Examples:

Example 1. Given the set of ordered pairs of R, show the representation of the below relation in the coordinate plane.
$$R = \{(-7,6), (-3,2), (0,-1), (1,-2), (4,-5)\}$$
Solution: To graph this relation, plot the points $(-7,6), (-3,2), (0,-1), (1,-2)$ and $(4,-5)$ on the coordinate plane.

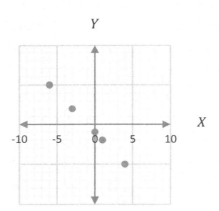

Example 2. Can a relation be a curve or a line?
Solution: Yes, a relation can be represented as a curve, line, or even discrete points on the coordinate plane, depending on the ordered pairs in the relation.

Example 3. What does it mean if points in a relation lie on a straight line?
Solution: If the points of a relation lie on a straight line, it indicates a linear relationship between the elements in the domain and range, which can often be described by a linear equation.

Domain and Range of Relation

- The domain and range are two fundamental concepts related to relations. The domain of a relation is the set of all first elements (or inputs) of the ordered pairs in the relation. The range, on the other hand, is the set of all second elements (or outputs) of the ordered pairs in the relation.

Examples:

Example 1. Consider the relation $R = \{(1,3), (2,4), (3,5)\}$. Determine the domain and range of the relation.

Solution: Given the relation $R = \{(1,3), (2,4), (3,5)\}$:

Domain: The domain is the set of all first elements in the ordered pairs of the relation. For relation R: Domain = $\{1,2,3\}$.

Range: The range is the set of all second elements in the ordered pairs of the relation. For relation R: Range = $\{3,4,5\}$.

Example 2. Find the domain and range of the following relation.
$$S = \{(-1,-2), (0,0), (1,-2), (5,-2), (1,0)\}$$

Solution: Given the relation $S = \{(-1,-2), (0,0), (1,-2), (5,-2), (1,0)\}$:

Domain: The domain is the set of all first elements in the ordered pairs of the relation. From relation S: Domain = $\{-1,0,1,5\}$.

Range: The range is the set of all second elements in the ordered pairs of the relation. From relation S: Range = $\{-2,0\}$.

Example 3. Determine the domain and range of the following relation.

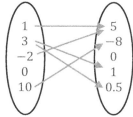

Solution: First, write the ordered pairs associated with the mapping.
$$R = \{(1,5), (3,1), (3,0.5), (-2,5), (10,-8)\}$$

Next, we see that the domain of R is $\{1,3,-2,10\}$, and the range is = $\{5,1,0.5,-8\}$.

Functions

- A function is a special type of relation that associates each element of a set (called the domain) with exactly one element of another set (called the range). function can be represented by an equation, a table, a graph, or a verbal description.

Examples:

Example 1. Given the set of ordered pairs $R = \{(1,2), (2,3), (3,4), (1,5)\}$, does R represent a function?

Solution: For a relation to be a function, each input (or x-value) must have exactly one unique output (or y-value). From R, we can see that the input 1 has two outputs: 2 and 5.

Thus, R does not represent a function.

Example 2. Given the set of ordered pairs $Q = \{(4,5), (5,6), (6,7)\}$, does Q represent a function?

Solution: For a relation to be a function, each input (or x-value) must have exactly one unique output (or y-value). We see that each input in Q has a unique output.

Thus, Q represents a function.

Example 3. Given the following map:

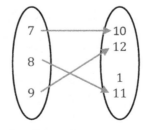

Based on the map, determine the function.

Solution: The map indicates that when $x = 7$, $y = 10$; when $x = 8$, $y = 11$; and when $x = 9$, $y = 12$.

Thus, the set of ordered pairs representing the function is $S = \{(7,10), (8,11), (9,12)\}$.

Identifying the Function from the Graph

- In mathematics, identifying a function from its graph involves examining the graph's shape, points, and behavior to determine the relationship between the input (x-axis) and output (y-axis) values. The most common method of verifying whether a graph represents a function is the vertical line test.
- Vertical Line Test:

    If a vertical line intersects a graph more than once, then the graph does not represent a function. If it intersects the graph only once or not at all, for any position of the line, then the graph represents a function.

    In such a way that Move a vertical line from the leftmost edge to the rightmost edge of the graph. If at any point the line intersects the graph more than once, the graph does not represent a function.

Example:

Given the following graph, determine whether the graph is a function or not.

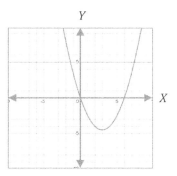

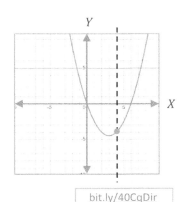

Solution: This graph represents a function, as it will only intersect a vertical line once no matter where you draw it. Such as the line drawn in the graph below and intersecting the graph at only one point.

Graphs of Basic Functions

- Classifying graphs of basic functions is crucial in understanding the behavior of functions and their vector representations. Here are the classifications of the graphs of some basic functions:

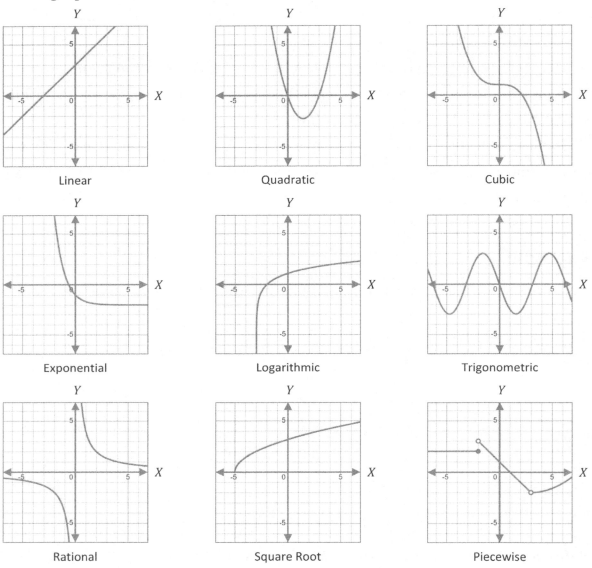

Linear	Quadratic	Cubic
Exponential	Logarithmic	Trigonometric
Rational	Square Root	Piecewise

- By understanding the classifications and characteristics of these basic functions, you can better analyze the behavior of functions, their vector representations, and transformations.

Chapter 13: Practices

✎ Identify Type of real numbers from a list of numbers.

1) $\sqrt{-4}$

2) $\frac{2}{3}$

3) $\frac{27}{1.5}$

4) $e - 1$

5) $1.310\overline{12}$

6) $\frac{\sqrt{4}}{7}$

7) 15

8) $1,123.58132134559\cdots$

✎ Mark the following points on the real number line.

9) 1.7

10) -4

11) $\frac{15}{3}$

12) $-\pi$

✎ Indicate the following points on the coordinate plane.

13) $A = (3,4)$

14) $B = (-1,2)$

15) $C = (-4,5)$

16) $D = (-3.5, -1)$

✎ Which set from A to B shows a relationship?

17) $A = \{a, b, c\}$
    $B = \{r, s\}$
    $R = \{(a,r), (a,r), (r,c)\}$

18) $A = \{-5, -1, 2, 3\}$
    $B = \{4\}$
    $S = \{(-5,4), (-1,4), (2,4), (3,4)\}$

19) $A = \{-1\}$
    $B = \{q, p, r\}$
    $Q = \{(-1,q), (-1,p), (-1,r)\}$

20) $A = \{7, 11\}$
    $B = \{-1, 1\}$
    $W = \{(1,11), (-1,7), (1,7)\}$

Effortless Math Education

✎ **Show the following relations on the coordinate plane.**

21) $F = \{(-2,3), (-2,1), (1,1), (-2,-2)\}$

22) $G = \{(x,y) | x^2 = 4, y \in \{-1,0,1\}\}$

23) $P = \{(x,y) | x = -1, y \in \mathbb{R}\}$

24) $Q = \{(x,y) | x \in \mathbb{R}, y < 1\}$

✎ **Determine the scope and range of the relationship in each case.**

25) $\{(x,y) | x = y, -1 < y \leq 1\}$

27) $\{(-7,2), (4,1), (-1,0), (2,3)\}$

26)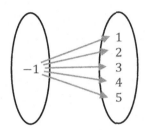

28)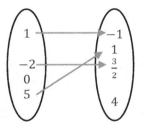

✎ **Specify which of the relations is the function.**

29) $R = \{(4,0), (-1,3), (1,5)\}$

31) $S = \{(1,1), (2,2), (4,4), (-1,-1)\}$

30)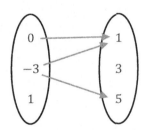

32)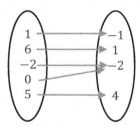

✎ **Given the following graphs, determine whether the graph is a function or not.**

33)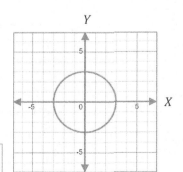

34)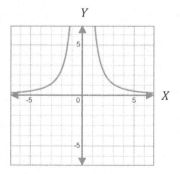

Effortless Math Education

Chapter 13: Answers

1) Imaginary number
2) Rational number
3) Integer
4) Irrational number
5) Rational number
6) Rational number
7) Integer
8) Irrational number

9)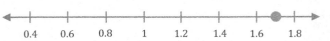

10)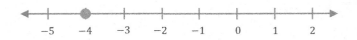

11)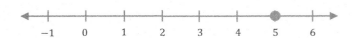

12)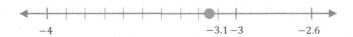

13) $A = (3,4)$
14) $B = (-1,2)$
15) $C = (-4,5)$
16) $D = (-3.5,-1)$

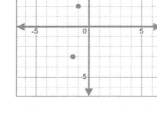

17) R is not a valid relation from A to B.
18) S is a valid relation from A to B
19) Q is a valid relation from A to B
20) W is not a valid relation from A to B. It is from B to A.

Effortless Math Education

EffortlessMath.com

21)

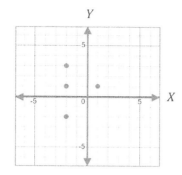

22)

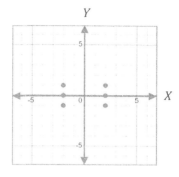

23)

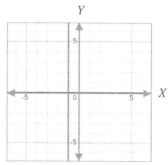

24)

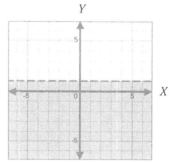

25) Domain: $(-1,1]$,

Range: $(-1,1]$

26) Domain: $\{-1\}$,

Range: $\{1,2,3,4,5\}$

27) Domain: $\{-7,-1,2,4\}$,

Range: $\{0,1,2,3\}$

28) Domain: $\{-2.1.5\}$,

Range: $\{-1,1,1.5\}$

29) It's a function.

30) It is NOT a function!

31) It's a function.

32) It's a function.

33) It is NOT a function!

34) It is a function.

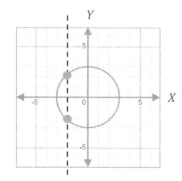

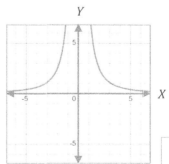

Chapter 14: Vectors in Two Dimension

Math topics that you'll learn in this chapter:

- ☑ Introduction to Vectors: Vectors in Two Dimensions
- ☑ Equality of Vectors in Two Dimensions
- ☑ Scalar Multiplication
- ☑ Vector addition and subtraction
- ☑ Representation of Addition and Subtraction
- ☑ Length of a Vector
- ☑ Dot Product and Cross Product
- ☑ Parallel vectors
- ☑ Orthogonal Vectors
- ☑ Parametric Equations and Graphs
- ☑ Applications of Vectors

Introduction to Vectors: Vectors in Two Dimensions

- Vectors are mathematical objects used to represent physical quantities that have both magnitude (length) and direction. A vector in two dimensions is often represented as an arrow with a specific length and direction or as an ordered pair of numbers (x, y) (or $\begin{pmatrix} x \\ y \end{pmatrix}$) corresponding to its horizontal and vertical components. These components can be thought of as displacements along the x and y axes. Vectors can be added, subtracted, multiplied by scalars, and even multiplied by other vectors using the dot or cross product.

Examples:

Example 1. Show vector $A = (2, 3)$ in coordinate plane.
Solution: Vector A has components $(2, 3)$, represented as an arrow starting at the origin and ending at the point $(2, 3)$ on the coordinate plane.

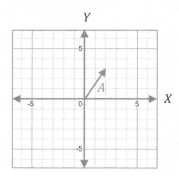

Example 2. Show vector $B = (-3, -5)$ in coordinate plane.
Solution: Vector B has components $(-3, -5)$, represented as an arrow starting at the origin and ending at the point $(-3, -5)$.

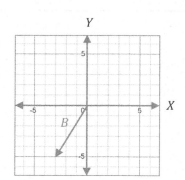

Equality of Vectors in Two Dimensions

- In two-dimensional space (often referred to as the plane), vectors are quantities that have both a magnitude (length) and direction.
- **Definition**: Two vectors in two dimensions are considered equal if and only if they have the same magnitude and direction, regardless of their initial points.
  - In other word, two vectors $A = (a_1, a_2)$ and $B = (b_1, b_2)$ are equal if $a_1 = b_1$ and $a_2 = b_2$.

Examples:

Example 1. Are the vectors $A = (4,6)$ and $B = (4,6)$ equal?

Solution: Yes, because both their x-components and y-components are the same, so $A = B$.

Example 2. Determine if the vectors $C = (7,3)$ and $D = (7,-3)$ are equal.

Solution: No, because while their x-components are the same, their y-components are different.

Example 3. Given vectors $E = (k, 5)$ and $F = (3,5)$, for what value of k are the vectors equal?

Solution: For E to be equal to F, k must be 3.

Example 4. Depict the vectors $G = (2,4)$ and $H = (2,-4)$ on the plane. Are they equal?

Solution: No, G and H are not equal because they point in opposite directions.

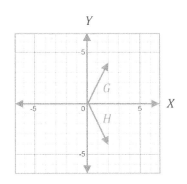

Scalar Multiplication

- In linear algebra, vectors can be scaled, or stretched/shrunk, using scalar multiplication. When a vector is multiplied by a scalar, each component of the vector is multiplied by that scalar.
- **Formula:** If v is a vector in two dimensions represented by $v = (x, y)$, and k is a scalar, then the scalar multiplication of v by k is given by: $kv = k(x, y) = (kx, ky)$.
- **Step-by-step calculation:**
  Step 1: Multiply the scalar k with the x-component of the vector.
  Step 2: Multiply the scalar k with the y-component of the vector.
  Step 3: The resulting vector is the scaled version of the original vector.
- Scalar multiplication can change the magnitude and direction of a vector. If the scalar is positive, the direction remains the same. If the scalar is negative, the vector's direction is reversed. If the scalar is zero, the vector collapses to the origin, resulting in the zero vector.

Examples:

Example 1. Given vector $v = (2,3)$ and scalar $k = 2$, find the vector kv.
Solution: We have: $kv = 2(2,3)$. So,
  Step 1: Multiply the scalar k with the x-component of the vector: $2 \times 2 = 4$.
  Step 2: Multiply the scalar k with the y-component of the vector: $2 \times 3 = 6$.
  Step 3: The resulting vector is the scaled version of the original vector.
$$kv = (4,6)$$

Example 2. Given vector $w = (-1,2)$ and scalar $c = -3$, find the vector cw.
Solution: $cw = -3(-1,2) = (-3 \times (-1), -3 \times 2) = (3,-6)$
See the figures below:

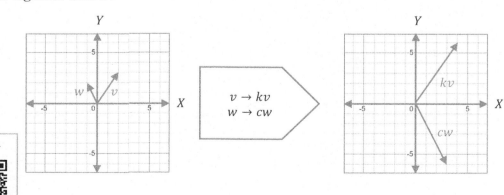

Vector Addition and Subtraction

- Vector addition and subtraction are two basic operations that can be performed on vectors. They allow us to combine or compare two vectors to obtain a new vector. These operations are particularly useful when dealing with physical quantities that have both a magnitude and a direction, such as force, velocity, or displacement.
- **Vector Addition:** When two vectors are added, they are placed head to tail, and the resulting vector (the sum) is drawn from the tail of the first vector to the head of the second vector.
- **Formula:** If $a = (x_1, y_1)$ and $b = (x_2, y_2)$, then: $a + b = (x_1 + x_2, y_1 + y_2)$.
- **Vector Subtraction:** Subtraction involves finding the vector that, when added to the second vector, will give the first vector. Geometrically, the difference between two vectors is the vector you must add to the second vector to get to the first vector.
- **Formula:** Using the vectors from above: $a - b = (x_1 - x_2, y_1 - y_2)$.

Examples:

Example 1. Given vectors $u = (2,4)$ and $v = (3,-1)$, find $u + v$.
Solution: $u + v = (1,2) + (3,-1) = (1 + 3, 2 + (-1)) = (4,1)$

Example 2. Let $A = (3,2)$ and $B = (1,-1)$. Then evaluate $A - B$.
Solution: $A - B = (3,2) - (2,-3) = (3 - 1, 2 - (-1)) = (2,3)$

See the figures below:

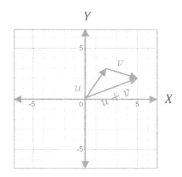
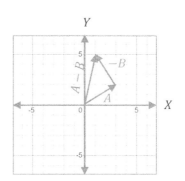

Representation of Addition and Subtraction

- In two-dimensional space, the parallelogram rule is a popular geometric method to visualize vector addition and subtraction. This method becomes especially useful when vectors are neither parallel nor perpendicular to each other.

- **Parallelogram Rule for Vector Addition**
  Step 1: Start by drawing both vectors with the same initial point.
  Step 2: Construct a parallelogram using the two vectors as adjacent sides.
  Step 3: The diagonal of the parallelogram originating from the common initial point represents the resultant vector or the sum of the two vectors.

- **Parallelogram Rule for Vector Subtraction**
  Step 1: Start by drawing both the minuend vector and the negative of the subtrahend vector with the same initial point.
  Step 2: As before, construct a parallelogram using these vectors as adjacent sides.
  Step 3: The diagonal of the parallelogram from the common initial point gives the resultant vector or the difference of the two vectors.

Example:

Given vectors $A = (4,1)$ and $B = (1,3)$, find $A + B$ and $B - A$ geometrically.
Solution: For evaluate of $C = A + B$, we have:

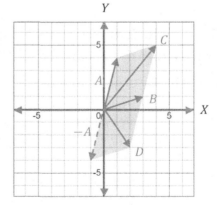

1. Plot both vectors with a common starting point.
2. Draw a parallelogram using these vectors as adjacent sides.
3. The diagonal from the common start point gives the resultant vector C, which can be computed algebraically as $(5,4)$.

For subtraction of $D = B - A$, we get:
1. Plot vector B and the negative of A, i.e., $-A$ from the same point.
2. Construct a parallelogram using B and $-A$ as adjacent sides.
3. The diagonal emerging from the common start point gives $B - A$, which can be computed algebraically as $(-3,2)$.

Length of a Vector

- The length (or magnitude) of a vector in two dimensions provides a scalar
- quantity representing "how much" of the vector there is, irrespective of its direction. Intuitively, if you think of the vector as an arrow drawn on a plane, the length of the vector is the length of the arrow.
- **Formula:** For a vector v in two dimensions with coordinates (x, y), its length (or magnitude), denoted by $|v|$, is given by the Pythagorean theorem:
$$|v| = \sqrt{x^2 + y^2}$$

Where:
- x is the horizontal component of the vector.
- y is the vertical component of the vector.

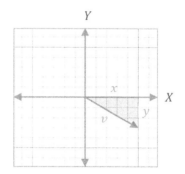

Examples:

Example 1. Find the length of the vector $a = (3,4)$.
Solution: Using the formula $|v| = \sqrt{x^2 + y^2}$ for the vector $v = (x, y)$. We have:
$|a| = \sqrt{3^2 + 4^2} = \sqrt{9 + 16} = \sqrt{25} = 5$
So, the length of vector a is 5 units.

Example 2. Determine the magnitude of the vector $b = (-5, 12)$.
Solution: Applying the formula, we get:
$|b| = \sqrt{(-5)^2 + 12^2} = \sqrt{25 + 144} = \sqrt{169} = 13$
Thus, the length of vector b is 13 units.

Example 1. Find the length of the vector m with coordinates $(-1, -7)$.
Solution: Use the formula of the length of vector. So, we get:
$|m| = \sqrt{(-1)^2 + (-7)^2} = \sqrt{1 + 49} = \sqrt{50} = 5\sqrt{2}$
Therefore, the length of vector m is $5\sqrt{2}$.

Dot Product and Cross Product

- In vector calculus, the dot product and cross product are two fundamental operations that help understand the relationships between two vectors.
- **Dot Product:** The dot product, sometimes called the scalar product, takes two vectors and returns a single scalar value. This value can be used to find the angle between two vectors, among other applications.
- **Formula for Dot Product:** If $A = (x_1, y_1)$ and $B = (x_2, y_2)$, the dot product $A \cdot B$ is calculated as: $A \cdot B = x_1 \times x_2 + y_1 \times y_2$.
- **Step-by-step Calculation for Dot Product**
  Step 1: Multiply the $x-$components of the two vectors.
  Step 2: Multiply the $y-$components of the two vectors.
  Step 3: Add the results of steps 1 and 2.
- **Cross Product:** In two dimensions, the cross product is a bit simpler than in three dimensions. The result is a scalar that represents the magnitude of the vector that would result in three dimensions, pointing out of the plane. (The cross product of two vectors is defined as a scalar equal to the determinant of the 2 × 2 matrix formed by their components.)
- **Formula for Cross Product:** $A \times B = x_1 \times y_2 - y_1 \times x_2$.
- **Step-by-step Calculation for Cross Product**
  Step 1: Multiply the $x-$component of the first vector by the $y-$component of the second vector.
  Step 2: Multiply the $y-$component of the first vector by the $x-$component of the second vector.
  Step 3: Subtract the result of step 2 from the result of step 1.

Examples:

Example 1. Given vectors $P = (2,3)$ and $Q = (4,-1)$, find $P \cdot Q$.
Solution: $P \cdot Q = 2 \times 4 + 3 \times (-1) = 8 + (-3) = 5$.

Example 2. Given vectors $R = (1,2)$ and $S = (3,4)$, find $R \times S$.
Solution: $R \times S = 1 \times 4 - 2 \times 3 = 4 - 6 = -2$.

Parallel Vectors

- Parallel vectors are vectors that have the same or opposite direction but can differ in magnitude. In two dimensions, parallel vectors can be easily identified based on their direction or by examining their components.
- **Identifying Parallel Vectors:**
  Two vectors are parallel if they are scalar multiples of each other, which means that one vector can be obtained by multiplying the other vector by a scalar.
- **Formula for Parallel Vectors:**
  Let's say we have two vectors $A = (x_1, y_1)$ and $B = (x_2, y_2)$. These vectors are parallel if there exists a scalar k such that: $A = k \times B$ or equivalently: $x_1 = kx_2$ and $y_1 = ky_2$.

  - To find a vector parallel to a given vector $E = (e_1, e_2)$, you can multiply its components by any nonzero scalar k.
  - The zero vector is considered parallel to any vector because it can be obtained by multiplying any vector by the scalar 0. However, it is the only vector that can be parallel to vectors of different directions.

Examples:

Example 1. Let $A = (2,4)$ and $B = (1,2)$. Are these vectors parallel?
Solution: Divide the corresponding components of the vectors: $2 \div 1 = 2$ and $4 \div 2 = 2$. Since the ratios are the same, the vectors are parallel.

Example 2. Let $C = (-3,6)$ and $D = (1,-2)$. Are these vectors parallel?
Solution: Divide the corresponding components of the vectors: $-3 \div 1 = -3$ and $6 \div (-2) = -3$. Since the ratios are the same, the vectors are parallel.

Example 3. Given vectors $P = (2,-3)$ and $Q = (4,6)$, determine if P and Q are parallel.
Solution: The ratio of the $x-$components is $2 \div 4 = \frac{1}{2}$ and the ratio of the $y-$components is $(-3) \div 6 = -\frac{1}{2}$. Since both ratios are not equal, vectors P and Q are not parallel.

Orthogonal Vectors

- Orthogonal vectors are vectors that are perpendicular to each other in a plane. In other words, the angle between them is 90°. A critical property of orthogonal vectors is that their dot product is zero. This characteristic provides a straightforward way to check for orthogonality, especially in two-dimensional space.
- **Identifying Orthogonal Vectors:**
  The key property to remember is that two vectors are orthogonal (or perpendicular) if and only if their dot product is zero. For two vectors $A = (x_1, y_1)$ and $B = (x_2, y_2)$, to be orthogonal, $A \cdot B$ should equal zero.
- **Step-by-step Calculation to Check for Orthogonal Vectors:**
  Step 1: Compute the dot product of the two vectors.
  Step 2: Check if the result is zero. If it is, the vectors are orthogonal.
  - In a coordinate system, two vectors are orthogonal when their slopes are negative reciprocals of each other or if one of the vectors is horizontal and the other is vertical.
  - A nonzero vector cannot be orthogonal to itself, as its dot product with itself will always be positive. However, the zero vector is orthogonal to any vector, including itself.
  - To find a vector orthogonal to a given vector $E = (e_1, e_2)$, you can swap its components and change the sign of one of them. That is, an orthogonal vector to E would be $(-e_2, e_1)$ or $(e_2, -e_1)$.

Examples:

Example 1. Given vectors $P = (3,2)$ and $Q = (-4,6)$, determine if P and Q are orthogonal.
Solution: First calculate dot product for P and Q:
$$P \cdot Q = (3 \times (-4)) + (2 \times 6) = -12 + 12 = 0$$
Since the dot product is zero, vectors P and Q are orthogonal.

Example 2. Let $M = (1, -2)$ and $N = (-2, 1)$. Are these vectors orthogonal?
Solution: Compute the dot product: $M \cdot N = (1 \times (-2)) + ((-2) \times 1) = -4 \neq 0$.
Since the dot product is non-zero, the vectors are not orthogonal.

Parametric Equations and Graphs

- Parametric equations are a set of equations that express the coordinates of a point in terms of a single parameter, usually denoted by t, called the parameter. These equations can be used to describe the motion of a particle, the path of an object, or the shape of a curve. In two-dimensional space, the position of a point P can be defined by two parametric equations, one for each coordinate:

$$x = f(t)$$
$$y = g(t)$$

  Where $f(t)$ and $g(t)$ are functions of the parameter t.

- When dealing with vectors, parametric equations are useful for representing the path of a vector as it moves through space. The vector $r(t) = (f(t), g(t))$ represents the position of the point P as a function of the parameter t.

- **Graphing with Parametric Equations**:
  To sketch the graph of a curve defined parametrically:
  Determine the range of t: You'll often be given an interval for t.
  Calculate Points: For several values of t within the range, calculate the corresponding x and y values.
  Sketch the Curve: Plot these points on the coordinate plane and sketch the curve.

- In order to convert parametric equations to a Cartesian equation, you can eliminate the parameter t from the parametric equations by solving one of the equations for t and substituting it into the other equation.

Example:

Given the parametric equations: $x(t) = t$, $y(t) = t^2$. Sketch the curve for $-2 \leq t \leq 2$.

Solution: Determine the range of t: t ranges from -2 to 2. Next, select a few values of t and calculate $x(t)$ and $y(t)$. For instance, when $t = -2$, $x(-2) = -2$ and $y(-2) = 4$. Thus, one point on the curve is $(-2, 4)$. Continue calculating points for various t values and plot them. Joining these points will give a parabolic curve opening upwards.

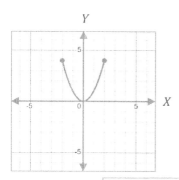

Applications of Vectors

- Vectors in two dimensions are fundamental in physics, engineering, computer graphics, and various other fields. They represent quantities that have both magnitude and direction in a plane. Here, we'll delve into some applications of vectors in two-dimensional space.
- **Displacement and Motion**: One of the primary applications of vectors is in representing displacement and motion. A displacement vector provides the shortest distance between two points along with the direction.
- **Force Resolution**: In physics, vectors are used to resolve forces into their components. A force acting at an angle can be resolved into two perpendicular components, often referred to as horizontal and vertical components.
- **Velocity and Acceleration**: Vectors are pivotal in representing velocity and acceleration. The direction of the velocity vector gives the direction of motion, and its magnitude gives the speed.

Examples:

Example 1. Suppose a person walks $4\ km$ east and then $3\ km$ north. Determine the resulting displacement vector.

Solution: Using the Cartesian plane, represent the eastward movement as vector $A = (4,0)$ and the northward movement as vector $B = (0,3)$.
The resultant displacement R is $A + B$, giving $R = (4,3)$.

Example 2. A car is moving with a velocity of $20\frac{m}{s}$ in the east direction and $15\frac{m}{s}$ in the north direction. Find the resultant velocity of the car.

Solution: We can represent the east and north velocities as vectors $E = (20,0)$ and $N = (0,15)$. The resultant velocity C is given by $C = A + B = (20,15)$. The magnitude of C is: $|C| = \sqrt{20^2 + 15^2} = 25\frac{m}{s}$.

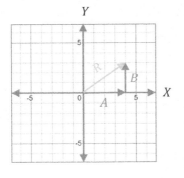

Chapter 14: Practices

✎ Show the following vectors in the coordinate plane.

1) $(0, -4)$

2) $(2, 0)$

3) $(-5, 3)$

4) $(3, 3)$

✎ Check the equality of vectors.

5) $u = (2, k)$, $v = (2a, 5)$

6) $A = (c + 1, 0)$, $B = (-1, d - 1)$

7) $F = \left(\frac{k}{2}, 2\right)$, $G = (1, 2)$

8) $v = (4, -3)$, $w = (5n - 1, -3)$

9)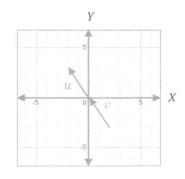

10)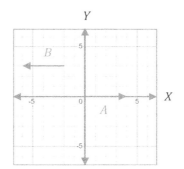

✎ Add and subtract.

11) $V = (3, -7)$ and $U = (2, 0)$

$V + U = $ ___ and $U - V = $ ___

12) $A = (-3, 4)$ and $B = (-2, -3)$

$A + B = $ ___ and $A - B = $ ___

13) $C = \left(\frac{1}{2}, 0.5\right)$ and $D = \left(\frac{3}{2}, 1\right)$

$D + C = $ ___ and $D - C = $ ___

14) $B = \left(3\sqrt{2}, -3\right)$ and $A = \left(\sqrt{8}, 3\right)$

$A + B = $ ___ and $A - B = $ ___

Determine addition and subtraction geometrically.

15) $V = (3,1)$ and $U = (2,5)$

$U + V$

16) $R = (4,-3)$ and $S = (3,2)$

$R - S$

17) $P = (-3,-1)$ and $Q = (1,3)$

$P - Q$

18) $A = (1,5)$ and $B = (1,-5)$

$A + B$

Evaluate.

19) $X = (1,-1)$, $c = -2$

$cX = $ ___

20) $W = (\sqrt{3}, 0)$, $\alpha = \sqrt{3}$

$\alpha W = $ ___

21) $U = (4,2)$, $k = -\frac{1}{2}$

$kU = $ ___

22) $V = (2,-1)$, $\beta = 1.5$

$\beta V = $

Find the lengths of the vectors.

23) $(-4, 3)$

24) $\left(-\frac{3}{5}, -0.8\right)$

25) $(1, -\sqrt{3})$

26) $(11, 2)$

Calculate the product.

27) $A = (1,0)$, $B = (1,0)$

$A.B = $ _____

28) $A = (4,-3)$, $B = \left(-\frac{1}{2}, -1\right)$

$A \times B = $ _____

29) $A = (-2,3)$, $B = \left(1, \frac{2}{3}\right)$

$A.B = $ _____

30) $A = (2,1)$, $B = (2,1)$

$A \times B = $ _____

In each case, find x such that the vectors are parallel.

31) $A = (2,4)$ and $B = (x, 8)$

32) $A = (3,-1)$ and $B = (-3, x)$

33) $A = (3,9)$ and $B = (x, 1)$

34) $A = (4,-3)$ and $B = (x, 6)$

Effortless Math Education

Specify orthogonal vectors.

35) $A = (0,1)$ and $B = (1,0)$

36) $A = (3,-2)$ and $B = (-1,-5)$

37) $C = (2,7)$ and $D = (-8,1)$

38) $C = (14,15)$ and $D = (-15,14)$

Given parametric equations, Sketch the curve for the given interval and determine the start and end points in each case.

39) $X = -2t$
$Y = t - 1$
$0 \leq t \leq 3$

40) $X = t^2 - 4$
$Y = t$
$-1 < t \leq 3$

Solve.

41) A boat goes 4 km north, then moves 10 km to the south. Finally, it goes 3 kilometers to the west and reaches its destination. How far is the destination from the origin?

Chapter 14: Answers

1) $(0, -4)$

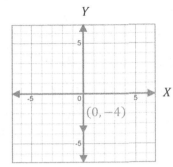

2) $(2, 0)$

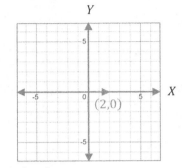

3) $(-5, 3)$

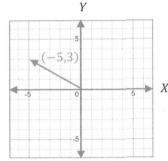

4) $(3, 3)$

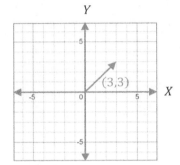

5) $a = 1, k = 5$

6) $c = -2, d = 1$

7) $k = 2$

8) $n = 1$

9) They are equal.

10) They are NOT equal.

11) $V + U = (5, -7)$

$U - V = (-1, 7)$

12) $A + B = (-5, 1)$

$A - B = (-1, 7)$

13) $D + C = (2, 1.5)$

$D - C = (1, 0.5)$

14) $A + B = (5\sqrt{2}, 0)$

$A - B = (-\sqrt{2}, 6)$

Effortless Math Education

EffortlessMath.com

15) $U + V = (5, 6)$

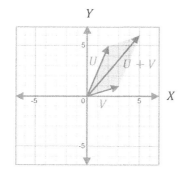

16) $R - S = (1, -5)$

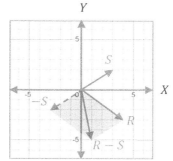

17) $P - Q = (-4, -4)$

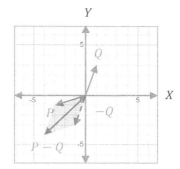

18) $A + B = (2, 0)$

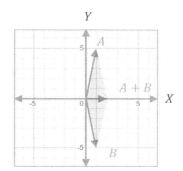

19) $(-2, 2)$

20) $(3, 0)$

21) $(-2, -1)$

22) $(3, 1.5)$

23) 5

24) 1

25) 2

26) $5\sqrt{5}$

27) 1

28) -5.5

29) 0

30) 0

31) 4

32) 1

33) $\frac{1}{3}$

34) -8

35) Two vectors are perpendicular to each other.

36) Are Not.

37) Are Not.

38) Two vectors are perpendicular to each other.

39)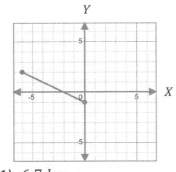

40)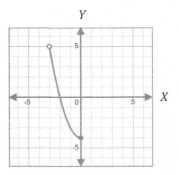

41) 6.7 km

CHAPTER 15
Analytic Geometry

Math topics that you'll learn in this chapter:

- ☑ Distance and Midpoint Formulas
- ☑ Circles
- ☑ Finding the Center and the Radius of Circles
- ☑ Parabolas
- ☑ Finding the Focus, Vertex, and Directrix of a Parabola
- ☑ Ellipses
- ☑ Hyperbolas
- ☑ Classifying a Conic Section (in Standard Form)
- ☑ Rotation of Axes and General Form of Conic Sections

Distance and Midpoint Formulas

- Distance and midpoint formulas are essential tools in vector analysis, especially in two-dimensional space. They allow us to find the length and the central point of a line segment connecting two vectors, or points, in the coordinate plane.
  - **Distance Formula**: The distance formula calculates the length of the line segment between two points (x_1, y_1) and (x_2, y_2) in the coordinate plane. The formula is derived from the Pythagorean theorem and is given by:
  $$d = \sqrt{(x_2 - x_1)^2 + (y_2 - y_1)^2}$$
  Where d is the distance between the two points.
  - **Midpoint Formula**: The midpoint formula calculates the central point of the line segment connecting two points (x_1, y_1) and (x_2, y_2). The formula is given by:
  $$M = \left(\frac{x_1 + x_2}{2}, \frac{y_1 + y_2}{2}\right)$$
  Where M is the midpoint of the line segment.
- These formulas are essential for vector analysis in two-dimensional space, providing valuable information about the geometric properties of line segments, which are the building blocks for more advanced vector applications, such as transformations and vector operations.

Examples:

Example 1. Find the midpoint of the line segment connecting points $A(3,2)$ and $B(7,5)$.
Solution: $M = \left(\frac{3+7}{2}, \frac{2+5}{2}\right) = (5, 3.5)$

The midpoint of the line segment connecting A and B is $(5, 3.5)$.

Example 2. Find the distance between the points $A(3,2)$ and $B(7,5)$.
Solution: $d = \sqrt{(7-3)^2 + (5-2)^2} = \sqrt{16+9} = \sqrt{25} = 5$

The distance between points A and B is 5 units.

Circles

- Equation of circles in standard form: $(x-h)^2 + (y-k)^2 = r^2$.
- Center: (h, k), Radius: r.
- General format: $ax^2 + by^2 + cx + dy + e = 0$.

Examples:

Write the standard form equation of each circle.

Example 1. Center: $(-9, -12)$, Radius: 4.

Solution: $(x-h)^2 + (y-k)^2 = r^2$ is the circle equation with a radius r, centered at (h, k). We have:

$h = -9$, $k = -12$ and $r = 4$.

Then: $\left(x - (-9)\right)^2 + \left(y - (-12)\right)^2 = (4)^2 \Rightarrow (x+9)^2 + (y+12)^2 = 16$.

Example 2. $x^2 + y^2 - 8x - 6y + 21 = 0$.

Solution: $(x-h)^2 + (y-k)^2 = r^2$ is the circle equation with a radius r, centered at (h, k). First move the loose number to the right side:

$x^2 + y^2 - 8x - 6y = -21$.

Group x-variables and y-variables together:

$(x^2 - 8x) + (y^2 - 6y) = -21$.

Convert x to square form:

$(x^2 - 8x + 16) + (y^2 - 6y) = -21 + 16 \Rightarrow (x-4)^2 + (y^2 - 6y) = -5$.

Convert y to square form:

$(x-4)^2 + (y^2 - 6y + 9) = -21 + 16 + 9 \Rightarrow (x-4)^2 + (y-3)^2 = 4$.

Then: $(x-4)^2 + (y-3)^2 = 2^2$.

Finding the Center and the Radius of Circles

- $(x - h)^2 + (y - k)^2 = r^2$

  Center: (h, k), Radius: r.

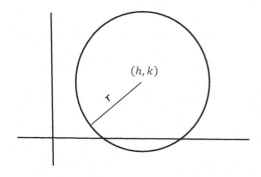

Examples:

Identify the center and radius.

Example 1. $x^2 + y^2 - 4y + 3 = 0$.

Solution: $(x - h)^2 + (y - k)^2 = r^2$ is the circle equation with a radius r, centered at (h, k). Rewrite $x^2 + y^2 - 4y + 3 = 0$ in the form of the standard circle equation:

Group x −variables and y −variables together:

$(x^2) + (y^2 - 4y) = -3$.

Convert x and y to square form:

$(x^2) + (y^2 - 4y + 4) - 4 = -3$.

Therefore:

$(x - 0)^2 + (y - 2)^2 = 1^2$.

Then:

Center: $(0, 2)$ and $r = 1$.

Example 2. $4x + x^2 - 6y = 24 - y^2$.

Solution: $(x - h)^2 + (y - k)^2 = r^2$ is the circle equation with a radius r, centered at (h, k). Rewrite $4x + x^2 - 6y = 24 - y^2$ in the form of the standard circle equation: $(x - (-2))^2 + (y - 3)^2 = (\sqrt{37})^2$.

Then: Center: $(-2, 3)$ and $r = \sqrt{37}$.

Parabolas

- The standard form of a parabola:

   When it opens up or down:

   $(x - h)^2 = 4p(y - k)$, Vertex: (h, k), Directrix: $y = k - p$, Focus: $(h, k + p)$.

   When it opens right or left:

   $(y - k)^2 = 4p(x - h)$, Vertex: (h, k), Directrix: $x = h - p$, Focus: $(h + p, k)$.

Examples:

Example 1. Write the equation of the parabola: Vertex: $(0,0)$ and Focus: $(0,4)$.

Solution: The standard form of a parabola:

$(x - h)^2 = 4p(y - k)$.

Vertex: $(h, k) = (0,0)$, then: $h = 0$, $k = 0$.

Focus: $(h, k + p) = (0,4)$, then:

$k + p = 4 \Rightarrow p = 4$.

Put in formula: $(x - 0)^2 = 4(4)(y - 0)$, then:

$x^2 = 16y$.

Example 2. Write the equation of the parabola: Vertex: $(2,3)$ and Focus: $(2,4)$.

Solution: The standard form of a parabola:

$(x - h)^2 = 4p(y - k)$.

Vertex: $(h, k) = (2,3)$, then: $h = 2$, $k = 3$.

Focus: $(h, k + p) = (2,4)$, then: $k + p = 4 \Rightarrow 3 + p = 4 \Rightarrow p = 1$.

Put in the standard form:

$(x - 2)^2 = 4(1)(y - 3)$, then: $(x - 2)^2 = 4(y - 3)$.

Finding the Focus, Vertex, and Directrix of a Parabola

- The standard form of a parabola:

When it opens up or down:

$(x - h)^2 = 4p(y - k)$, Vertex: (h, k), Directrix: $y = k - p$, Focus: $(h, k + p)$.

When it opens right or left:

$(y - k)^2 = 4p(x - h)$, Vertex: (h, k), Directrix: $x = h - p$, Focus: $(h + p, k)$.

- The x value of the vertex of an up-down facing parabola of the form:

$y = ax^2 + bx + c$ is: $x_v = -\frac{b}{2a}$.

Examples:

Example 1. Find the vertex of parabola. $y = x^2 + 4x$

Solution: The parabola params are: $a = 1$, $b = 4$ and $c = 0$.

$x_v = -\frac{b}{2a} \Rightarrow x_v = -\frac{4}{2(1)} = -2$.

Use x_v to find y_v: $y_v = ax^2 + bx + c$, then:

$y_v = (1)(-2)^2 + (4)(-2) + 0 \Rightarrow y_v = -4$.

Therefore, the vertex of the parabola is: $(-2, -4)$.

Example 2. Write the vertex form equation of a parabola. $y = x^2 - 6x + 5$

Solution: First, evaluate the x value of the vertex from the formula $x_v = -\frac{b}{2a}$. Then: $x_v = -\frac{(-6)}{2(1)} = 3$. To find the y value of the vertex, substitute $x_v = 3$ in the equation: $y_v = (3)^2 - 6(3) + 5 = -4$. Now, plug the vertex $(x_v, y_v) = (3, -4)$ into the vertex formula of parabola and simplify:

$(x - 3)^2 = 4p(y - (-4)) \Rightarrow x^2 - 6x + 9 = 4p(y + 4) \Rightarrow x^2 - 6x + 9 = 4py + 16p$.

Rewrite the obtained equation as $4py = x^2 - 6x + (9 - 16p)$. Then, compare it's with the given equation and obtain the value of p. Therefore:

$4p = 1 \Rightarrow p = \frac{1}{4}$. Finally,

$p = \frac{1}{4} \Rightarrow (x - 3)^2 = 4\left(\frac{1}{4}\right)(y + 4) \Rightarrow (x - 3)^2 = (y + 4)$.

Ellipses

- Horizontal: $\dfrac{(x-h)^2}{a^2} + \dfrac{(y-k)^2}{b^2} = 1$

- Vertical: $\dfrac{(x-h)^2}{b^2} + \dfrac{(y-k)^2}{a^2} = 1$

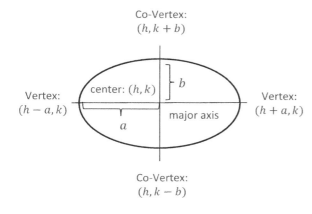
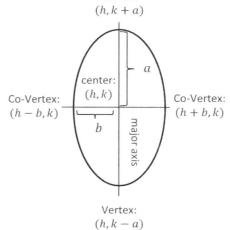

Horizontal foci: $(h+c, k), (h-c, k)$

Vertical foci: $(h, k+c), (h, k-c)$

- Horizontal Ellipse Vertices: the vertices are the two points on the ellipse that intersect the major axis for an ellipse with the major axis parallel to the x-axis, the vertices are: $(h+a, k), (h-a, k)$
- Horizontal Ellipse Foci: $(h+c, k), (h-c, k)$, where $c = \sqrt{a^2 - b^2}$ is the distance from the center (h, k) to a focus.

Example:

Find vertices of $\dfrac{x^2}{169} + \dfrac{y^2}{64} = 1$.

Solution: Rewrite $\dfrac{x^2}{169} + \dfrac{y^2}{64} = 1$ in the form of the standard ellipse equation:

$\dfrac{(x-h)^2}{a^2} + \dfrac{(y-k)^2}{b^2} = 1 \Rightarrow \dfrac{(x-0)^2}{13^2} + \dfrac{(y-0)^2}{8^2} = 1$.

Then: $(h, k) = (0,0)$, $a = 13$ and $b = 8$.

To find the vertices, we have:

$(h+a, k) \to (0+13, 0) = (13, 0)$,

$(h-a, k) \to (0-13, 0) = (-13, 0)$.

Hyperbolas

Up/down Hyperbola:

$$\frac{(y-k)^2}{a^2} - \frac{(x-h)^2}{b^2} = 1$$

center: (h, k)

foci: $(h, k \pm c)$

$c^2 = a^2 + b^2$

vertices: $(h, k \pm a)$

transverse axis: $x = h$

(Parallel to y-axis)

asymptotes: $y - k = \pm \frac{a}{b}(x - h)$

Left/right Hyperbola:

$$\frac{(x-h)^2}{a^2} - \frac{(y-k)^2}{b^2} = 1$$

center: (h, k)

foci: $(h \pm c, k)$

$c^2 = a^2 + b^2$

vertices: $(h \pm a, k)$

transverse axis: $y = k$

(Parallel to x-axis)

asymptotes: $y - k = \pm \frac{b}{a}(x - h)$

Example:

Find the center and foci of $-x^2 + y^2 - 18x - 14y - 132 = 0$.

Solution: Rewrite in standard form. Add 132 to both sides:

$-x^2 + y^2 - 18x - 14y = 132$.

Factor out the coefficient of square terms:

$(y^2 - 14y) - (x^2 + 18x) = 132$.

Convert x and y to square form:

$(y^2 - 14y + 49) - (x^2 + 18x + 81) = 132 - 81 + 49 \Rightarrow (y - 7)^2 - (x + 9)^2 = 100$.

Divide by 100: $-\frac{(x+9)^2}{100} + \frac{(y-7)^2}{100} = 1 \Rightarrow \frac{(y-7)^2}{10^2} - \frac{(x-(-9))^2}{10^2} = 1$.

Then: $(h, k) = (-9, 7)$, $a = 10$, $b = 10$ and center is: $(-9, 7)$.

Foci: $(-9, 7 + c), (-9, 7 - c)$. Compute c: $c = \sqrt{10^2 + 10^2} = 10\sqrt{2}$.

Then: $(-9, 7 + 10\sqrt{2}), (-9, 7 - 10\sqrt{2})$.

Classifying a Conic Section (in Standard Form)

Conic section	Standard form of equation		
Parabola	$y = a(x - h)^2 + k$	$x = a(y - k)^2 + h$	$a = 4p$
Circle	$(x - h)^2 + (y - k)^2 = r^2$		
Ellipse	$\frac{(x-h)^2}{a^2} + \frac{(y-k)^2}{b^2} = 1$	$\frac{(y-k)^2}{a^2} + \frac{(x-h)^2}{b^2} = 1$	
Hyperbola	$\frac{(x-h)^2}{a^2} - \frac{(y-k)^2}{b^2} = 1$	$\frac{(y-k)^2}{a^2} - \frac{(x-h)^2}{b^2} = 1$	

Examples:

Example 1. Write this equation in standard form. $-x^2 + 8x + y - 17 = 0$.

Solution: It's a parabola. Rewrite in standard form: $-x^2 + 8x + y - 17 = 0$.

Rewrite as: $y = x^2 - 8x + 17$, complete the square $x^2 - 8x + 17 = (x - 4)^2 + 1$.

Then: $y = (x - 4)^2 + 1$. Subtract 1 from both sides: $y - 1 = (x - 4)^2$.

Rewrite in standard form: $4 \cdot \frac{1}{4}(y - 1) = (x - 4)^2$.

Example 2. Write this equation in standard form. $x^2 - 4y^2 + 6x - 8y + 1 = 0$.

Solution: It's hyperbola. First subtract 1 from both sides:

$x^2 - 4y^2 + 6x - 8y + 1 = 0 \Rightarrow x^2 - 4y^2 + 6x - 8y = -1$.

Factor out the coefficient of square terms: $(x^2 + 6x) - 4(y^2 + 2y) = -1$.

Divide by the coefficient of square terms: $\frac{1}{4}(x^2 + 6x) - (y^2 + 2y) = -\frac{1}{4}$.

Convert x and y to square form: $\frac{1}{4}(x^2 + 6x + 9) - (y^2 + 2y + 1) = -\frac{1}{4} + \frac{1}{4}(9) - 1$.

Convert y to square form: $\frac{1}{4}(x + 3)^2 - (y + 1)^2 = -\frac{1}{4} + \frac{1}{4}(9) - 1$.

Then: $\frac{1}{4}(x + 3)^2 - (y + 1)^2 = 1 \Rightarrow \frac{(x+3)^2}{4} - \frac{(y+1)^2}{1} = 1 \Rightarrow \frac{(x-(-3))^2}{2^2} - \frac{(y-(-1))^2}{1^2} = 1$.

Rotation of Axes and General Form of Conic Sections

- Rotation of axes is a transformation used to simplify the analysis of conic sections, such as ellipses, hyperbolas, and parabolas. By rotating the coordinate axes, we can transform the equation of a conic section into a simpler form that reveals its key characteristics.
- **Rotation of Axes**: To rotate the coordinate axes through an angle θ, we use the following transformation formulas:
$$x' = x \cos \theta - y \sin \theta$$
$$y' = x \sin \theta + y \cos \theta$$
where (x, y) are the original coordinates and (x', y') are the coordinates after rotation.
- Rotation of axes is a technique used to simplify the equation of a conic section by aligning the coordinate axes with the axes of symmetry of the conic section. This process eliminates the cross-term involving both x and y from the equation, resulting in a simpler form that can be easily analyzed.
- **General Form of Conic Sections**: After rotation, the equation of a conic section can be written in the standard form:
$$Ax'^2 + Bx'y' + Cy'^2 + Dx' + Ey' + F = 0$$
where $A, B, C, D, E,$ and F are constants.

Examples:

Example 1. Rotate the point $P(3,4)$ by an angle of $45°$ counterclockwise.

Solution: Using the rotation of axes formulas, we have:
$$x' = 3 \cos 45° - 4 \sin 45° = 3\left(\frac{\sqrt{2}}{2}\right) - 4\left(\frac{\sqrt{2}}{2}\right) = -\frac{\sqrt{2}}{2}$$
$$y' = 3 \sin 45° + 4 \cos 45° = 3\left(\frac{\sqrt{2}}{2}\right) + 4\left(\frac{\sqrt{2}}{2}\right) = \frac{7\sqrt{2}}{2}$$

The rotated point is $(-22, 272)$.

Example 2. Given the equation $3x^2 - 4xy + 3y^2 + 2x - y - 1 = 0$, rotate the axes to simplify the equation.

Solution: We can use the rotation formulas to substitute into the given equation. The rotation angle can be found by solving $\tan 2\theta = \frac{B}{A-C}$, where B is the coefficient of the xy term in the original equation. After substituting and simplifying, we get: $5x'^2 + 4x' - 2y' - 1 = 0$

This simplified equation reveals that the conic section is a parabola.

Chapter 15: Practices

✎ Find midpoint and distance between given points.

1) $(0,0)$ and $(2,7)$
2) $(-3,-1)$ and $(1,2)$
3) $(0,2)$ and $(0,-2)$
4) $(-2,-3)$ and $(2,3)$
5) $(7,2)$ and $(5,-1)$
6) $(2,-4)$ and $(5,0)$
7) $(3,-2)$ and $(3,-4)$
8) $(2,1)$ and $(1,2)$

✎ Write the standard form equation of each circle.

9) $y^2 + 2x + x^2 = 24y - 120$
10) $x^2 + y^2 - 2y - 15 = 0$
11) $8x + x^2 - 2y = 64 - y^2$
12) Center: $(-5,-6)$, Radius: 9
13) Center: $(-12,-5)$, Area: 4π
14) Center: $(-11,-14)$, Area: 16π
15) Center: $(-3,2)$, Circumference: 2π
16) Center: $(15,14)$, Circumference: $2\pi\sqrt{15}$

✎ Identify the center and radius of each.

17) $(x-2)^2 + (y+5)^2 = 10$
18) $x^2 + (y-1)^2 = 4$
19) $(x-2)^2 + (y+6)^2 = 9$
20) $(x+14)^2 + (y-5)^2 = 16$

✎ Write the equation of the following parabolas.

21) Vertex $(0,0)$ and Focus $(0,2)$
22) Vertex $(3,2)$ and Focus $(3,4)$
23) Vertex $(1,1)$ and Focus $(1,6)$
24) Vertex $(-1,2)$ and Focus $(-1,5)$
25) Vertex $(2,2)$ and Focus $(2,6)$
26) Vertex $(0,1)$ and Focus $(0,2)$
27) Vertex $(2,1)$ and Focus $(4,1)$
28) Vertex $(5,0)$ and Focus $(9,0)$

✎ **Write the vertex form equation of each parabola.**

29) $y = x^2 + 8x$

30) $y = x^2 - 6x + 5$

31) $y + 6 = (x + 3)^2$

32) $y = x^2 + 10x + 33$

✎ **Identify the vertices, co-vertices, and foci.**

33) $\frac{x^2}{36} + \frac{y^2}{16} = 1$

34) $\frac{x^2}{49} + \frac{y^2}{169} = 1$

35) $\frac{(x+5)^2}{81} + \frac{(y-1)^2}{144} = 1$

36) $\frac{(x-3)^2}{49} + \frac{(y-9)^2}{4} = 1$

37) $\frac{x^2}{64} + \frac{(y-8)^2}{9} = 1$

38) $\frac{x^2}{64} + \frac{(y-6)^2}{121} = 1$

✎ **Identify the vertices, foci, and direction of the opening of each.**

39) $\frac{y^2}{25} - \frac{x^2}{16} = 1$

40) $\frac{x^2}{121} - \frac{y^2}{36} = 1$

41) $\frac{x^2}{121} - \frac{y^2}{81} = 1$

42) $\frac{x^2}{81} - \frac{y^2}{4} = 1$

43) $\frac{(x+2)^2}{169} - \frac{(y+8)^2}{4} = 1$

44) $\frac{(y+8)^2}{36} - \frac{(x+2)^2}{25} = 1$

✎ **Classify each conic section and write its equation in standard form.**

45) $3x^2 + 30x + y + 79 = 0$

46) $x^2 + y^2 + 4x - 2y - 18 = 0$

47) $49x^2 + 9y^2 + 392x + 343 = 0$

48) $-9x^2 + y^2 - 72x - 153 = 0$

49) $-2y^2 + x - 20y - 49 = 0$

50) $-x^2 + 10x + y - 21 = 0$

✎ **Which conic sections are each of the following equations?**

51) $3x^2 - 4xy + 3y^2 = 0$

52) $x^2 + 2xy + y^2 = 9$

53) $4x^2 + 6xy + 4y^2 = 0$

54) $x^2 + xy = 4$

55) $x^2 - 2xy + y^2 = 4$

56) $x^2 - 2xy - y^2 = 1$

Effortless Math Education

Chapter 15: Answers

1) $M = \left(1, \frac{7}{2}\right)$ and $d = \sqrt{53}$

2) $M = \left(-1, \frac{1}{2}\right)$ and $d = 5$

3) $M = (0,0)$ and $d = 4$

4) $M = (0,0)$ and $d = \sqrt{50}$

5) $M = \left(6, \frac{1}{2}\right)$ and $d = \sqrt{13}$

6) $M = \left(\frac{7}{2}, -2\right)$ and $d = 5$

7) $M = (3, -3)$ and $d = 2$

8) $M = \left(\frac{3}{2}, \frac{3}{2}\right)$ and $d = \sqrt{2}$

9) $(x+1)^2 + (y-12)^2 = 25$

10) $x^2 + (y-1)^2 = 16$

11) $(x+4)^2 + (y-1)^2 = 81$

12) $(x+5)^2 + (y+6)^2 = 81$

13) $(x+12)^2 + (y+5)^2 = 4$

14) $(x+11)^2 + (y+14)^2 = 16$

15) $(x+3)^2 + (y-2)^2 = 1$

16) $(x-15)^2 + (y-14)^2 = 15$

17) Center: $(2, -5)$, Radius: $\sqrt{10}$

18) Center: $(0, 1)$, Radius: 2

19) Center: $(2, -6)$, Radius: 3

20) Center: $(-14, 5)$, Radius: 4

21) $x^2 = 8y$

22) $(x-3)^2 = 8(y-2)$

23) $(x-1)^2 = 20(y-1)$

24) $(x+1)^2 = 12(y-2)$

25) $(x-2)^2 = 16(y-2)$

26) $x^2 = 4(y-1)$

27) $(y-1)^2 = 8(x-2)$

28) $y^2 = 16(x-5)$

29) $y = (x+4)^2 - 16$

30) $y = (x-3)^2 - 4$

31) $y = (x+3)^2 - 6$

32) $y = (x+5)^2 + 8$

33) Vertices: $(6,0), (-6,0)$

   Co−vertices: $(0,4), (0,-4)$

   Foci: $(2\sqrt{5}, 0), (-2\sqrt{5}, 0)$

34) Vertices: $(0,13), (0,-13)$

   Co−vertices: $(7,0), (-7,0)$

   Foci: $(0, 2\sqrt{30}), (0, -2\sqrt{30})$

35) Vertices: $(-5, 13), (-5, -11)$

   Co−vertices: $(4, 1), (-14, 1)$

   Foci: $(-5, 1 \pm 3\sqrt{7})$

36) Vertices: $(10, 9), (-4, 9)$

   Co−vertices: $(3, 11), (3, 7)$

   Foci: $(3 \pm 3\sqrt{5}, 9)$

37) Vertices: $(8,8)$, $(-8,8)$

Co−vertices: $(0,11)$, $(0,5)$

Foci: $(\sqrt{55}, 8)$, $(-\sqrt{55}, 8)$

38) Vertices: $(0,17)$, $(0,-5)$

Co−vertices: $(8,6)$, $(-8,6)$

Foci: $(0, 6 \pm \sqrt{57})$

39) Vertices: $(0,5)$, $(0,-5)$

Foci: $(0, \sqrt{41})$, $(0, -\sqrt{41})$

Opens up/down

40) Vertices: $(11,0)$, $(-11,0)$

Foci: $(\sqrt{157}, 0)$, $(-\sqrt{157}, 0)$

Opens left/right

41) Vertices: $(11,0)$, $(-11,0)$

Foci: $(\sqrt{202}, 0)$, $(-\sqrt{202}, 0)$

Opens left/right

42) Vertices: $(9,0)$, $(-9,0)$

Foci: $(\sqrt{85}, 0)$, $(-\sqrt{85}, 0)$

Opens left/right

43) Vertices: $(11,-8)$, $(-15,-8)$

Foci: $(-2 \pm \sqrt{173}, -8)$

Opens left/right

44) Vertices: $(-2,-2)$, $(-2,-14)$

Foci: $(-2, -8 \pm \sqrt{61})$

Opens up/down

45) Parabola, $4(-\frac{1}{12})(y - (-4)) = (x - (-5))^2$

46) Circle, $(x - (-2))^2 + (y - 1)^2 = (\sqrt{23})^2$

47) Ellipse, $\frac{(x-(-4))^2}{3^2} + \frac{(y)^2}{7^2} = 1$

48) Hyperbola, $\frac{(y)^2}{3^2} - \frac{(x-(-4))^2}{1^2} = 1$

49) Parabola, $(4)\left(\frac{1}{8}\right)(x - (-1)) = (y - (-5))^2$

50) Parabola, $(4)\left(\frac{1}{4}\right)(y - (-4)) = (x - 5)^2$

51) Ellipse

52) Circle

53) Hyperbola

54) Parabola

55) Ellipse

56) Hyperbola

CHAPTER

16 Matrices

Math topics that you'll learn in this chapter:

- ☑ Introduction to Matrices
- ☑ Matrix Addition and Subtraction
- ☑ Scalar Multiplication
- ☑ Matrix Multiplication
- ☑ Determinants of Matrices
- ☑ Inverse of a Matrix
- ☑ Solving Systems of Equations with Matrices

Introduction to Matrices

- Matrices are two-dimensional arrays and are used to analyze numerical data of tables, linear equations and …
- A matrix is a rectangular array of numbers, which is represented as follows:

$$A = \begin{bmatrix} a_{11} & a_{12} & \cdots & a_{1n} \\ a_{21} & a_{22} & & a_{2n} \\ \vdots & & \ddots & \vdots \\ a_{m1} & a_{m2} & \cdots & a_{mn} \end{bmatrix}$$

Each number in the matrix is called an entry.
- The number of horizontal rows and the number of vertical columns of a matrix is called the dimension of it. The dimension of the matrix A is $m \times n$.
- A matrix whose number of rows is equal to the number of columns is called a square matrix.

Examples:

Example 1. Solve $\begin{bmatrix} -1 & a+2 \\ 4 & 2 \\ 1 & -1 \end{bmatrix} = \begin{bmatrix} -1 & 0 \\ 2b-a & 2 \\ 1 & -1 \end{bmatrix}$ for a and b.

Solution: Since two matrices are equal, each of the corresponding arrays are equal. Therefore: $a + 2 = 0 \Rightarrow a = -2$.

In addition: $2b - a = 4$. So $a = -2$, then:
$2b - a = 4 \Rightarrow 2b - (-2) = 4 \Rightarrow 2b = 2 \Rightarrow b = 1$.

Example 2. The following table shows the age and shoe size of each student in a class. Write the matrix corresponding to the table.

Student	Size	Age
1	37	11
2	38	12
3	27	10
4	39	10
5	35	11

Solution: Put each student's number as a row of the matrix and age and shoe size as its column. Therefore, the matrix corresponding to the table is a matrix of dimension 5×2. As follow:

$$S = \begin{bmatrix} 37 & 11 \\ 38 & 12 \\ 27 & 10 \\ 39 & 10 \\ 35 & 11 \end{bmatrix}$$

bit.ly/401yGV9

Find more at

EffortlessMath.com

Matrix Addition and Subtraction

- A matrix (plural: matrices) is a rectangular array of numbers or variables arranged in rows and columns.
- We can add or subtract two matrices if they have the same dimensions. For addition or subtraction, add or subtract the corresponding entries, and place the result in the corresponding position in the resultant matrix.

Examples:

Example 1. $[1 \quad -4 \quad 6] + [2 \quad -3 \quad -9] =$

Solution: Add the elements in the matching positions:

$[1+2 \quad -4+(-3) \quad 6+(-9)] = [3 \quad -7 \quad -3]$.

Example 2. $\begin{bmatrix} 2 & 4 \\ -5 & -1 \\ -2 & -6 \end{bmatrix} + \begin{bmatrix} 1 & 0 \\ 0 & 7 \\ 3 & 5 \end{bmatrix} =$

Solution: Add the elements in the matching positions:

$\begin{bmatrix} 2+1 & 4+0 \\ (-5)+0 & (-1)+7 \\ (-2)+3 & (-6)+5 \end{bmatrix} = \begin{bmatrix} 3 & 4 \\ -5 & 6 \\ 1 & -1 \end{bmatrix}$.

Example 3. $\begin{bmatrix} 1 & -1 \\ 2 & 0 \end{bmatrix} - \begin{bmatrix} 4 & 0 \\ 2 & -1 \end{bmatrix} =$

Solution: Subtract the elements in the matching positions:

$\begin{bmatrix} 1-4 & -1-0 \\ 2-2 & 0-(-1) \end{bmatrix} = \begin{bmatrix} -3 & -1 \\ 0 & 1 \end{bmatrix}$.

Example 4. $\begin{bmatrix} -1 & 2 & 0 \\ 3 & -2 & 7 \\ 0 & 1 & -1 \end{bmatrix} - \begin{bmatrix} 0 & 2 & 4 \\ 1 & 0 & -1 \\ 1 & 0 & -1 \end{bmatrix} =$

Solution: Subtract the elements in the matching positions:

$\begin{bmatrix} -1-0 & 2-2 & 0-4 \\ 3-1 & -2-0 & 7-(-1) \\ 0-1 & 1-0 & -1-(-1) \end{bmatrix} = \begin{bmatrix} -1 & 0 & -4 \\ 2 & -2 & 8 \\ -1 & 1 & 0 \end{bmatrix}$.

Scalar Multiplication

- Scalar multiplication is a fundamental operation in linear algebra, used extensively in the study of matrices and their applications. In scalar multiplication, a scalar (a single number) is multiplied with each element of a matrix to create a new matrix of the same size. This operation can be used in a variety of contexts, such as scaling a vector in a certain direction or transforming a matrix in some specific way.
- **Definition**: Given a matrix A with entries a_{ij} and a scalar c, the scalar multiplication cA is the matrix obtained by multiplying each entry a_{ij} of A by c. Mathematically, this is expressed as: $(cA)_{ij} = c \cdot a_{ij}$.
  for all entries a_{ij} in the matrix A.
  - Note that multiplying any matrix by the scalar 0 will result in the zero matrix of the same size as the original matrix.

Examples:

Example 1. Consider the matrix A and scalar c defined as follows:
$$A = \begin{bmatrix} 2 & 4 \\ 1 & 3 \end{bmatrix}, c = 2$$
Get the corresponding scalar multiplication.

Solution: We obtain the scalar multiplication cA by multiplying each entry in A by c: $cA = 2 \times \begin{bmatrix} 2 & 4 \\ 1 & 3 \end{bmatrix} = \begin{bmatrix} 2 \times 2 & 2 \times 4 \\ 2 \times 1 & 2 \times 3 \end{bmatrix} = \begin{bmatrix} 4 & 8 \\ 2 & 6 \end{bmatrix}$.

Example 2. Consider the matrix B and scalar d defined as follows:
$$B = \begin{bmatrix} -1 & 5 & 0 \\ 2 & 1 & -3 \end{bmatrix}, d = -1$$
Get the corresponding scalar multiplication.

Solution: We obtain the scalar multiplication dB by multiplying each entry in B by d: $dB = \begin{bmatrix} (-1) \times (-)1 & (-1) \times 5 & (-1) \times 0 \\ (-1) \times 2 & (-1) \times 1 & (-1) \times (-3) \end{bmatrix} = \begin{bmatrix} 1 & -5 & 0 \\ -2 & -1 & 3 \end{bmatrix}$.

Example 3. Let's consider the matrix C and scalar e defined as follows:
$$C = \begin{bmatrix} -4 & 1 & 7 \end{bmatrix}, e = 0$$
Find the scalar multiplication eC.

Solution: We obtain the scalar multiplication eC by multiplying each entry in C by e: $eC = 0 \times \begin{bmatrix} -4 & 1 & 7 \end{bmatrix} = \begin{bmatrix} 0 & 0 & 0 \end{bmatrix}$.

Matrix Multiplication

- **Step 1:** Make sure that it's possible to multiply the two matrices (The number of columns in the 1st one should be the same as the number of rows in the second one.)
- **Step 2:** The elements of each row of the first matrix should be multiplied by the elements of each column in the second matrix.
- **Step 3:** Add the products.

Examples:

Example 1. $\begin{bmatrix} -1 & -3 \\ -4 & 0 \end{bmatrix} \begin{bmatrix} -3 & -2 \\ 4 & 4 \end{bmatrix} =$

Solution: Multiply the rows of the first matrix by the columns of the second matrix.

$\begin{bmatrix} (-1)(-3)+(-3)(4) & (-1)(-2)+(-3)(4) \\ (-4)(-3)+(0)(4) & (-4)(-2)+(0)(4) \end{bmatrix} = \begin{bmatrix} -9 & -10 \\ 12 & 8 \end{bmatrix}.$

Example 2. $\begin{bmatrix} -1 & -5 & -2 \\ 5 & 0 & 4 \end{bmatrix} \begin{bmatrix} 4 \\ 0 \\ 2 \end{bmatrix} =$

Solution: Multiply the rows of the first matrix by the columns of the second matrix.

$\begin{bmatrix} (-1)(4)+(-5)(0)+(-2)(2) \\ (5)(4)+(0)(0)+(4)(2) \end{bmatrix} = \begin{bmatrix} -8 \\ 28 \end{bmatrix}.$

Example 3. $\begin{bmatrix} 1 & 0 & -1 \\ 2 & -1 & 1 \end{bmatrix} \begin{bmatrix} 1 & 2 \\ 2 & -1 \\ 3 & 1 \end{bmatrix} =$

Solution: Multiply the rows of the first matrix by the columns of the second matrix.

$\begin{bmatrix} (1)(1)+(0)(2)+(-1)(3) & (1)(2)+(0)(-1)+(-1)(1) \\ (2)(1)+(-1)(2)+(1)(3) & (2)(2)+(-1)(-1)+(1)(1) \end{bmatrix} = \begin{bmatrix} -2 & 1 \\ 3 & 6 \end{bmatrix}.$

Determinants of Matrices

$$\begin{bmatrix} a & b \\ c & d \end{bmatrix} \quad |A| = ad - bc$$

$$\begin{bmatrix} a & b & c \\ d & e & f \\ g & h & i \end{bmatrix} \quad |A| = a(ei - fh) - b(di - fg) + c(dh - eg)$$

Examples:

Example 1. Evaluate the determinant of matrix. $\begin{bmatrix} 1 & -2 \\ -5 & 0 \end{bmatrix}$

Solution: Use the matrix determinant:

$|A| = ad - bc.$

Therefore:

$|A| = (1)(0) - (-2)(-5) = -10.$

Example 2. Evaluate the determinant of matrix. $\begin{bmatrix} 2 & 6 & 3 \\ 0 & 5 & 1 \\ 4 & 7 & 4 \end{bmatrix}$

Solution: Use the matrix determinant:

$|A| = a(ei - fh) - b(di - fg) + c(dh - eg).$

Then:

$|A| = 2(5 \times 4 - 7 \times 1) - 6(0 \times 4 - 4 \times 1) + 3(0 \times 7 - 5 \times 4) = -10.$

Example 3. Evaluate the determinant of matrix. $\begin{bmatrix} 1 & 2 \\ -1 & -1 \end{bmatrix}$

Solution: Use the matrix determinant: $|A| = ad - bc.$

Therefore:

$|A| = (1)(-1) - (2)(-1) = 1.$

Inverse of a Matrix

- For an arbitrary matrix A with the following two conditions:
  - Be a square matrix.
  - Be a non-singular matrix. that's mean $|A| \neq 0$.
- There exists a matrix B such that:
  - With matrix A having the same dimension.
  - $BA = AB = I$, where I is the identity matrix.
- The inverse of matrix A is denoted by A^{-1} ($A^{-1} \neq \frac{1}{A}$). For a 2×2 matrix:

$$A = \begin{bmatrix} a & b \\ c & d \end{bmatrix} \Rightarrow A^{-1} = \frac{1}{|A|} \begin{bmatrix} d & -b \\ -c & a \end{bmatrix}$$

$$A = \begin{bmatrix} a_{11} & a_{12} & a_{13} \\ a_{21} & a_{22} & a_{23} \\ a_{31} & a_{32} & a_{33} \end{bmatrix} \Rightarrow A^{-1} = \frac{1}{|A|} \begin{bmatrix} \begin{vmatrix} a_{22} & a_{23} \\ a_{32} & a_{33} \end{vmatrix} & \begin{vmatrix} a_{13} & a_{12} \\ a_{33} & a_{32} \end{vmatrix} & \begin{vmatrix} a_{12} & a_{13} \\ a_{22} & a_{23} \end{vmatrix} \\ \begin{vmatrix} a_{23} & a_{21} \\ a_{33} & a_{31} \end{vmatrix} & \begin{vmatrix} a_{11} & a_{13} \\ a_{31} & a_{33} \end{vmatrix} & \begin{vmatrix} a_{13} & a_{11} \\ a_{23} & a_{21} \end{vmatrix} \\ \begin{vmatrix} a_{21} & a_{22} \\ a_{31} & a_{32} \end{vmatrix} & \begin{vmatrix} a_{12} & a_{11} \\ a_{32} & a_{31} \end{vmatrix} & \begin{vmatrix} a_{11} & a_{12} \\ a_{21} & a_{22} \end{vmatrix} \end{bmatrix}$$

Examples:

Example 1. Show that $A = \begin{bmatrix} 2 & 1 \\ -1 & 0 \end{bmatrix}$ and $B = \begin{bmatrix} 0 & -1 \\ 1 & 2 \end{bmatrix}$ are inverses of one another.

Solution: For two matrices to be invertible, they must $BA = AB = I$. Therefore:
$A \times B = \begin{bmatrix} 2 & 1 \\ -1 & 0 \end{bmatrix} \begin{bmatrix} 0 & -1 \\ 1 & 2 \end{bmatrix} = \begin{bmatrix} 2 \times 0 + 1 \times 1 & 2 \times (-1) + 1 \times 2 \\ (-1) \times 0 + 0 \times 1 & (-1) \times (-1) + 0 \times 2 \end{bmatrix} = \begin{bmatrix} 1 & 0 \\ 0 & 1 \end{bmatrix} = I,$
$B \times A = \begin{bmatrix} 0 & -1 \\ 1 & 2 \end{bmatrix} \begin{bmatrix} 2 & 1 \\ -1 & 0 \end{bmatrix} = \begin{bmatrix} 0 \times 2 + (-1) \times (-1) & 0 \times 1 + (-1) \times 0 \\ 1 \times 2 + 2 \times (-1) & 1 \times 1 + 2 \times 0 \end{bmatrix} = \begin{bmatrix} 1 & 0 \\ 0 & 1 \end{bmatrix} = I.$

A and B are inverses of each other.

Example 2. Find the inverse of the matrix: $C = \begin{bmatrix} -1 & 3 \\ 0 & 2 \end{bmatrix}$.

Solution: Since C is a square matrix, calculate the determinant of the matrix. Then: $|A| = \left| \begin{bmatrix} a & b \\ c & d \end{bmatrix} \right| = ad - bc \Rightarrow |C| = (-1) \times 2 - 3 \times 0 = -2$.

Now, using this formula $A = \begin{bmatrix} a & b \\ c & d \end{bmatrix} \Rightarrow A^{-1} = \frac{1}{|A|} \begin{bmatrix} d & -b \\ -c & a \end{bmatrix}$. We have:

$C^{-1} = \frac{1}{|C|} \begin{bmatrix} 2 & -3 \\ 0 & -1 \end{bmatrix} \Rightarrow C^{-1} = -\frac{1}{2} \begin{bmatrix} 2 & -3 \\ 0 & -1 \end{bmatrix} = \begin{bmatrix} -1 & \frac{3}{2} \\ 0 & \frac{1}{2} \end{bmatrix}.$

Solving Systems of Equations with Matrices

- Any system of linear equations can be written as a matrix equation, $AX = B$ where A is the coefficient matrix, X is the variable matrix and B is the constant matrix.
- To solve a system of linear equations with a matrix equation, use the following steps:

Step 1: Rewrite the system of equations in standard form.

Step 2: Write the system as a matrix equation.

Step 3: Obtain the determinant of the matrix of coefficients and solve for $X = A^{-1}B$.

Example:

What is the value of y in the following system of equations?
$$2x - 1 = 3y$$
$$y = 4 + x$$

Solution: First the system of equations in standard form. As follow:
$2x - 3y = 1$
$x - y = -4$,

Write the system as a matrix equation:
$2x - 3y = 1$
$x - y = -4$ $\Rightarrow \begin{bmatrix} 2 & -3 \\ 1 & -1 \end{bmatrix} \begin{bmatrix} x \\ y \end{bmatrix} = \begin{bmatrix} 1 \\ -4 \end{bmatrix}$.

Let $A = \begin{bmatrix} 2 & -3 \\ 1 & -1 \end{bmatrix}$, obtain the determinant of A. Then, $|A| = 2 \times (-1) - (-3) \times 1 = 1$. Therefore:

$A^{-1} = \frac{1}{|A|} \begin{bmatrix} -1 & 3 \\ -1 & 2 \end{bmatrix} = \begin{bmatrix} -1 & 3 \\ -1 & 2 \end{bmatrix}$.

Solve $X = A^{-1}B$. It means that:
$X = \begin{bmatrix} x \\ y \end{bmatrix} = \begin{bmatrix} -1 & 3 \\ -1 & 2 \end{bmatrix} \begin{bmatrix} 1 \\ -4 \end{bmatrix} = \begin{bmatrix} (-1) \times 1 + 3 \times (-4) \\ (-1) \times 1 + 2 \times (-4) \end{bmatrix} = \begin{bmatrix} -13 \\ -9 \end{bmatrix}$.

Finally, the value of y is equal to -9.

Chapter 16: Practices

Solve for a and b.

1) $\begin{bmatrix} -1 & -2 \\ 2 & 6 \\ 1 & a+5 \end{bmatrix} = \begin{bmatrix} -1 & -2 \\ 2 & 2b-a \\ 1 & -1 \end{bmatrix}$

2) $\begin{bmatrix} 4 & -2 \\ 2 & a+4 \end{bmatrix} = \begin{bmatrix} 4 & 2a+b \\ 2 & a+4 \end{bmatrix} = \begin{bmatrix} 4 & 2a+b \\ 2 & 7 \end{bmatrix}$

Solve.

3) $\begin{bmatrix} 2 & 1 \\ -1 & 3 \end{bmatrix} - \begin{bmatrix} 2 & 5 \\ -7 & -2 \end{bmatrix} =$

4) $\begin{bmatrix} 6 & 4 \\ -9 & 7 \end{bmatrix} + \begin{bmatrix} 5 & 3 \\ -4 & 1 \end{bmatrix} =$

5) $\begin{bmatrix} 2 & 0 \\ -1 & 1 \end{bmatrix} - \begin{bmatrix} 4 & -2 \\ 2 & 1 \end{bmatrix} =$

6) $\begin{bmatrix} 6 & -7 \\ -3 & 11 \end{bmatrix} + \begin{bmatrix} 10 & -11 \\ 12 & 18 \end{bmatrix} =$

7) $\begin{bmatrix} -1 & 2 & -1 \\ 2 & -1 & 0 \end{bmatrix} - \begin{bmatrix} 2 & -5 & -4 \\ 1 & 1 & -3 \end{bmatrix} =$

8) $\begin{bmatrix} 8 & 12 \\ 14 & 21 \end{bmatrix} + \begin{bmatrix} 8 & -15 \\ 10 & -7 \end{bmatrix} =$

9) $\begin{bmatrix} 12 \\ 9 \\ 5 \end{bmatrix} + \begin{bmatrix} 18 \\ -14 \\ 19 \end{bmatrix} =$

10) $\begin{bmatrix} 14 \\ -16 \\ 13 \\ 21 \end{bmatrix} + \begin{bmatrix} -16 \\ 8 \\ -5 \\ -18 \end{bmatrix} =$

Evaluate.

11) $(-1) \times \begin{bmatrix} 2 & 1 & -3 \\ 2 & 0 & -1 \end{bmatrix}$

12) $0 \times \begin{bmatrix} 1 & 5 \\ 7 & -2 \end{bmatrix}$

13) $\left(\frac{1}{2}\right) \times \begin{bmatrix} 1 & 5 & -3 \\ 2 & -8 & 1 \\ 6 & -4 & 0 \end{bmatrix}$

14) $(-3) \times \begin{bmatrix} 2 \\ -1 \\ 4 \end{bmatrix}$

15) $2 \times \begin{bmatrix} -1 & 2 & 0 \end{bmatrix}$

16) $(-3) \times \begin{bmatrix} 0 & 2 \\ \frac{1}{3} & 1 \\ 4 & -2 \end{bmatrix}$

Effortless Math Education

✎ Solve.

17) $\begin{bmatrix} -1 & 0 & 3 \end{bmatrix} \begin{bmatrix} 1 \\ 2 \\ -1 \end{bmatrix} =$

18) $\begin{bmatrix} -1 \\ 6 \\ -6 \end{bmatrix} \begin{bmatrix} 8 & 5 & 4 \end{bmatrix} =$

19) $\begin{bmatrix} 0 & 2 \\ 2 & -1 \end{bmatrix} \begin{bmatrix} -2 & 1 \\ 1 & 4 \end{bmatrix} =$

20) $\begin{bmatrix} 2 & 4 & 3 \\ 4 & 3 & 2 \end{bmatrix} \begin{bmatrix} 4 & 3 \\ 5 & 5 \\ 2 & 5 \end{bmatrix} =$

21) $\begin{bmatrix} 2 & 5 \\ -4 & -3 \end{bmatrix} \begin{bmatrix} 1 & -5 \\ 3 & 2 \end{bmatrix} =$

22) $\begin{bmatrix} 1 & -2 \\ -4 & 5 \end{bmatrix} \begin{bmatrix} 4 & 3 \\ 4 & 0 \end{bmatrix} =$

23) $\begin{bmatrix} 3 & 1 & 2 \\ -5 & 6 & 5 \end{bmatrix} \begin{bmatrix} 3 \\ 5 \\ 2 \end{bmatrix} =$

24) $\begin{bmatrix} -1 & 2 & 5 \\ 0 & -2 & -1 \end{bmatrix} \begin{bmatrix} 5 & 1 \\ 2 & -2 \\ 0 & 1 \end{bmatrix} =$

✎ Evaluate the determinant of each matrix.

25) $\begin{bmatrix} 2 & 3 \\ -7 & -1 \end{bmatrix} =$

26) $\begin{bmatrix} 3 & 1 & 5 \\ -1 & -4 & 1 \\ 5 & 3 & 0 \end{bmatrix} =$

27) $\begin{bmatrix} 4 & 6 \\ 8 & 1 \end{bmatrix} =$

28) $\begin{bmatrix} 9 & 2 & -1 \\ 3 & -1 & -5 \\ 2 & -2 & 1 \end{bmatrix} =$

29) $\begin{bmatrix} -3 & 9 \\ 4 & 5 \end{bmatrix} =$

30) $\begin{bmatrix} 2 & 9 & -1 \\ -1 & 4 & -2 \\ 1 & -4 & 1 \end{bmatrix} =$

31) $\begin{bmatrix} -6 & 12 \\ 3 & 0 \end{bmatrix} =$

32) $\begin{bmatrix} 3 & -4 & 1 \\ 4 & 2 & -8 \\ 6 & -3 & -2 \end{bmatrix} =$

33) $\begin{bmatrix} -1 & 1 & 7 \\ 4 & -2 & 7 \\ 0 & 2 & 1 \end{bmatrix} =$

34) $\begin{bmatrix} 6 & 5 & 1 \\ 1 & -4 & 2 \\ 7 & -2 & -2 \end{bmatrix} =$

✎ Find the inverse of the matrix.

35) $C = \begin{bmatrix} -1 & -4 \\ 0 & -2 \end{bmatrix}$

36) $C = \begin{bmatrix} 2 & 3 & -4 \\ 0 & -1 & -2 \\ 2 & 4 & 0 \end{bmatrix}$

37) $C = \begin{bmatrix} -2 & 1 \\ 4 & 2 \end{bmatrix}$

38) $C = \begin{bmatrix} -2 & 1 & -1 \\ 0 & 4 & -4 \\ 0 & 2 & -4 \end{bmatrix}$

What is the value of x and y in the following system of equations?

39) $\begin{cases} 2x + 2y = 14 \\ -10x - 2y = -54 \end{cases}$

40) $\begin{cases} -2x + 8y = -6 \\ -2x + 4y = -6 \end{cases}$

Chapter 16: Answers

1) $a = -6$ and $b = 0$

2) $a = 3$ and $b = -8$

3) $\begin{bmatrix} 0 & -4 \\ 6 & 5 \end{bmatrix}$

4) $\begin{bmatrix} 11 & 7 \\ -13 & 8 \end{bmatrix}$

5) $\begin{bmatrix} -2 & 2 \\ -3 & 0 \end{bmatrix}$

6) $\begin{bmatrix} 16 & -18 \\ 9 & 29 \end{bmatrix}$

7) $\begin{bmatrix} -3 & 7 & 3 \\ 1 & -2 & 3 \end{bmatrix}$

8) $\begin{bmatrix} 16 & -3 \\ 24 & 14 \end{bmatrix}$

9) $\begin{bmatrix} 30 \\ -5 \\ 24 \end{bmatrix}$

10) $\begin{bmatrix} -2 \\ -8 \\ 8 \\ 3 \end{bmatrix}$

11) $\begin{bmatrix} -2 & -1 & 3 \\ -2 & 0 & 1 \end{bmatrix}$

12) $\begin{bmatrix} 0 & 0 \\ 0 & 0 \end{bmatrix}$

13) $\begin{bmatrix} \frac{1}{2} & \frac{5}{2} & -\frac{3}{2} \\ 1 & -4 & \frac{1}{2} \\ 3 & -2 & 0 \end{bmatrix}$

14) $\begin{bmatrix} -6 \\ 3 \\ -12 \end{bmatrix}$

15) $\begin{bmatrix} -2 & 4 & 0 \end{bmatrix}$

16) $\begin{bmatrix} 0 & -6 \\ -1 & -3 \\ -12 & 6 \end{bmatrix}$

17) $[-4]$

18) $\begin{bmatrix} -8 & -5 & -4 \\ 48 & 30 & 24 \\ -48 & -30 & -24 \end{bmatrix}$

19) $\begin{bmatrix} 2 & 8 \\ -5 & -2 \end{bmatrix}$

20) $\begin{bmatrix} 34 & 41 \\ 35 & 37 \end{bmatrix}$

21) $\begin{bmatrix} 17 & 0 \\ -13 & 14 \end{bmatrix}$

22) $\begin{bmatrix} -4 & 3 \\ 4 & -12 \end{bmatrix}$

23) $\begin{bmatrix} 18 \\ 25 \end{bmatrix}$

24) $\begin{bmatrix} -1 & 0 \\ -4 & 3 \end{bmatrix}$

25) 19

26) 81

27) −44

28) −121

29) −51

30) −17

31) −36

32) 52

33) 68

34) 178

35) $C^{-1} = \begin{bmatrix} -1 & 2 \\ 0 & -\frac{1}{2} \end{bmatrix}$

36) $C^{-1} = \begin{bmatrix} -2 & 4 & \frac{5}{2} \\ 1 & -2 & -1 \\ -\frac{1}{2} & \frac{1}{2} & \frac{1}{2} \end{bmatrix}$

37) $C^{-1} = \begin{bmatrix} -\frac{1}{4} & \frac{1}{8} \\ \frac{1}{2} & \frac{1}{4} \end{bmatrix}$

38) $C^{-1} = \begin{bmatrix} -\frac{1}{2} & \frac{1}{8} & 0 \\ 0 & \frac{1}{2} & -\frac{1}{2} \\ 0 & \frac{1}{4} & -\frac{1}{2} \end{bmatrix}$

39) $x = 5$ and $y = 2$

40) $x = 3$ and $y = 0$

Time to Test

Time to refine your math skill with a practice test.

In this section, there are two complete CLEP Precalculus Tests. Take these tests to simulate the test day experience. After you've finished, score your test using the answer keys.

Before You Start

- You'll need a pencil and a calculator to take the test.
- For each question, there are four possible answers. Choose which one is best.
- It's okay to guess. There is no penalty for wrong answers.
- Use the answer sheet provided to record your answers.
- **Calculator is permitted for Section I CLEP Precalculus Test.**
- After you've finished the test, review the answer key to see where you went wrong.

Good luck!

CLEP Precalculus Practice Test 1

2024

Total number of questions: 48

Time: 90 minutes

Calculator is permitted for Section I Test.

CLEP Precalculus Practice Test 1 Answer Sheet

Remove (or photocopy) this answer sheet and use it to complete the practice test.

CLEP Precalculus Practice Test 1 Answer Sheet	
Section I	**Section II**
1 Ⓐ Ⓑ Ⓒ Ⓓ	1 Ⓐ Ⓑ Ⓒ Ⓓ
2 Ⓐ Ⓑ Ⓒ Ⓓ	2 Ⓐ Ⓑ Ⓒ Ⓓ
3 Ⓐ Ⓑ Ⓒ Ⓓ	3 Ⓐ Ⓑ Ⓒ Ⓓ
4 Ⓐ Ⓑ Ⓒ Ⓓ	4 Ⓐ Ⓑ Ⓒ Ⓓ
5 Ⓐ Ⓑ Ⓒ Ⓓ	5 Ⓐ Ⓑ Ⓒ Ⓓ
6 Ⓐ Ⓑ Ⓒ Ⓓ	6 Ⓐ Ⓑ Ⓒ Ⓓ
7 Ⓐ Ⓑ Ⓒ Ⓓ	7 Ⓐ Ⓑ Ⓒ Ⓓ
8 Ⓐ Ⓑ Ⓒ Ⓓ	8 Ⓐ Ⓑ Ⓒ Ⓓ
9 Ⓐ Ⓑ Ⓒ Ⓓ	9 Ⓐ Ⓑ Ⓒ Ⓓ
10 Ⓐ Ⓑ Ⓒ Ⓓ	10 Ⓐ Ⓑ Ⓒ Ⓓ
11 Ⓐ Ⓑ Ⓒ Ⓓ	11 Ⓐ Ⓑ Ⓒ Ⓓ
12 Ⓐ Ⓑ Ⓒ Ⓓ	12 Ⓐ Ⓑ Ⓒ Ⓓ
13 Ⓐ Ⓑ Ⓒ Ⓓ	13 Ⓐ Ⓑ Ⓒ Ⓓ
14 Ⓐ Ⓑ Ⓒ Ⓓ	14 Ⓐ Ⓑ Ⓒ Ⓓ
15 Ⓐ Ⓑ Ⓒ Ⓓ	15 Ⓐ Ⓑ Ⓒ Ⓓ
16 Ⓐ Ⓑ Ⓒ Ⓓ	16 Ⓐ Ⓑ Ⓒ Ⓓ
17 Ⓐ Ⓑ Ⓒ Ⓓ	17 Ⓐ Ⓑ Ⓒ Ⓓ
18 Ⓐ Ⓑ Ⓒ Ⓓ	18 Ⓐ Ⓑ Ⓒ Ⓓ
19 Ⓐ Ⓑ Ⓒ Ⓓ	19 Ⓐ Ⓑ Ⓒ Ⓓ
20 Ⓐ Ⓑ Ⓒ Ⓓ	20 Ⓐ Ⓑ Ⓒ Ⓓ
21 Ⓐ Ⓑ Ⓒ Ⓓ	21 Ⓐ Ⓑ Ⓒ Ⓓ
22 Ⓐ Ⓑ Ⓒ Ⓓ	22 Ⓐ Ⓑ Ⓒ Ⓓ
23 Ⓐ Ⓑ Ⓒ Ⓓ	23 Ⓐ Ⓑ Ⓒ Ⓓ
24 Ⓐ Ⓑ Ⓒ Ⓓ	
25 Ⓐ Ⓑ Ⓒ Ⓓ	

Section I: Multiple-Choice

Time limit: 50 minutes

The use of an online graphing calculator (non- CAS) is allowed for this section.

1) What is the range for $f(x) = x^2 + 2$?

   A. $\mathbb{R}$

   B. $(-2, +\infty)$

   C. $(2, +\infty)$

   D. $[2, +\infty)$

2) Triangle ABC has a right angle.

   Angle ABC is $20°$.

   $AB = 16\ cm$

   What is the length of BC? (Nearest tenth)

   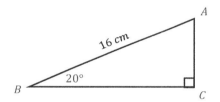

   A. 20

   B. 15

   C. 9.5

   D. 5.5

3) What is the graph of linear inequality, $y < -2x - 2$?

A.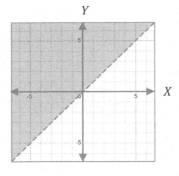

B.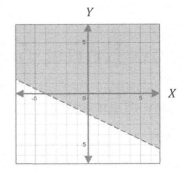

C.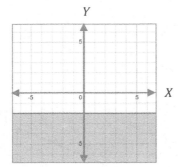

D.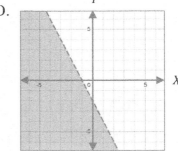

4) In an arithmetic sequence where the 3rd sequence is 13 and the 7th sequence is 25, what is the sum of the 10th sequence of this series?

5) Which statement best describes these two functions?

$$f(x) = 2x^2 - 4x$$
$$g(x) = (x-1)^2 - 1$$

A. They have no common points.

B. They have same $x-$intercepts.

C. The maximum of $f(x)$ is the same as the minimum of $g(x)$.

D. They have same minimum.

6) Which graph represents the function $-\log(1-x)$?

A.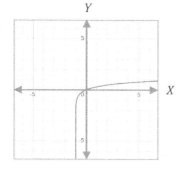

B.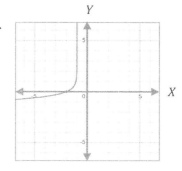

C.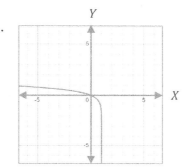

D.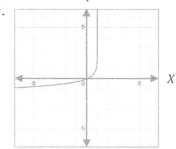

7) f is an exponential function defined by $f(x) = a2^{bx-1} - 1$, where a and b are positive constants. If $f(1) = 1$ and $f(2) = 15$, what is the value of $a + b$?

   A. 0.5

   B. 1.5

   C. 3

   D. 3.5

8) What is the value of $\cos 30°$?

   A. $\frac{\sqrt{2}}{2}$

   B. $\frac{1}{2}$

   C. $-\frac{1}{2}$

   D. $\frac{\sqrt{3}}{2}$

9) Find the function represented by the following graph.

   A. $f(x) = 2x^2 + 4x - 3$

   B. $f(x) = -2x^2 + 4x - 3$

   C. $f(x) = 2x^2 - 4x - 3$

   D. $f(x) = 2x^2 + 4x + 3$

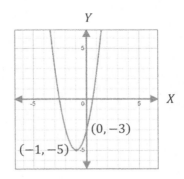

10) What is the equation of a circle with center $(-1, 2)$ and perimeter 4π?

    A. $(x + 1)^2 + (y - 2)^2 = 4\pi$

    B. $(x + 1)^2 + (y - 2)^2 = 4$

    C. $(x - 1)^2 + (y + 2)^2 = 2$

    D. $(x - 1)^2 + (y + 2)^2 = 2\pi$

11) If $ABCDEF$ is a regular hexagon, find the value of $\overrightarrow{AB} + \overrightarrow{AC} + \overrightarrow{AE} + \overrightarrow{AF}$.

    A. $\vec{O}$

    B. $\overrightarrow{AD}$

    C. $2\overrightarrow{AD}$

    D. $4\overrightarrow{AB}$

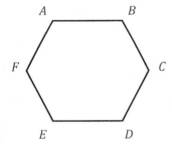

12) What is the vertex of the parabola $y = (x - 2)^2 + 3$?

    A. $(-2, 3)$

    B. $(-2, -3)$

    C. $(2, 3)$

    D. $(2, -3)$

13) For which value of a, the function $f(x) = \begin{cases} \frac{2\sin^2 x - \sin x - 1}{\cos^2 x} & ; x \neq \frac{\pi}{2} \\ a & ; x = \frac{\pi}{2} \end{cases}$ is continuous at $x = \frac{\pi}{2}$?

A. 1.5

B. 1

C. −1

D. −1.5

14) For every $n \in \mathbb{N}$, $\lim\limits_{n \to +\infty} \frac{2^{2n+1} - 2^{1-2n}}{2^{2n+1} + 3 \times 2^{1-2n}} = ?$

A. 1

B. $\frac{1}{3}$

C. $-\frac{1}{3}$

D. −1

15) A woman on the top of a tower, standing on the beach, finds that a boat coming towards her takes 8 minutes for the angle of depression to change from 25° to 50°. How soon will the boat reach the beach?

A. 3 minutes

B. 5 minutes

C. 8 minutes

D. 12 minutes

16) What is the domain and range of the function $f(x) = \frac{2}{\sec(x-\pi)}$?

A. Domain: $\mathbb{R}$, Range: $[-2,2]$

B. Domain: $\mathbb{R} - \{\frac{\pi}{2}, \pi\}$, Range: $\mathbb{R}$

C. Domain: $\left(-\infty, \frac{\pi}{2}\right) \cup \left(\frac{\pi}{2}, \pi\right) \cup (\pi, +\infty)$, Range: $(-2,2)$

D. Domain: $(-\infty, +\infty)$, Range: $[-1,1]$

17) What is the number of discontinuity points of function $f(x) = [x] \sin \pi x$ where $|x| \leq 2$?

   A. 3

   B. 2

   C. 1

   D. 0

18) What is the center and radius of a circle with the following equation?
$$(x-4)^2 + (y+7)^2 = 3$$

   A. $(4,7)$ and $\sqrt{3}$

   B. $(4,-7)$ and 3

   C. $(4,7)$ and 3

   D. $(4,-7)$ and $\sqrt{3}$

19) In $\triangle ABC$, $\angle C = 90°$ and $AB = x$, $BC = y$, $CA = z$; then the value of $(\sec B \cdot \tan A)$ is:

   A. $\frac{x}{z}$

   B. $\frac{z}{x}$

   C. $\frac{y}{x}$

   D. $\frac{x}{y}$

20) If $e^{\ln 4} = x$, what is the value of x?

   A. e

   B. 4

   C. 2

   D. e^4

21) The minimum value of $4\sin^2\alpha + 5\cos^2\alpha$ is:

   A. 4

   B. 5

   C. 1

   D. 0

22) If $f(x) = \frac{1}{2}x - 1$ and $g(x) = -2$, which graph corresponds to the function of $(fog)(x)$?

   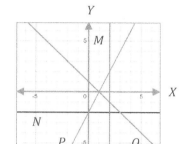

   A. M

   B. P

   C. O

   D. N

23) What is the value of x in the following equation?

$$log_4(x+2) - log_4(x-2) = 1$$

24) Two right-angled triangles are shown below.

NO is 12 cm

MN is 6 cm

Angle NMP is 60°

Find the size of angle MNO.

A. 30°

B. 60°

C. 90°

D. 120°

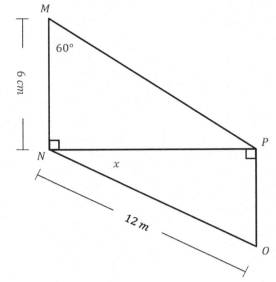

25) How many x-intercepts do the graph of $y = \frac{x-1}{1-x^2}$ have?

A. 0

B. 1

C. 2

D. 3

Section II: Multiple-Choice

Time limit: 40 minutes

No calculator is allowed for this section.

1) Which of the following is equivalent to the expression $3\ln(x) + 4\ln(y)$ for all values of x and y for which both expressions are defined?

   A. $\ln(x^3 y^4)$

   B. $\ln(x^4 y^3)$

   C. $7\ln(xy)$

   D. $\ln(x^7 y)$

2) According to the graph of the given function, what is the value of $\int_{-1}^{5} f(x)\,dx$?

   A. 10

   B. 12

   C. 13

   D. 14

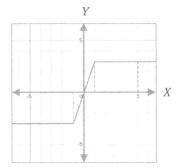

3) If $\tan\theta = \frac{5}{12}$ and $\sin\theta < 0$, then $\cos\theta = ?$

   A. $\frac{12}{13}$

   B. $-\frac{5}{13}$

   C. $-\frac{12}{13}$

   D. $\frac{13}{12}$

4) If $x = 3\left(\log_2 \frac{1}{32}\right)$, what is the value of x?

   A. -15

   B. $\frac{3}{5}$

   C. 15

   D. $-\frac{3}{5}$

$$f(x) = \frac{1}{(x-3)^2 + 4(x-3) + 4}$$

5) For what value of x is the function $f(x)$ above undefinded?

   A. -1

   B. 1

   C. -3

   D. 3

6) Which function represents this graph?

   A. $y = 2x^2 - 2$

   B. $y = -\frac{1}{2}x^2 + 2$

   C. $y = -2x^2 + 2$

   D. $y = -\frac{1}{2}x^2 - 2$

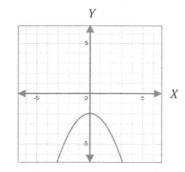

7) If $(fog)(x) = x - 1$, how might $f(x)$ and $g(x)$ be defined?

   A. $f(x) = x + 1$ and $g(x) = -x - 2$

   B. $f(x) = -x + 1$ and $g(x) = x - 2$

   C. $f(x) = x + 1$ and $g(x) = x + 2$

   D. $f(x) = -x + 1$ and $g(x) = -x + 2$

8) Find the radius of a circle with the following equation:
$$x^2 + y^2 - 6x + 4y + 4 = 0$$

9) Which graph reperesents the inverse of $y = -x$?

A.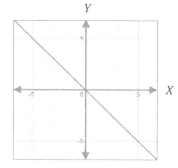

B.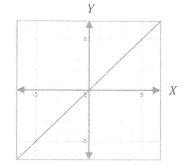

C.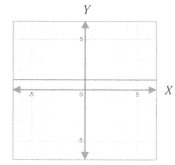

D.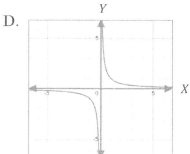

10) What is the equation of the horizontal asymptote of the function $f(x) = \frac{x+3}{x^2+1}$?

A. $y = 0$

B. $x = -3$

C. $x^2 = -1$

D. No horizontal asymptote

11) Which one is $\overrightarrow{NM} + \overrightarrow{PM}$ in figure?

A. $\overrightarrow{NP}$

B. $\overrightarrow{MO}$

C. $\overrightarrow{PN}$

D. $\overrightarrow{OM}$

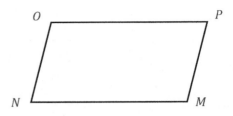

12) What is the value of $sin\left(\frac{11\pi}{4}\right)$?

13) Which of the following is true for $0° < \theta < 90°$?

A. $sin\,\theta > sin^2\,\theta$

B. $sin\,\theta < sin^2\,\theta$

C. $sin\,\theta \leq sin^2\,\theta$

D. $sin\,\theta \geq sin^2\,\theta$

14) Which statement best describes these two functions?

$$f(x) = 2x^2 - x + 3$$
$$g(x) = -x^2 + 2x + 1$$

A. The maximum of $f(x)$ is less than the minimum of $g(x)$.

B. The minimum of $f(x)$ is less than the maximum of $g(x)$.

C. The maximum of $f(x)$ is greater than the minimum of $g(x)$.

D. The minimum of $f(x)$ is greater than the maximum of $g(x)$.

15) According to the following graph, there is a curve $y = a\,sec(bx) + c$, for the interval $0 \leq x \leq 2\pi$. Based on the graph, what are the values of a, b, and c?

A. $a = 1, b = \pi, c = 0$

B. $a = 2, b = \frac{\pi}{2}, c = 1$

C. $a = -1, b = \pi, c = 0$

D. $a = -2, b = \frac{\pi}{2}, c = 1$

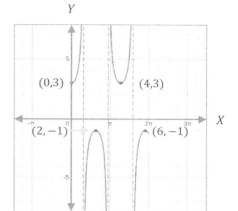

16) Which answer choice describes how the graph of $f(x) = e^x$ was transformed to create the graph of $g(x) = e^{x+1}$?

A. A horizontal shift down

B. A vertical shift up

C. A horizontal shift to the left

D. A vertical shift down

17) What is the inverse of the function $f(x) = 5 \cdot \left(\frac{1}{2}\right)^x$?

A. $f^{-1}(x) = \frac{\ln 2}{\ln \frac{x}{5}}$

B. $f^{-1}(x) = \ln \frac{x}{5} - \ln 2$

C. $f^{-1}(x) = \log_2 \frac{x}{5}$

D. $f^{-1}(x) = -\log_2 \frac{x}{5}$

18) If $x\,tan\,30° = y\,sec\,60°$, then $\frac{x^4}{y^4}$ is equal to:

A. 2^2

B. 4^2

C. 6^2

D. 12^2

19) If $\cos x \cdot \cos y + \sin x \cdot \sin y = 1$, then $\sin x - \sin y$ is:

A. -2

B. 0

C. 1

D. 2

20) What is the equation (in standard form) of the following graph?

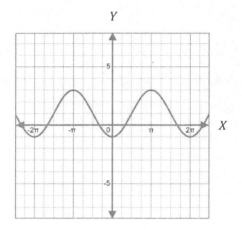

A. $y = 2 \sin\left(x + \frac{\pi}{2}\right)$

B. $y = 2 \sin\left(x - \frac{\pi}{2}\right) + 1$

C. $y = 2 \sin\left(x + \frac{\pi}{2}\right) + 1$

D. $y = 2 \sin\left(x - \frac{\pi}{2}\right) - 1$

21) The value of $\cos(60° + \theta) - \sin(30° - \theta)$ is:

A. 1

B. 0

C. $2 \cos \theta$

D. $2 \sin \theta$

22) If $\alpha + \beta = 120°$ and $\alpha:\beta = 1:3$, then the ratio of $\sin\beta$ to $\sin\alpha$ is:

23) If $f(x) = x - |x - 2|$, what is the product of $\int_0^4 f(x)\,dx$?

   A. 2

   B. 3

   C. 4

   D. 5

End of CLEP Precalculus Practice Test 1

CLEP Precalculus Practice Test 2

2024

Total number of questions: 48

Time: 90 minutes

Calculator is permitted for Section I Test.

CLEP Precalculus Practice Test 2 Answer Sheet

Remove (or photocopy) this answer sheet and use it to complete the practice test.

CLEP Precalculus Practice Test 2 Answer Sheet	
Section I	Section II
1 Ⓐ Ⓑ Ⓒ Ⓓ	1 Ⓐ Ⓑ Ⓒ Ⓓ
2 Ⓐ Ⓑ Ⓒ Ⓓ	2 Ⓐ Ⓑ Ⓒ Ⓓ
3 Ⓐ Ⓑ Ⓒ Ⓓ	3 Ⓐ Ⓑ Ⓒ Ⓓ
4 Ⓐ Ⓑ Ⓒ Ⓓ	4 Ⓐ Ⓑ Ⓒ Ⓓ
5 Ⓐ Ⓑ Ⓒ Ⓓ	5 Ⓐ Ⓑ Ⓒ Ⓓ
6 Ⓐ Ⓑ Ⓒ Ⓓ	6 Ⓐ Ⓑ Ⓒ Ⓓ
7 Ⓐ Ⓑ Ⓒ Ⓓ	7 Ⓐ Ⓑ Ⓒ Ⓓ
8 Ⓐ Ⓑ Ⓒ Ⓓ	8 Ⓐ Ⓑ Ⓒ Ⓓ
9 Ⓐ Ⓑ Ⓒ Ⓓ	9 Ⓐ Ⓑ Ⓒ Ⓓ
10 Ⓐ Ⓑ Ⓒ Ⓓ	10 Ⓐ Ⓑ Ⓒ Ⓓ
11 Ⓐ Ⓑ Ⓒ Ⓓ	11 Ⓐ Ⓑ Ⓒ Ⓓ
12 Ⓐ Ⓑ Ⓒ Ⓓ	12 Ⓐ Ⓑ Ⓒ Ⓓ
13 Ⓐ Ⓑ Ⓒ Ⓓ	13 Ⓐ Ⓑ Ⓒ Ⓓ
14 Ⓐ Ⓑ Ⓒ Ⓓ	14 Ⓐ Ⓑ Ⓒ Ⓓ
15 Ⓐ Ⓑ Ⓒ Ⓓ	15 Ⓐ Ⓑ Ⓒ Ⓓ
16 Ⓐ Ⓑ Ⓒ Ⓓ	16 Ⓐ Ⓑ Ⓒ Ⓓ
17 Ⓐ Ⓑ Ⓒ Ⓓ	17 Ⓐ Ⓑ Ⓒ Ⓓ
18 Ⓐ Ⓑ Ⓒ Ⓓ	18 Ⓐ Ⓑ Ⓒ Ⓓ
19 Ⓐ Ⓑ Ⓒ Ⓓ	19 Ⓐ Ⓑ Ⓒ Ⓓ
20 Ⓐ Ⓑ Ⓒ Ⓓ	20 Ⓐ Ⓑ Ⓒ Ⓓ
21 Ⓐ Ⓑ Ⓒ Ⓓ	21 Ⓐ Ⓑ Ⓒ Ⓓ
22 Ⓐ Ⓑ Ⓒ Ⓓ	22 Ⓐ Ⓑ Ⓒ Ⓓ
23 Ⓐ Ⓑ Ⓒ Ⓓ	23 Ⓐ Ⓑ Ⓒ Ⓓ
24 Ⓐ Ⓑ Ⓒ Ⓓ	
25 Ⓐ Ⓑ Ⓒ Ⓓ	

EffortlessMath.com

Section I: Multiple-Choice

Time limit: 50 minutes

The use of an online graphing calculator (non-CAS) is allowed for this section.

1) What is the domain and range of the function $f(x) = 2 - 3\sin\left(2x - \frac{\pi}{3}\right)$?

   A. Domain: $\left[\frac{\pi}{3}, +\infty\right)$, Range: $[-1, 5]$

   B. Domain: $(-\infty, +\infty)$, Range: $[-5, 1]$

   C. Domain: $\mathbb{R} - \frac{\pi}{3}$, Range: $[-5, 1]$

   D. Domain: $\mathbb{R}$, Range: $[-1, 5]$

2) If $f(x) = x + 6$ and $g(x) = -x^2 - 2x - 1$, what is $(g - f)(x)$?

   A. $x^2 + 3x + 7$

   B. $-x^2 + 3x - 7$

   C. $-x^2 - 3x - 7$

   D. $x^2 - 3x + 7$

3) Which statement best describes the equation $y = \frac{1}{\cos\left(x - \frac{\pi}{2}\right)} + 4$?

   A. The function has vertical asymptote at $x = n\frac{\pi}{2}$; n is an integer.

   B. The function has horizontal asymptote at $y = 5$ and $y = 3$.

   C. It represents a secant function, $y = \sec x$, translated $\frac{\pi}{2}$ units to the left.

   D. It represents a cosine function, $y = \csc x$, translated 4 units upwards.

4) What is the inverse of $f(x) = 1 - \sin(x)$?

   A. $f^{-1}(x) = \sin(1 - x)$

   B. $f^{-1}(x) = \arcsin(1 - x)$

   C. $f^{-1}(x) = 1 - \arcsin(x)$

   D. $f^{-1}(x) = \arcsin(x - 1)$

5) Which function is best represented by this graph?

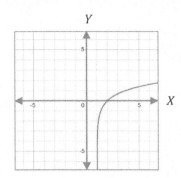

A. $ln(x)$

B. $ln(x+1)$

C. $ln(x-1)$

D. $ln(x)-1$

6) A ladder leans against a wall forming a 60° angle between the ground and the ladder. If the bottom of the ladder is 30 feet away from the wall, how long is the ladder?

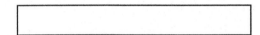

7) The diagram shows two right-angled triangles.

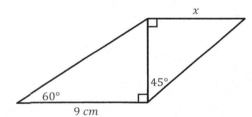

Find the value of x.

A. $\frac{9}{\sqrt{2}}$

B. 9

C. $9\sqrt{2}$

D. $9\sqrt{3}$

8) What is the inverse of $f(x) = cos^2\left(\frac{1}{2}x - 1\right)$?

   A. $f^{-1}(x) = 2\,arccos(x)$
   B. $f^{-1}(x) = 2\sqrt{arccos(x)} + 2$
   C. $f^{-1}(x) = 2\,arccos(\sqrt{x}) + 2$
   D. $f^{-1}(x) = 2\,tan(\sqrt{x}) - 2$

9) Which graph corresponds to $y = (x+1)^2 - 2$?

A.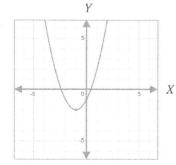

B.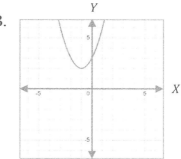

C.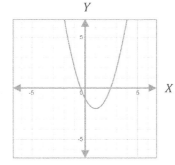

D.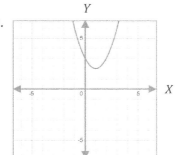

10) Find the value of x in this equation: $log(5x+2) = log(3x-1)$.

11) What are the coordinates at the minimum point of $f(x) = x^2 + 2x - 1$?

   A. $(-1, 2)$

   B. $(1, -2)$

   C. $(-1, -2)$

   D. $(1, 2)$

12) The graph of the function with equation $f(x) = \frac{ax^2 + 7x}{2x^2 + bx + c}$ has only one vertical asymptote as $x = 2$. If $f(3) = 6$, what is the asymptotic equation of it?

   A. $y = -1$

   B. $y = -\frac{1}{2}$

   C. $y = \frac{1}{2}$

   D. $y = \frac{3}{2}$

13) If $f(x) = 2x^3 + 4$ and $g(x) = \frac{1}{x}$, what is the value of $f(g(x))$?

   A. $\frac{1}{2x^3 + 4}$

   B. $\frac{2}{x^3} + 4$

   C. $2x^3 + 4 + \frac{1}{x}$

   D. $2x^2 + \frac{4}{x}$

14) Solve this equation for x: $e^{2x} = 12$.

   A. $\frac{1}{2} ln(12)$

   B. $ln(12)$

   C. $ln(2)$

   D. $\frac{1}{2} ln(2)$

15) Which best describes the graph of $\frac{x^2}{49} + \frac{y^2}{16} = 1$?

   A. Hyperbola

   B. Circle

   C. Parabola

   D. Elipse

16) What is the parent graph of the following function and what transformations have taken place on it?
$$y = 2 - (2 + 4x - x^2):$$

   A. The parent graph is $y = -x^2$, which is shifted 4 units down and shifted 2 units left.

   B. The parent graph is $y = x^2$, which is shifted 4 units and shifted 2 units right.

   C. The parent graph is $y = -x^2$, which is shifted 2 units right and shifted 4 units up.

   D. The parent graph is $y = x^2$, which is shifted 2 units right and shifted 4 units down.

17) The function g is an exponential function of the form $g(x) = ab^x$. Based on the values given in the table, which of the following expressions defines $g^{-1}(x)$?

x	0	1	2
$g(x)$	4	8	16

   A. $4 \log_2 x$

   B. $2 \log_4 x$

   C. $\log_2 \left(\frac{x}{4}\right)$

   D. $\log_4 \left(\frac{x}{2}\right)$

18) The graph illustrates how the number of presentations made by a convention presenter relates to the number of cookies she had left to give away.

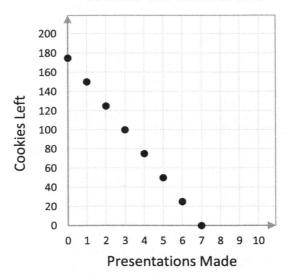

Cookies at Presentation

What does the x −intercept of the graph represent?

A. The initial number of cookies the presenter had before making any presentations.

B. The point at which the presenter stopped giving away cookies during the presentations.

C. The rate at which the presenter made presentations per unit of time.

D. The maximum number of presentations the presenter made before running out of cookies.

19) What is the domain and range of the radical function $y = 3\sqrt{2x + 4} + 8$?

A. Domain $x \geq -2$, range $f(x) \geq 8$

B. Domain $-\infty \leq x \leq +\infty$, range $-\infty \leq x \leq +\infty$

C. Domain $x \geq -2$, range $-\infty \leq x \leq +\infty$

D. Domain $x > -2$, range $f(x) \geq 8$

20) How many are the zeros of the function $f(x) = x^3 + 6x^2 + 8x$?

21) Find the equation of the graphed Hyperbola:

A. $\frac{(x+3)^2}{4} - \frac{(y-4)^2}{9} = 1$

B. $\frac{(x-3)^2}{4} - \frac{(y+4)^2}{9} = 1$

C. $\frac{(y+4)^2}{4} - \frac{(x-3)^2}{9} = 1$

D. $\frac{(y-4)^2}{4} - \frac{(x+3)^2}{9} = 1$

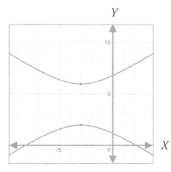

22) If $\sec\theta + \cos\theta = 2$, then the value of $\sin^3\theta + \cos^3\theta$ is:

A. 8

B. 2

C. 1

D. 0

23) ABC is a right-angled triangle, right angled at B and $\angle A = 45°$ and $AB = 10\ cm$, then the ratio of sides BC and CA is:

A. $\sqrt{2} : 1$

B. $1 : \sqrt{2}$

C. $\sqrt{2} : \sqrt{3}$

D. $\sqrt{2} : 3$

24) Find a positive coterminal angle to angle $125°$.

25) Let $f(x) = \begin{cases} (x-1)[x] & ; |x-1| < 1 \\ x^2 + ax + b & ; |x-1| \geq 1 \end{cases}$ be a continuous function on the domain. What is the value of a?

A. $-\frac{3}{2}$

B. -1

C. 1

D. $\frac{5}{2}$

Section II: Multiple-Choice

Time limit: 40 minutes

No calculator is allowed for this section.

1) The diagram shows a right-angled triangle ABC. What is the length of BC.

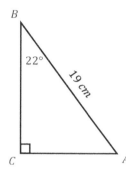

Angle	Sine	Cosine	Tangent
22°	0.375	0.927	0.404
68°	0.927	0.375	2.475

A. $47\ cm$

B. $17.6\ cm$

C. $7.7\ cm$

D. $7.1\ cm$

2) What is the domain and range of function: $f(x) = \frac{1}{x+2}$?

A. $\{-2\}$ and $\mathbb{R}$

B. $\mathbb{R}$ and $\mathbb{R} - \{0\}$

C. $\mathbb{R} - \{2\}$ and $\mathbb{R} - \{0\}$

D. $-\infty < x < +\infty$ and $\mathbb{R}$

3) If $\frac{1}{2} log_{2x} 64 = 3$, what is the value of x?

4) The value of $4(\sin 45° \cos 15°)$ is:

A. 1

B. $\sqrt{3}$

C. $\sqrt{3} + 1$

D. Not defined.

5) Which graph corresponds to $f(x) = \tan\left(x - \frac{\pi}{2}\right) + 2$, when $0 \le x \le \pi$?

A.
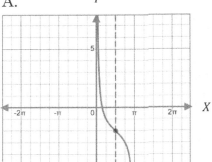

B.
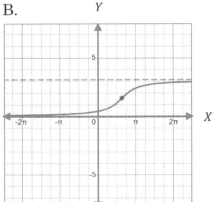

C.
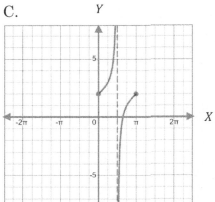

D.
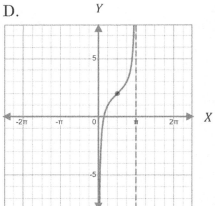

6) Convert the radian measure $\frac{2\pi}{3}$ to degree measure.

   A. 120°

   B. 60°

   C. 90°

   D. 150°

7) Find the equation of the given parabola:

   A. $y = x^2 + 4x - 1$

   B. $y = -x^2 - 4x$

   C. $y = -2x^2 - 4x + 2$

   D. $y = -x^2 + 4$

   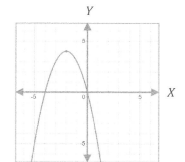

8) Which function is the invers of $f(x) = ln\sqrt{x}$?

   A. e^x

   B. $x^{\frac{1}{2}}$

   C. e^{2x}

   D. $\frac{1}{f(x)}$

9) If $f(x) = 2x^3 + x$ and $g(x) = x - 2$, what is the value of $(f - g)(1)$?

   A. 1

   B. 2

   C. 3

   D. 4

10) The graph of a function $f(x)$ is a transformed trigonometric function. Which of the following represents the function $f(x)$?

A. $f(x) = 3\cos\left(2\left(x - \frac{\pi}{2}\right)\right) - 1$

B. $f(x) = -3\cos\left(2\left(x + \frac{\pi}{2}\right)\right) - 1$

C. $f(x) = -3\sin\left(2\left(x - \frac{\pi}{2}\right)\right) - 1$

D. $f(x) = 3\sin\left(2\left(x + \frac{\pi}{2}\right)\right) - 1$

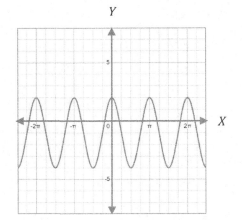

11) Which graph represents the inverse of $y = sin\left(x - \frac{\pi}{3}\right)$ over the interval $\left[-\frac{\pi}{6}, \frac{5\pi}{6}\right]$?

A.
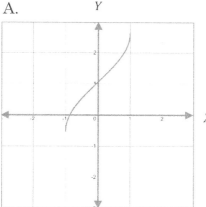

B.
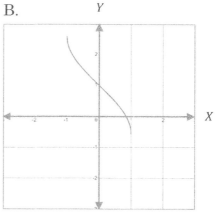

C.
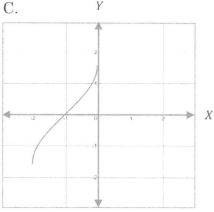

D.
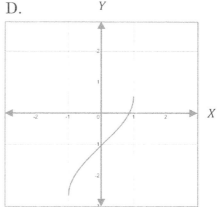

12) Which statement describes the equation $x = y^2 + 2y - 4$?

A. It is a vertical parabola.

B. It is a vertical hyperbola.

C. It is a horizontal parabola.

D. It is a horizontal hyperbola.

13) If $2(sin^2\theta - cos^2\theta) = -1$, θ is a positive acute angle, then the value of θ is:

A. 60°

B. 45°

C. 30°

D. 22.5°

14) Find the slope of the line passing through the points $(-4,3)$ and $(-9,7)$.

A. $-\frac{4}{5}$

B. $\frac{4}{5}$

C. $\frac{5}{4}$

D. $-\frac{5}{4}$

15) In circular measure, the value of 15° is:

A. $\frac{\pi}{12}$

B. $\frac{\pi}{8}$

C. $\frac{\pi}{4}$

D. $\frac{\pi}{6}$

16) Which statement best describes these two functions?

$$f(x) = cos\, x + 4$$
$$g(x) = 2 - sin^2 x$$

A. They have no common points.

B. They have the same x-intercepts.

C. The maximum of $f(x)$ is the same as the maximum of $g(x)$.

D. They have the same minimum.

17) What is the sum of the first 7 terms of the series 1,3,9,⋯?

   A. 729

   B. 2187

   C. 1093

   D. 364

18) The angles of depression of two boats from the top of a lighthouse are 30° and 45° towards the east. If the boats are 200 meters apart, the height of the lighthouse is:

   A. 100 meter

   B. $100\sqrt{3}$ meter

   C. 200 meter

   D. $100(1+\sqrt{3})$ meter

19) What is the slope of a line that is perpendicular to the line $4x - 2y = 14$?

   A. 2

   B. −2

   C. $\frac{1}{2}$

   D. $-\frac{1}{2}$

20) Which function is the inverse of $g(x) = \ln x^2$?

   A. $\frac{1}{\ln x^2}$

   B. $\sqrt{e^x}$

   C. $e^{\sqrt{x}2}$

   D. $\pm\sqrt{e^x}$

21) The graph shows the height in feet of a stone ball above the ground t seconds after it was launched from the ground.

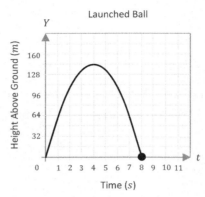

Which function is best represented by the graph of this situation?

A. $y = -9t^2 + 72t$

B. $y = -9t^2 - 72t$

C. $y = -9t^2 + 144t - 576$

D. $y = -9t^2 - 144t - 576$

22) If $cos\left(\frac{\pi x}{2}\right) = x^2 - x + 1$, then the value of x is:

A. -1

B. 0

C. 1

D. None of these

23) Which function represents this graph?

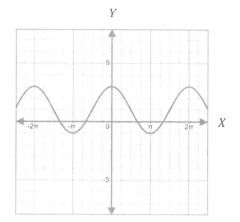

A. $y = 2\sec(x)$

B. $y = \cos(x) + 1$

C. $y = \tan(2x) - 1$

D. $y = 2\cos(x) + 1$

End of CLEP Precalculus Practice Test 2

CLEP Precalculus Practice Tests Answer Keys

Now, it's time to review your results to see where you went wrong and what areas you need to improve.

CLEP Precalculus Practice Test 1					CLEP Precalculus Practice Test 2				
Section I		**Section II**			**Section I**		**Section II**		
1	D	21	A	1	A	21	B	1	D	21	D	1	B	21	A
2	B	22	D	2	B	22	2:1	2	C	22	C	2	C	22	B
3	D	23	$\frac{10}{3}$	3	C	23	C	3	D	23	B	3	1	23	D
4	205	24	D	4	A			4	B	24	485°	4	C		
5	B	25	A	5	B			5	C	25	A	5	D		
6	D			6	D			6	60			6	A		
7	D			7	D			7	D			7	B		
8	D			8	3			8	C			8	C		
9	A			9	A			9	A			9	D		
10	B			10	A			10	No			10	B		
11	B			11	D			11	C			11	A		
12	C			12	$\frac{\sqrt{2}}{2}$			12	B			12	C		
13	D			13	A			13	B			13	C		
14	A			14	D			14	A			14	A		
15	B			15	B			15	D			15	A		
16	A			16	C			16	D			16	A		
17	D			17	D			17	C			17	C		
18	D			18	D			18	D			18	D		
19	A			19	B			19	A			19	D		
20	B			20	B			20	3			20	D		

CLEP Precalculus Practice Tests Answers and Explanations

CLEP Precalculus Practice Tests 1 Explanations

Section I

1) Choice D is correct.

Since x^2 is never negative, $x^2 + 2$ is never less than 2.

Hence, the range of $f(x)$ is "all real numbers where $f(x) \geq 2$".

2) Choice B is correct.

In a right triangle ABC, where $\angle C = 90°$, $AB = 16\,cm$, and $\angle B = 20°$, we can calculate the length of the side BC using the cosine function. The cosine of an angle in a right triangle is the ratio of the length of the side adjacent to the angle to the length of the hypotenuse. Here, the side BC is adjacent to $\angle B$ and AB is the hypotenuse. Therefore, rearranging the formula, we can express BC as follows: $BC = cos(B) \times AB$. Plugging in the values:

$BC = cos\,20° \times 16\,cm \approx 0.9397 \times 16\,cm \approx 15.03\,cm$

So, the length of side BC is approximately $15\,cm$.

3) Choice D is correct.

To draw the graph of $y < -2x - 2$, you first need to graph the line: $y = -2x - 2$.

Since there is a less than ($<$) sign, draw a dashed line.

The slope is -2 and y-intercept is -2.

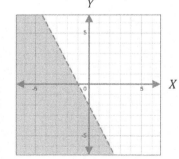

Then, choose a testing point and substitute the value of x and y from that point into the inequality. The easiest point to test is the origin: $(0,0)$,

$(0,0) \to y < -2x - 2 \to 0 < -2(0) - 2 \to 0 < -2$.

This is incorrect! 0 is not less than -2. So, the left side of the line is the solution to this inequality.

4) The solution is 205.

To find any term in an arithmetic sequence, use this formula:

$a_n = a_1 + d(n-1)$.

We have $a_3 = 13$ and $a_7 = 25$.

Therefore:

$a_3 = a_1 + d(3-1) \to a_1 + 2d = 13$ and $a_7 = a_1 + d(7-1) \to a_1 + 6d = 25$.

Solve the following equation:

$\begin{cases} a_1 + 2d = 13 \\ a_1 + 6d = 25 \end{cases}$

Subtracting the second equation from the first equation, we have: $(a_1 + 6d) - (a_1 + 2d) = 25 - 13$.

Simplify to: $a_1 + 6d - a_1 - 2d = 25 - 13 \to 4d = 12 \to d = 3$.

By substituting $d = 3$ in the first equation, we get:

$a_1 + 2d = 13 \to a_1 + 2 \times 3 = 13 \to a_1 = 7$.

Then, use this formula: $S_n = \frac{n}{2}(2a_1 + d(n-1))$.

Therefore:

$S_{10} = \frac{10}{2}(2 \times 7 + 3(10-1)) \to S_{10} = 5(14 + 27) \to S_{10} = 205$.

5) Choice B is correct.

Draw the graph corresponding to each function. Rewrite:

$f(x) = 2x^2 - 4x \to f(x) = 2(x^2 - 2x)$

$\to f(x) = 2(x-1)^2 - 2$

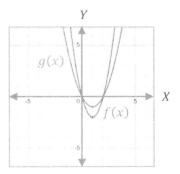

According to a standard form of a parabola, $(1, -2)$ is the vertex. In addition, if $f(x) = 0$, then:

$2x^2 - 4x = 0 \to 2x(x-2) = 0 \to x = 0, x = -2$,

So, $(0,0)$ and $(2,0)$ are $x-$intercepts for $f(x)$.

Correspondingly, we have for $g(x)$, $(1, -1)$ as its vertex and $(0,0)$ and $(2,0)$ are $x-$intercepts.

Therefore, they have same $x-$intercepts.

6) **Choice D is correct.**

We know that the graph $y = f(x - k); k > 0$, is shifted k units to the right of the graph $y = f(x)$ and $k < 0$, is shifted k units to the left.

In addition, the function $y = f(x)$ is symmetric to the function $y = f(-x)$, with respect to the y-axis and symmetric to the function $y = -f(x)$ and to the x-axis.

Now, $y = \log(-x)$ is symmetric to $y = \log x$ with respect to the x-axis as follows:

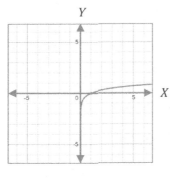
$y = \log x$

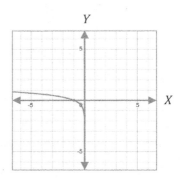
$y = \log(-x)$

On the other hand, $y = \log(1 - x)$ is shifted 1 unit to the right, since $y = \log -(x - 1)$.

Finally, $y = -\log(1 - x)$ is symmetric respect to the

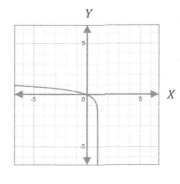
$y = \log(1 - x)$

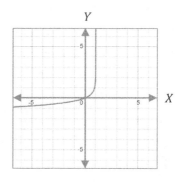
$y = -\log(1 - x)$

7) **Choice D is correct.**

By using $f(1) = 1 \rightarrow f(1) = a2^{b \times 1 - 1} - 1 = a2^{b-1} - 1 = 1 \rightarrow a2^{b-1} = 2$,

and $f(2) = 15 \rightarrow f(2) = a2^{b \times 2 - 1} - 1 = a2^{2b-1} - 1 = 1 \rightarrow a2^{2b-1} = 16$,

The following system of equations is obtained.

$$\begin{cases} a2^{b-1} = 2 \\ a2^{2b-1} = 16 \end{cases} \rightarrow \begin{cases} a2^b = 4 \\ a2^{2b} = 32 \end{cases} \rightarrow \begin{cases} 2^b = \frac{4}{a} \\ a(2^b)^2 = 32 \end{cases}$$

Substitute the first equation into the second equation. So,

$$a(2^b)^2 = 32 \rightarrow a\left(\frac{4}{a}\right)^2 = 32 \rightarrow \frac{16}{a} = 32 \rightarrow a = \frac{1}{2}.$$

Now, by substituting $a = \frac{1}{2}$ in the first equation, we have:

$$a = \frac{1}{2} \rightarrow \frac{1}{2} \times 2^{b-1} = 2 \rightarrow 2^{b-1} = 4 \rightarrow 2^{b-1} = 2^2 \rightarrow b - 1 = 2 \rightarrow b = 3.$$

Therefore, $a + b = \frac{1}{2} + 3 = \frac{1+6}{2} = \frac{7}{2} = 3.5$.

8) Choice D is correct.

The value of $\cos 30° = \frac{\sqrt{3}}{2}$.

9) Choice A is correct.

The standard form of a parabola is:

$(y - k) = 4p(x - h)^2$.

The coordinate $(-1, -5)$ is vertex.

Now, we have: $(y + 5) = 4p(x + 1)^2$.

Put $(0, -3)$ in equation. Then:

$(-3 + 5) = 4p(0 + 1)^2 \rightarrow 2 = 4p \rightarrow p = \frac{1}{2}$.

Finally:

$(y + 5) = 4p(x + 1)^2 \rightarrow (y + 5) = 4\frac{1}{2}(x + 1)^2 \rightarrow (y + 5) = 2(x + 1)^2$.

Then simplify to:

$(y + 5) = 2(x + 1)^2 \rightarrow y + 5 = 2(x^2 + 2x + 1) \rightarrow y = 2x^2 + 4x - 3$.

10) Choice B is correct.

The equation of a circle in standard form is:

$(x - h)^2 + (y - k)^2 = r^2$, where r is the radius of circle and $(-1, 2)$ is the center.

Considering that perimeter of circle is 4π, then $P = 2r\pi \rightarrow 4\pi = 2r\pi \rightarrow r = 2$.

Therefore: $(x + 1)^2 + (y - 2)^2 = 2^2 \rightarrow (x + 1)^2 + (y - 2)^2 = 4$.

11) Choice B is correct.

Since the quadrilateral $ABDE$ is rectangle, we have: $\vec{AB} + \vec{AE} = \vec{AD}$. Also, $ACDF$ is rectangle. So, $\vec{AC} + \vec{AF} = \vec{AD}$. Now, by substituting we get:

$$\vec{AB} + \vec{AC} + \vec{AE} + \vec{AF} = (\vec{AB} + \vec{AE}) + (\vec{AC} + \vec{AF})$$
$$= \vec{AD} + \vec{AD} = 2\vec{AD}$$

12) Choice C is correct.

The standard form of a up/down parabola is:

$(y - k) = 4p(x - h)^2$.

Rewrite to standard form:

$y = (x-2)^2 + 3 \rightarrow y - 3 = (x-2)^2 \rightarrow (y-3) = 4 \cdot \frac{1}{4}(x-2)^2$.

Therefore, the vertex is equal to $(2,3)$.

13) Choice D is correct.

For the function to be continuous at point $x = \frac{\pi}{2}$, it is necessary that $f\left(\frac{\pi}{2}\right) = \lim\limits_{x \to \frac{\pi}{2}} f(x)$. We know that $f\left(\frac{\pi}{2}\right) = a$. So, we have: $\lim\limits_{x \to \frac{\pi}{2}} f(x) = \lim\limits_{x \to \frac{\pi}{2}} \frac{2\sin^2 x - \sin x - 1}{\cos^2 x} = \frac{0}{0}$.

We remove the ambiguity of the limit by using trigonometric rules. Next,

$$\lim\limits_{x \to \frac{\pi}{2}} f(x) = \lim\limits_{x \to \frac{\pi}{2}} \frac{2\sin^2 x - \sin x - 1}{\cos^2 x} = \lim\limits_{x \to \frac{\pi}{2}} \frac{(2\sin x + 1)(\sin x - 1)}{1 - \sin^2 x}$$

$$= \lim\limits_{x \to \frac{\pi}{2}} \frac{(2\sin x + 1)(\sin x - 1)}{-(\sin x + 1)(\sin x - 1)} = \lim\limits_{x \to \frac{\pi}{2}} -\frac{2\sin x + 1}{\sin x + 1} = -\frac{3}{2} = -1.5$$

14) Choice A is correct.

Put $+\infty$ in the function equation as,

If $n \to +\infty$, then $\begin{cases} 2^{1-2n} = \frac{1}{2^{-1+2n}} \to 0 \\ 2^{2n+1} \to +\infty \end{cases}$. So, $\lim\limits_{n \to +\infty} \frac{2^{2n+1} - 2^{1-2n}}{2^{2n+1} + 3 \times 2^{1-2n}} = \frac{\infty}{\infty}$.

Next, by factoring we get:

$$\lim\limits_{n \to +\infty} \frac{2^{2n+1} - 2^{1-2n}}{2^{2n+1} + 3 \times 2^{1-2n}} = \lim\limits_{n \to +\infty} \frac{2^{1-2n}(2^{4n} - 1)}{2^{1-2n}(2^{4n} + 3)} = \lim\limits_{n \to +\infty} \frac{2^{4n} - 1}{2^{4n} + 3} \sim \lim\limits_{n \to +\infty} \frac{2^{4n}}{2^{4n}} = 1.$$

15) Choice B is correct.

Given the angles and the time it takes for the angle of depression to change; we can use the tangent of the angles of depression to determine the time it will take for the boat to reach the beach.

$$\begin{aligned} h &= (x+8)\tan 25° \\ h &= x\tan 50° \end{aligned} \rightarrow x\tan 50° = (x+8)\tan 25° \rightarrow x = \frac{8\tan 25°}{\tan 50° - \tan 25°} \approx 5$$

Therefore, the correct option is B, 5 minutes.

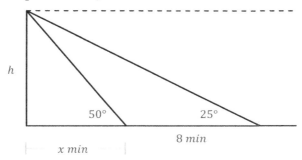

16) Choice A is correct.

Since the secant function $sec(x) = \frac{1}{cos(x)}$, rewrite the given function as: $f(x) = 2\cos(x - \pi)$.

Determine the Domain:

The domain of a function is the set of all possible input values (often denoted as x-values) that will give a valid output from a particular function. The cosine function, $cos(x)$, is defined for all real numbers. Thus, the function $2\cos(x - \pi)$ is also defined for all real numbers since it's just a cosine function that's been scaled and shifted. So, the domain of this function is all real numbers $\mathbb{R}$, or in interval notation, $(-\infty, +\infty)$.

Determine the Range:

The range of a function is the set of all possible output values (often denoted as y-values) which are valid for a given input to the function. The cosine function yields all values of y in the interval $[-1, 1]$, because the cosine of any angle is always between -1 and 1 inclusive.

Since $f(x) = 2\cos(x - \pi)$, the range of $f(x)$ will be all real numbers in the interval $[-2, 2]$ because the function is the cosine function scaled vertically by a factor of 2 as:

$-1 \leq \cos(x - \pi) \leq 1 \rightarrow -2 \leq 2\cos(x - \pi) \leq 2$

In summary, the domain of the function $f(x) = \frac{2}{\sec(x-\pi)}$ is all real numbers, and the range is $[-2, 2]$.

17) Choice D is correct.

For the existence of term $[x]$, it is enough to check the continuity at integer points. Since the sine function $\sin \pi x$ is equal to zero at integer points, the limit and value of the function are equal at these points. Therefore, the number of discontinuity points is zero.

18) Choice D is correct.

The equation of a circle in standard form is:
$(x - h)^2 + (y - k)^2 = r^2$.

Where the center is at: (h, k) and its radius is r.

Then, for the circle with equation $(x - 4)^2 + (y + 7)^2 = 3$, the center is at $(4, -7)$ and its radius is $\sqrt{3}$ ($r^2 = 3 \rightarrow r = \sqrt{3}$).

19) Choice A is correct.

In a right triangle ABC with $\angle C = 90°$, we can express $\sec B$ and $\tan A$ using the sides of the triangle: $\sec B = \frac{1}{\cos B}$. In right triangle ABC, $\cos B = \frac{adjacent}{hypotenuse} = \frac{y}{x}$.

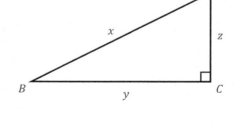

Hence, $\sec B = \frac{x}{y}$. Similarly, $\tan A = \frac{opposite}{adjacent} = \frac{y}{z}$

in the triangle. Hence, the value of $(\sec B \cdot \tan A) = \left(\frac{x}{y}\right)\left(\frac{y}{z}\right) = \frac{x}{z}$.

20) Choice B is correct.

If $a^y = x$, then: $\log_a x = y$.

Therefore: $e^{\ln 4} = x \to \ln x = \ln 4$.

Since $\log_a b = \log_a c \to b = c$.

Accordingly: $\ln x = \ln 4 \to x = 4$.

21) Choice A is correct.

The expression, $y = 4 \sin^2 \alpha + 5 \cos^2 \alpha$, can be written as follow:
$$4(\sin^2 \alpha + \cos^2 \alpha) + \cos^2 \alpha = 4 + \cos^2 \alpha$$

Here, the function $y = 4 + \cos^2 \alpha$, will always be greater than or equal to 4. Because the value of the function cosine is $-1 \leq \cos \alpha \leq 1$, then $0 \leq \cos^2 \alpha \leq 1$. So, the value of the function $y = 4 + \cos^2 \alpha$ is $4 \leq 4 + \cos^2 \alpha \leq 5 \to 4 \leq y \leq 5$. Therefore, the minimum value is 4 (Choice A).

22) Choice D is correct.

Considering that $(fog)(x) = f(g(x))$, then:

$f(g(x)) = f(-2) = \frac{1}{2}(-2) - 1 = -2$.

Therfore, line N corresponds to the answer.

23) The solution is $\frac{10}{3}$.

We know that:

$\log_a b - \log_a c = \log_a \frac{b}{c}$ and $\log_a b = c \to b = a^c$.

Then:

$\log_4(x+2) - \log_4(x-2) = 1 \to \log_4 \frac{x+2}{x-2} = 1 \to \frac{x+2}{x-2} = 4^1 = 4 \to x+2 = 4(x-2)$

Therefore:

$x + 2 = 4x - 8 \to 4x - x = 8 + 2 \to 3x = 10 \to x = \frac{10}{3}$.

24) Choice D is correct.

According to the contents of the given diagram and those two triangles MNP and NPO are common on the NP side. We evaluate the tangent of the angle 60 degrees for triangle MNP and the cosine of angle x for the triangle NPO. We get:

For $\triangle MNP$: $\tan \angle NMP = \frac{NP}{MN} \to NP = MN \times \tan 60° \to NP = 6\sqrt{3}$

For $\triangle NPO$: $\cos \angle ONP = \frac{NP}{NO} \to NP = NO \times \cos x \to NP = 12 \cos x$

Next, we have: $12 \cos x = 6\sqrt{3}$, then $\cos x = \frac{\sqrt{3}}{2}$. Since, the sum of the internal angles of each triangle is 180 degrees. So, $0 < x < 90°$. Hence, $x = 30°$. Therefore, the measure of angle $\angle MNO$ is $\angle MNP + \angle PNO = 90° + x = 90° + 30° = 120°$ degrees.

25) Choice A is correct.

By definition, the x-intercept is the point where a graph crosses the x-axis. If $y = 0$ is put into the equation, it would become:

$y = \frac{x-1}{1-x^2} \rightarrow \frac{x-1}{1-x^2} = 0 \rightarrow x - 1 = 0 \rightarrow x = 1$.

However, we know that the function is not defined for $x = 1$ and $x = -1$, as these values would result is division by zero.

Therefore, the graph of $y = \frac{x-1}{1-x^2}$ would not have x-intercepts.

Section II:

1) Choice A is correct.

Simplifying $3\ln(x) + 4\ln(y)$ using logarithmic properties:
$$3\ln(x) + 4\ln(y) = \ln(x^3) + \ln(y^4) = \ln(x^3 y^4)$$
Thus, the answer is A. $\ln(x^3 y^4)$.

2) Choice B is correct.
$$\int_{-1}^{5} f(x)\, dx = \int_{-1}^{0} f(x)\, dx + \int_{0}^{1} f(x)\, dx + \int_{1}^{5} f(x)\, dx = 4 \times 3 = 12$$

3) Choice C is correct.

According to the trigonometric circle and $\tan\theta = \frac{opposite}{adjacent}$, and since, $\sin\theta < 0$ and $\tan\theta > 0$, therefore, $\cos\theta < 0$.

Considering, $\tan\theta = \frac{5}{12}$, then:
$$c = \sqrt{5^2 + 12^2} = \sqrt{25 + 144} = \sqrt{169} = 13,$$
$$\cos\theta = \frac{adjacent}{hypotenuse} \rightarrow \cos\theta = -\frac{12}{13}$$

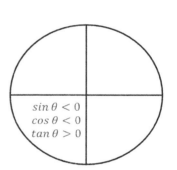

4) Choice A is correct.

We know $\log_a \frac{x}{y} = \log_a x - \log_a y$.

So: $x = 3\left(\log_2 \frac{1}{32}\right) \rightarrow x = 3(\log_2 1 - \log_2 32)$.

In addition, we know $\log_a 1 = 0$.

Therefore:

$x = -3\log_2 32$.

Considering:

$\log_a x^b = b \times \log_a x$, and $\log_a a = 1$.

Then:

$\log_2 32 = \log_2 2^5 = 5\log_2 2 = 5$.

Finally, we have:

$x = -3\log_2 32 \rightarrow x = -3 \times 5 \rightarrow x = -15$.

5) Choice B is correct.

The function $f(x)$ is undefined when the denominator of $\frac{1}{(x-3)^2+4(x-3)+4}$ is equal to zero. The expression $(x-3)^2 + 4(x-3) + 4$ is a perfect square.

$(x-3)^2 + 4(x-3) + 4 = ((x-3) + 2)^2$ can be rewritten as $(x-1)^2$.

The expression $(x-1)^2$ is equal to zero if $x = 1$.

Therefore, the value of x, for which $f(x)$ is undefined, is 1.

6) Choice D is correct.

According to the graph, the function is a parabola that open downward and $(0, -2)$ is the vertex. Now, we have:

$(y - k) = 4p(x - h)^2 \to (y - 2) = 4p(x - 0)^2 \to y = 4px^2 - 2$, where $p < 0$.

Since all points of the graph must be satisfy in the equation. Therefore, for point $(2, -4)$, we have:

$y = 4px^2 - 2 \to -4 = 4p(2)^2 - 2 \to 16p = -2 \to p = -\frac{1}{8}$.

Finally:

$y = 4\left(-\frac{1}{8}\right)x^2 - 2 \to y = -\frac{1}{2}x^2 - 2$.

7) Choice D is correct.

Since $(f \circ g)(x) = f(g(x))$, then:

$f(-x - 2) = (-x - 2) + 1 = -x - 1$, this is NOT true!

$f(x - 2) = -(x - 2) + 1 = -x + 2 + 1 = -x + 3$, this is NOT true!

$f(x + 2) = (x + 2) + 1 = x + 3$, this is NOT true!

$f(-x + 2) = -(-x + 2) + 1 = x - 2 + 1 = x - 1$, this is true!

8) The solution is $r = 3$.

The standard form of circle equation is:

$(x - h)^2 + (y - k)^2 = r^2$ where the radius of the circle is r, and it's centered at (h, k).

First, move the loose number to the right side:

$x^2 + y^2 - 6x + 4y = -4$.

Group x −variables and y −variables together:

$(x^2 - 6x) + (y^2 + 4y) = -4$.

Convert x to square form:

$(x^2 - 6x + 9) + y^2 - 6y = -4 + 9 \to (x-3)^2 + (y^2 + 4y) = -4 + 9$.

Convert y to square form:

$(x-3)^2 + (y^2 + 4y + 4) = -4 + 9 + 4 \to (x-3)^2 + (y+2)^2 = 9$.

Then, the equation of the circle in standard form is:

$(x-3)^2 + (y+2)^2 = 3^2$.

The center of the circle is at $(3, -2)$ and its radius is 3.

9) Choice A is correct.

First, $y = -x$.

Then, replace all x's with y and all y's with x: $x = -y$.

Now, solve for y:

$x = -y \to -x = y$.

Actually, the inverse of $y = -x$ is itself. In othr words, the invers of a graph is asymetric to $y = x$.

10) Choice A is correct.

In a rational function, if the denominator has a bigger degree than the numerator, the horizontal asymptote is the x −axes or the line $y = 0$.

In the function $f(x) = \frac{x+3}{x^2+1}$, the degree of numerator is 1 (x to the power of 1) and the degree of the denominator is 2 (x to the power of 2). The horizontal asymptote is the line $y = 0$.

11) Choice D is correct.

According to the figure,

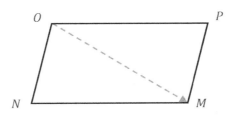

We have:

$\overrightarrow{NM} + \overrightarrow{PM} = \overrightarrow{NM} - \overrightarrow{NO} = \overrightarrow{OM}$

12) The solution is $\frac{\sqrt{2}}{2}$.

We know that $sin\left(\frac{11\pi}{4}\right) = sin\left(\frac{11\pi}{4} - 2\pi\right) = sin\left(\frac{3\pi}{4}\right) = sin\left(\frac{\pi}{4}\right) = \frac{\sqrt{2}}{2}$.

13) Choice A is correct.

Let's check each option.

For θ in $(0°, 90°)$, $0 < sin\,\theta < 1$, so it's clear that $sin\,\theta$ is always greater than $sin^2\,\theta$. Therefore, the correct answer is A, $sin\,\theta > sin^2\,\theta$.

14) Choice D is correct.

Considering that $f(x)$ opens upward and $g(x)$.

Rewrite:

$f(x) = 2x^2 - x + 3 \to f(x) = 2\left(x - \frac{1}{4}\right)^2 + \frac{23}{8}$.

So:

$f(x) > \frac{23}{8}$.

On the other hand:

$g(x) = -x^2 + 2x + 1 \to g(x) = -(x-1)^2 + 2$.

Which means that $g(x) < 0$.

Therefore, $g(x) < f(x)$ is for every x.

15) Choice B is correct.

For this purpose, first consider the graph of the secant function.

We could then evaluate these values as follows: The distance between the two parts of the graph in the secant function is 2 (The horizontal box specified in the graph). a is the amplitude of the function. Since in the given graph this difference is 4 units, so the amplitude is half of this difference.

That is, $a = 2$.

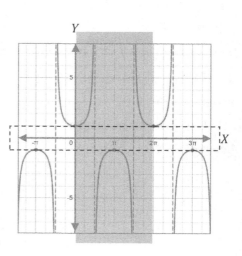

b determines the period of the function (period $= \frac{2\pi}{b}$). The vertical box shown in the secant graph, which is 2π units on the x −axis and correspond to this box on the graph of the content of the question, is 3 units. So, we get, $4 = \frac{2\pi}{b} \to b = \frac{\pi}{2}$.

c, which equals 1 here, represents the vertical shift of the function. Therefore, our function should be shifted up by 1 unit. Because, the middle horizontal line between the two parts of the secant graph is the x −axis. In the graph of problem, the corresponding horizontal line is shifted up by one unit. So, $d = +1$. We would

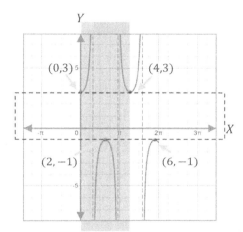

then compare this to the provided graph. If the graph fits these characteristics, then option B is the correct answer.

16) Choice C is correct.

Remember that for the function $y = f(x - k)$, if $k > 0$, the function is shifted to the right and if $k < 0$, it is shifted to the left. Rewrite, $g(x) = e^{x+1} = e^{x-(-1)}$. Therefore, the function $g(x)$ is shifted by 1 unit to the left. The choice C is correct.

17) Choice D is correct.

First, replace $f(x)$ with y: $y = 5 \cdot \left(\frac{1}{2}\right)^x$. Then, replace all x's with y and all y's with x: $x = 5 \cdot \left(\frac{1}{2}\right)^y$. Now, solve for y:

$$x = 5 \cdot \left(\frac{1}{2}\right)^y \to \frac{x}{5} = \left(\frac{1}{2}\right)^y \to \ln\left(\frac{x}{5}\right) = \ln\left(\frac{1}{2}\right)^y \to \ln\left(\frac{x}{5}\right) = y \ln\left(\frac{1}{2}\right)$$

$$\to \ln\left(\frac{x}{5}\right) = -y \ln 2 \to y = -\frac{\ln\left(\frac{x}{5}\right)}{\ln 2}.$$

Finally, replace y with: $f^{-1}(x) = -\frac{\ln\left(\frac{x}{5}\right)}{\ln 2}$ or $f^{-1}(x) = -\log_2\left(\frac{x}{5}\right)$.

18) Choice D is correct.

Let's first simplify both sides of the equation. We know that $\tan 30° = \frac{\sqrt{3}}{3}$, and $\sec 60° = 2$. So, we can write the given equation $x \tan 30° = y \sec 60°$ as $x\frac{\sqrt{3}}{3} = 2y$, or equivalently $\frac{x}{y} = 2\sqrt{3}$. Now, let's calculate $\frac{x^4}{y^4}$, which is equal to $\frac{x^4}{y^4} = \left(\frac{x}{y}\right)^4 = \left(2\sqrt{3}\right)^4 = 16 \times 9 = 144 = 12^2$.

19) Choice B is correct.

The given equation, $\cos x \cdot \cos y + \sin x \cdot \sin y = 1$, can be rewritten using the cosine of the difference of two angles identity, i.e., $\cos(x - y) = \cos x \cdot \cos y + \sin x \cdot \sin y$. So, we have $\cos(x - y) = 1$. The equation $\cos(x - y) = 1$ has solutions when $x - y$ equals to 0 or any multiple of 2π (because the cosine of 0 or any multiple of 2π is 1). Let's assume $x - y = 0$ (the simplest solution). This gives us $x = y$. Substitute $y = x$ into the second equation to find $\sin x - \sin y = \sin x - \sin x = 0$.

20) Choice B is correct.

We're looking for a sine function since the graph appears to start at its midpoint and moves upwards, indicative of the sine function. The graph has an amplitude of 2 which tells us that the coefficient in front of the sine function is 2. The period of the graph is 2π which is standard for sine and cosine functions, so we don't need to adjust for period in the function. The graph is shifted $\frac{\pi}{2}$ units to the right, indicating a phase shift. The phase shift in the sine function is opposite to what it looks like. Hence, the function is $y = 2 \sin\left(x - \frac{\pi}{2}\right)$. The graph is also shifted up by 1 unit. This tells us that we're dealing with a vertical shift. This adds +1 outside the function. So, the equation of the graph is $y = 2 \sin\left(x - \frac{\pi}{2}\right) + 1$.

Therefore, the correct answer is: B. $y = 2 \sin\left(x - \frac{\pi}{2}\right) + 1$.

21) Choice B is correct.

We can use the addition and subtraction formula for sine and cosine to solve this problem.

$cos(60° + \theta) = cos\, 60°\, cos\, \theta - sin\, 60°\, sin\, \theta = \left(\frac{1}{2}\right) cos\, \theta - \left(\frac{\sqrt{3}}{2}\right) sin\, \theta$

$sin(30° - \theta) = sin\, 30°\, cos\, \theta - cos\, 30°\, sin\, \theta = \left(\frac{1}{2}\right) cos\, \theta - \left(\frac{\sqrt{3}}{2}\right) sin\, \theta$

Subtracting these two expressions, we obtain:

$cos(60° + \theta) - sin(60° - \theta) = \left(\frac{1}{2}\right) cos\, \theta - \left(\frac{\sqrt{3}}{2}\right) sin\, \theta - \left[\left(\frac{1}{2}\right) cos\, \theta - \left(\frac{\sqrt{3}}{2}\right) sin\, \theta\right]$

$= \left(\frac{1}{2}\right) cos\, \theta - \left(\frac{\sqrt{3}}{2}\right) sin\, \theta - \left(\frac{1}{2}\right) cos\, \theta + \left(\frac{\sqrt{3}}{2}\right) sin\, \theta$

$= 0$

22) The solution is $2:1$.

Given $\alpha + \beta = 120°$ and $\alpha:\beta = 1:3$, we can solve for α and β first. Since $\alpha:\beta = 1:3$, let $\alpha = x$ and $\beta = 3x$. Then, from the given $\alpha + \beta = 120°$, we get:

$x + 3x = 120° \rightarrow 4x = 120° \rightarrow x = 30°$

So, $\alpha = 30°$ and $\beta = 3 \times 30° = 90°$.

Now, we need to find the ratio of $sin\, \beta$ to $sin\, \alpha$: $\frac{sin\, \beta}{sin\, \alpha} = \frac{sin\, 90°}{sin\, 30°}$. $sin\, 90°$ is 1 and $sin\, 30°$ is $\frac{1}{2}$, therefore the ratio is: $\frac{sin\, \beta}{sin\, \alpha} = \frac{1}{\frac{1}{2}} = \frac{2}{1}$.

23) Choice C is correct.

$\int_0^4 (x - |x - 2|)\, dx = \int_0^4 x\, dx - \int_0^4 |x - 2|\, dx = \frac{4 \times 4}{2} - \left(\frac{2 \times 2}{2} + \frac{2 \times 2}{2}\right) = 8 - 4 = 4$

CLEP Precalculus Practice Tests 2 Explanations

Section I

1) Choice D is correct.

The function is $f(x) = 2 - 3\sin\left(2x - \frac{\pi}{3}\right)$.

Determine the Domain:

The domain of a function is the set of all possible input values (often denoted as x-values) which will provide a valid output from a particular function. For the sine function (and all its transformations), the domain is all real numbers. This is because any real number can be inputted into the sine function, and it will yield a real number output. The $\left(2x - \frac{\pi}{3}\right)$ part inside the sine function doesn't restrict the domain as it is a linear transformation that also allows all real numbers. So, the domain of this function is all real numbers, or in interval notation, $(-\infty, +\infty)$.

Determine the Range:

The range of a function is the set of all possible output values (often denoted as y-values) which are valid for a given input to the function. The sine function has a range of $[-1, 1]$ on its own, but there are transformations applied to it in this function.

The $3\sin\left(2x - \frac{\pi}{3}\right)$ part stretches the range to $[-3, 3]$ because the amplitude (or peak value) of the sine wave is multiplied by 3:

$-1 \leq \sin\left(2x - \frac{\pi}{3}\right) \leq 1 \rightarrow -3 \leq 3\sin\left(2x - \frac{\pi}{3}\right) \leq 3$

As the same way, we get:

$-3 \leq 3\sin\left(2x - \frac{\pi}{3}\right) \leq 3 \rightarrow -3 \leq -3\sin\left(2x - \frac{\pi}{3}\right) \leq 3$

$$\to 2 - 3 \leq 2 - 3\sin\left(2x - \frac{\pi}{3}\right) \leq 2 + 3$$

$$\to -1 \leq f(x) \leq 5$$

So, the range becomes $[-1, 5]$. So, the domain is $(-\infty, +\infty)$ and the range is $[-1, 5]$.

2) Choice C is correct.

For two function $f(x)$ and $g(x)$, we know that $(f - g)(x) = f(x) - g(x)$. Therefore:

$(g - f)(x) = g(x) - f(x) \to (-x^2 - 2x - 1) - (x + 6) = -x^2 - 3x - 7$.

3) Choice D is correct.

Rewrite the given equation as follows. We know that $\cos\left(x - \frac{\pi}{2}\right) = \sin x$, so we have: $y = \frac{1}{\sin x} + 4$. Since $\frac{1}{\sin x} = \csc x$, we get: $y = \csc x + 4$. Now, you see that the equation is the cosecant function, translated 4 units upward. The cosecant function is the reciprocal of the sine function and has vertical asymptotes where the sine function is zero. That is, the vertical lines $x = n\pi$ are asymptotes, where n is an integer. Therefore, the correct answer is:

D. It represents a cosine function, $y = \csc x$, translated 4 units upwards.

4) Choice B is correct.

To find the inverse of $f(x) = 1 - \sin(x)$, we first set $f(x)$ equal to y, resulting in $y = 1 - \sin(x)$. Then we swap x and y to find the inverse: $x = 1 - \sin(y)$. Solving this for y involves several steps:

1. We isolate the sin function: $\sin(y) = 1 - x$.
2. Next, we need to reverse the sine operation by applying the *arcsin* to both sides, remembering that *arcsin* is the inverse function of sine: $y = \arcsin(1 - x)$.

So, the correct answer is B, $f^{-1}(x) = \arcsin(1 - x)$.

5) Choice C is correct.

The function $f(x) = ln(x)$ with domain $x > 0$ and range $-\infty < f(x) < +\infty$ has an x-intercept with coordinates $(1,0)$ where $x = 0$ is a vertical asymptote.

Its graph as follow:

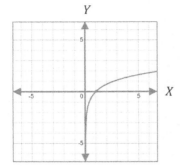

On the other hand, we know that the graph $y = f(x - k); k > 0$, is shifted k units to the right of the graph $y = f(x)$ and if $k < 0$, is shifted k units to the left.

Now, in the example graph, x-intercept with coordinates $(2,0)$ and vertical asymptote with equation $x = 1$ is shifted 1 unit to the right. Therefore, the function $y = ln(x - 1)$ is represented by example graph.

6) The solution is $60\ ft$.

Consider the relationship among all sides of the special right triangle $30° - 60° - 90°$ is provided in this triangle:

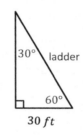

In this triangle, the opposite side of the $30°$ angle is half of the hypotenuse. Draw the shape of this question: The ladder is the hypotenuse.

$cos\ 60° = \frac{adjacent}{hypotenuse} \rightarrow \frac{1}{2} = \frac{30}{ladder} \rightarrow ladder = 60.$

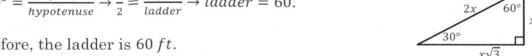

Therefore, the ladder is $60\ ft$.

7) Choice D is correct.

Given the quadrilateral $ABCD$ with diameter BD drawn, $\angle BAD = 60°$, $AB = 9\ cm$, and $\angle DBC = 45°$, the length of side DC can be found as follows:

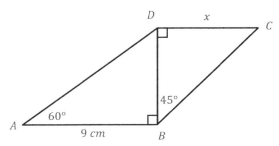

Firstly, note that because BD is the diameter, which is the common side of two right-angled triangles ABD with right angle at $\angle ABD$ and BDC with right angled at $\angle BDC$. By using the tangent of the angle BAD, find the length of the side BD. So, we get:

$$tan \angle BAD = \frac{BD}{AB} \rightarrow tan\ 60° = \frac{BD}{9} \rightarrow BD = 9\sqrt{3}$$

Now, to find $x = DC$, it is enough to evaluate the tangent of $45°$. Hence,

$$tan \angle DBC = \frac{DC}{BD} \rightarrow tan\ 45° = \frac{x}{9\sqrt{3}} \rightarrow x = 9\sqrt{3}$$

Therefore, the length of side x is $9\sqrt{3}\ cm$.

8) Choice C is correct.

To find the inverse of the function $f(x) = cos^2\left(\frac{1}{2}x - 1\right)$, we start by setting $f(x)$ equal to y: $y = cos^2\left(\frac{1}{2}x - 1\right)$. We swap x and y to find the inverse: $x = cos^2\left(\frac{1}{2}y - 1\right)$. Next, we take the square root of both sides:

$$x = cos^2\left(\frac{1}{2}y - 1\right) \rightarrow x = \left(cos\left(\frac{1}{2}y - 1\right)\right)^2$$
$$\rightarrow \sqrt{x} = cos\left(\frac{1}{2}y - 1\right)$$

Finally, we take the $arccos$ of both sides: $\frac{1}{2}y - 1 = arccos(\sqrt{x})$. Now, isolate y:

$$\frac{1}{2}y - 1 = arccos(\sqrt{x}) \rightarrow \frac{1}{2}y = arccos(\sqrt{x}) + 1$$
$$y = 2\ arccos(\sqrt{x}) + 2$$

So, the correct answer is C, $f^{-1}(x) = 2\arccos(\sqrt{x}) + 2$.

9) Choice A is correct.

The answer is on the following graph:

A quadratic function in the vertex form is: $y = a(x-h)^2 + k$ with (h, k) as the vertex. The vertex of $y = (x+1)^2 - 2$ is $(-1, -2)$.

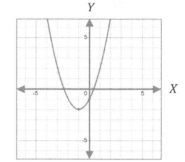

Substitute zero for x and solve for y:

$y = (0+1)^2 - 2 = -1$.

The y−intercept is $(0, -1)$.

Now, you can simply graph the quadratic function. Notice that quadratic function is a U-shaped curve. (You can plug in values of x and solve for y to get some points on the graph.)

10) There is no solution.

When the logarithms have the same base: $f(x) = g(x)$, then: $x = y$,

$\log(5x+2) = \log(3x-1) \rightarrow (5x+2) = (3x-1)$

$5x + 2 - 3x + 1 = 0 \rightarrow 2x = -3 \rightarrow x = -\frac{3}{2}$

Verify Solution: $\log\left(5\left(-\frac{3}{2}\right) + 2\right) = \log\left(\frac{-15}{2} + 2\right) = \log\left(-\frac{11}{2}\right) = \log(-5.5)$.

Logarithms of negative numbers are not defined. Therefore, there is no solution for this equation.

11) Choice C is correct.

Rewrite: $f(x) = x^2 + 2x - 1 \rightarrow f(x) = (x^2 + 2x + 1) - 2 \rightarrow f(x) = (x+1)^2 - 2$.

This means that $(-1, -2)$ is the minimum point.

12) Choice B is correct.

Since the function has only one vertical asymptote, then $x = 2$ is the double root of the denominator. So:

$2x^2 + bx + c = 2(x-2)^2 \rightarrow 2x^2 + bx + c = 2(x^2 - 4x + 4)$

$\rightarrow 2x^2 + bx + c = 2x^2 - 8x + 8 \rightarrow b = -8$, and $c = 8$.

Therefore $f(x) = \frac{ax^2+7x}{2x^2-8x+8}$. Also $f(3) = 6$, then:

$f(3) = \frac{a(3)^2+7(3)}{2(3)^2-8(3)+8} = \frac{9a+21}{18-24+8} = \frac{9a+21}{2} = 9a + 21 = 12 \to a = -1$.

Finally, for find the horizontal asymptote we get:

$$\lim_{n \to +\infty} f(x) = \lim_{n \to +\infty} \frac{-x^2 + 7x}{2x^2 - 8x + 8} = -\frac{1}{2}$$

13) Choice B is correct.

To find $f(g(x))$, substitute x with $\frac{1}{x}$ in the function $f(x)$. Then:

$f(g(x)) = f\left(\frac{1}{x}\right) = 2 \times \left(\frac{1}{x}\right)^3 + 4 = \frac{2}{x^3} + 4$.

14) Choice A is correct.

If $f(x) = g(x)$, then: $ln(f(x)) = ln(g(x)) \to ln(e^{2x}) = ln(12)$.

Use logarithm rule:

$log_a x^b = b \, log_a x \to ln(e^{2x}) = 2x \, ln(e) \to (2x) \, ln(e) = ln(12)$.

Since: $ln(e) = 1$, then: $(2x) \, ln(e) = ln(12) \to 2x = ln(12) \to x = \frac{ln(12)}{2}$.

15) Choice D is correct.

Considering the classification of conic sections, the equation is a standard form of horizontal ellipse:

$\frac{(x-h)^2}{a^2} + \frac{(y-k)^2}{b^2} = 1$, where $a > b$.

16) Choice D is correct.

Rewrite:

$y = 2 - (2 + 4x - x^2) \to y = x^2 - 4x \to y = (x - 2)^2 - 4$.

This means that the parent graph is $y = x^2$, which is shifted 2 units right and shifted 4 units down.

17) Choice C is correct.

First, determine the values of a and b for the function $g(x) = ab^x$.

From $g(0) = 4$, we get $a = 4$ because $g(0) = ab^0 = a$.

To find b, use $g(1) = 8$: $4b = 8$, so $b = 2$.

The function becomes $g(x) = 4 \times 2^x$.

Find $g^{-1}(x)$, which is the inverse of g. Let $y = g(x)$ or $y = 4 \times 2^x$.

Swap x and y: $x = 4 \times 2^y$. Solve for y in terms of x: $\frac{x}{4} = 2^y$.

Taking the logarithm base 2: $y = log_2\left(\frac{x}{4}\right)$.

Therefore, $g^{-1}(x) = log_2\left(\frac{x}{4}\right)$. The correct answer is C. $log_2\left(\frac{x}{4}\right)$.

18) Choice D is correct.

The x−intercept of a graph is the point where the line or curve intersects the x−axis. In this context, the x−axis represents the number of presentations made by the convention presenter, and the y−axis represents the number of cookies she had left to give away. Therefore, the x−intercept represents the point at which the number of presentations made by the presenter is zero, i.e., the initial state before any presentations were made. At this point, the presenter had all the cookies she started with and had not given away any yet. Hence, the x−intercept of the graph represents the initial number of cookies the presenter had before making any presentations.

19) Choice A is correct.

For domain: Find non-negative values for radicals: $2x + 4 \geq 0$.

Domain of functions: $2x + 4 \geq 0 \rightarrow 2x \geq -4 \rightarrow x \geq -2$.

Domain of the function $y = 3\sqrt{2x + 4} + 8$: $x \geq -2$.

For range: The range of a radical function of the form $c\sqrt{ax + b} + k$ is: $f(x) \geq k$.

For the function $y = 3\sqrt{2x + 4} + 8$, the value of k is 8. Then: $f(x) \geq 8$.

Range of the function $y = 3\sqrt{2x + 4} + 8$: $f(x) \geq 8$.

20) The solution is 3.

Frist, factor the function: $f(x) = x^3 + 6x^2 + 8x = x(x + 4)(x + 2)$.

To find the zeros, $f(x)$ should be zero.

$f(x) = x(x + 4)(x + 2) = 0$.

Therefore, the zeros are: $x = 0$,
$(x + 4) = 0 \to x = -4$, $(x + 2) = 0 \to x = -2$.

21) Choice D is correct.

According to the graph, we have the standard form of an up/down hyperbola with center $(-3,4)$, semi-axis 2 and semi-conjugate-axis 3. Then:
$$\frac{(y-k)^2}{a^2} - \frac{(x-h)^2}{b^2} = 1 \to \frac{(y-4)^2}{4} - \frac{(x+3)^2}{9} = 1$$

22) Choice C is correct.

Since $\sec\theta = \frac{1}{\cos\theta}$, we have: $\sec\theta + \cos\theta = 2 \to \frac{1}{\cos\theta} + \cos\theta = 2$. Multiply both sides of the equation by $\cos\theta$. So, $1 + \cos^2\theta = 2\cos\theta$. Now, rewrite the equation as: $\cos^2\theta - 2\cos\theta + 1 = 0$. Therefore, we get: $(\cos\theta - 1)^2 = 0$, and $\cos\theta - 1 = 0 \to \cos\theta = 1$. Next, evaluate the value of $\sec\theta$: $\sec\theta = \frac{1}{\cos\theta} \to \sec\theta = 1$.

Finally, substitute the obtained value into the expression $\sin^3\theta + \cos^3\theta$ and calculate it.
$\sin^3\theta + \cos^3\theta = (0)^3 + (1)^3 = 0 + 1 = 1$
Therefore, the correct answer is C, 1.

23) Choice B is correct.

In a right-angled triangle ABC with $\angle B = 90°$ and $\angle A = 45°$, the ratio of the opposite side of the angle A to the hypotenuse of the triangle is $\frac{BC}{CA}$, which is equivalent to sine of the angle A (The same requested item in case of question). For $\angle A = 45°$, we have $\sin 45° = \frac{1}{\sqrt{2}}$. So, we get:

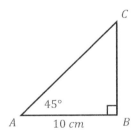

$\sin \angle A = \frac{BC}{CA} \to \frac{BC}{CA} = \frac{1}{\sqrt{2}}$. The correct answer is B.

24) The solution is 485°.

To find the coterminal angle to angle 125°:

$125° + 360° = 485°$

$125° - 360° = -235°$

25) Choice A is correct.

First, we rewrite the function as,

$$f(x) = \begin{cases} (x-1)[x] & ; -1 < x-1 < 1 \\ x^2 + ax + b & ; x-1 \geq 1 \text{ or } x-1 \leq -1 \end{cases}.$$

Also,

$$f(x) = \begin{cases} x^2 + ax + b & ; x \leq 0 \\ (x-1)[x] & ; 0 < x < 2 \\ x^2 + ax + b & ; x \geq 2 \end{cases}$$

So, for the function to be continuous, it must be continuous in $x = 0$ and $x = 2$. Therefore:

$x = 0 \to \begin{array}{l} f(0) = \lim\limits_{x \to 0^-} f(x) = b \\ \lim\limits_{x \to 0^+} f(x) = \lim\limits_{x \to 0^+} (x-1)[x] = (0-1)[0^+] = 0 \end{array} \to b = 0$

$x = 2 \to \begin{array}{l} \lim\limits_{x \to 2^-} f(x) = \lim\limits_{x \to 0^+} (x-1)[x] = (2-1)[2^-] = 1 \\ f(2) = \lim\limits_{x \to 2^+} f(x) = 4 + 2a + b \end{array} \to 4 + 2a + b = 1$

Finally, we get: $4 + 2a = 1 \to a = -\frac{3}{2}$.

Section II

1) Choice B is correct.

Given that triangle ABC is right-angled at C with hypotenuse $AB = 19\ cm$ and $\angle B = 22°$ degrees, you want to find the length of side BC. The length of side BC can be calculated using the cosine of $\angle B$ (which is the ratio of the adjacent side to the hypotenuse in a right-angled triangle). We know that $cos(B) = \frac{BC}{AB}$, so:

$BC = AB \times cos(B) \rightarrow BC = 19\ cm \times cos\ 22°$

$\rightarrow BC = 19\ cm \times 0.927$

$\rightarrow BC = 17.613\ cm$

Therefore, the length of side BC is approximately $17.6\ cm$.

2) Choice C is correct.

The function is not defined for $x = -2$, as this value would result is division by zero.

Hence the domain of $f(x)$ is: all real numbers except -2.

Range: No matter how large or small x becomes, $f(x)$ will never be equal to zero.

Therefore, the range of $f(x)$ is all real numbers except zero.

3) The solution is 1.

Use algorithm rule:

$log_a x^b = b\ log_x x \rightarrow \frac{1}{2} log_{2x} 64 = log_{2x} 64^{\frac{1}{2}}$.

In addition:

$log_a b = c \rightarrow a^c = b$.

Now, we have:

$\frac{1}{2} log_{2x} 64 = 3 \rightarrow log_{2x} 64^{\frac{1}{2}} = 3 \rightarrow log_{2x} 8 = 3 \rightarrow (2x)^3 = 8$.

Finally, simplify:

$8x^3 = 8 \rightarrow x^3 = 1 \rightarrow x = 1$.

4) Choice C is correct.

To find the value of $sin\,45°\,cos\,15°$, we can use the trigonometric identity: $sin(A)\,cos(B) = \frac{1}{2}[sin(A+B) + sin(A-B)]$. Applying this identity, we have:

$sin\,45°\,cos\,15° = \frac{1}{2}[sin(45° + 15°) + sin(45° - 15°)] = \frac{1}{2}[sin\,60° + sin\,30°]$

$= \frac{1}{2}\left[\frac{\sqrt{3}}{2} + \frac{1}{2}\right] = \frac{\sqrt{3}+1}{4}$

Therefore, the value of $4(sin\,45°\,cos\,15°)$ is $4\left(\frac{\sqrt{3}+1}{4}\right) = \sqrt{3} + 1$.

5) Choice D is correct.

The standard form of the tangent function is $f(x) = a\,tan(b(x-c)) + d$, where:

b determines the period of the function (period $= \frac{\pi}{b}$ for tan).

c is the phase shift (how much the function is shifted horizontally).

d is the vertical shift (how much the function is shifted vertically).

a is the vertical stretch or compression factor (not required for this problem).

Given that:

The period is π, which suggests that $b = 1$ (since $\frac{\pi}{b} = \pi$).

The phase shift is 1 unit to the right, so $c = \frac{\pi}{2}$.

The vertical shift is 2 units up, so $d = 2$.

We consider function $y = tan\,x$ and apply the above steps to reach the desired graph.

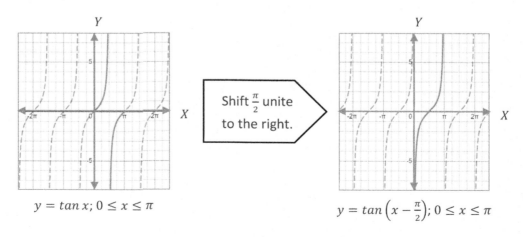

Now, we shift the obtained graph up 2 units.

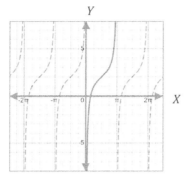

$y = tan\left(x - \frac{\pi}{2}\right) + 2; 0 \leq x \leq \pi$

The red part of the graph is the desired answer and corresponds to choice D.

6) Choice A is correct.

Use this formula: $Degrees = Radian \times \frac{180}{\pi}$,

$Degrees = \frac{2\pi}{3} \times \frac{180}{\pi} = \frac{360\pi}{3\pi} = 120$

7) Choice B is correct.

The standard form of a up/down parabola is:

$(y - k) = 4p(x - h)^2$.

According to the graph, vertex is equal to $(-2, 4)$, and since the graph opens downward, $p < 0$.

On the other hand, $(0,0)$ also applies to the function. Then:

$(y - k) = 4p(x - h)^2 \to (y - 4) = 4p(x + 2)^2$.

Therefore:

$(0 - 4) = 4p(0 + 2)^2 \to -4 = 4p \times 4 \to 16p = -4 \to p = -\frac{1}{4}$.

Finally:

$(y - 4) = 4\left(-\frac{1}{4}\right)(x + 2)^2 \to y - 4 = -x^2 - 4x - 4 \to y = -x^2 - 4x$.

8) Choice C is correct.

Rewrite as:

$x = \ln\sqrt{y} \to x = \ln y^{\frac{1}{2}}.$

We know:

$\log_a x^b = b \log_a x.$

Then:

$x = \ln y^{\frac{1}{2}} \to x = \frac{1}{2}\ln y.$

Multiply both sides with 2:

$2x = \ln y.$

Using, $y = \log_a x \to x = a^y.$

Which means that $e^{2x} = y.$

Finally:

$y = e^{2x} \to f^{-1}(x) = e^{2x}.$

9) Choice D is correct.

Since $(f - g)(x) = f(x) - g(x)$, then:

$(f - g)(x) = (2x^3 + x) - (x - 2) = 2x^3 + 2.$

Therefore, replace x with 1:

$(f - g)(1) = 2(1)^3 + 2 = 4.$

10) Choice B is correct.

The general form of a sinusoidal function is given by $f(x) = a\sin(b(x - c)) + d$ or $f(x) = a\cos(b(x - c)) + d$, where:

1. a is the amplitude of the function.
2. b determines the period of the function (period $= \frac{2\pi}{b}$).
3. c is the phase shift (how much the function is shifted horizontally).
4. d is the vertical shift (how much the function is shifted vertically).

Given that:

5. Amplitude is 3 (so $a = 3$)

6. Period is π (so $b = 2$, since $\frac{2\pi}{b} = \pi$)

7. Phase shift is $\frac{\pi}{2}$ units to the right (so, $c = \frac{\pi}{2}$)

8. Vertical shift is 1 unit down (so $d = -1$)

The function reaches its minimum at $x = 0$. Since the cosine function reaches its maximum at $x = 0$ and we are dealing with a minimum, we need a negative cosine function. Substituting all these values into the equation, we get:

$$f(x) = -3\cos\left(2\left(x + \frac{\pi}{2}\right)\right) - 1$$

So, the correct answer is option B: $f(x) = -3\cos\left(2\left(x + \frac{\pi}{2}\right)\right) - 1$.

11) Choice A is correct.

To find the right choice, we consider graph $y = \sin\left(x - \frac{\pi}{3}\right)$. Figure below.

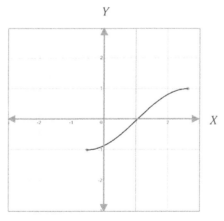

$$y = \sin\left(x - \frac{\pi}{3}\right); -\frac{\pi}{6} \leq x \leq \frac{5\pi}{6}$$

Considering that in the given interval the function is one to one, then the inverse level of the function was determined.

In the next step, we determine the image of this graph relative to line $y = x$. figure below.

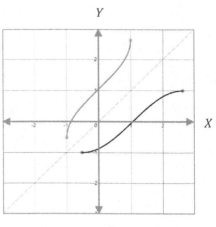

$$y = \arcsin(x) + \frac{\pi}{3}; -1 \leq x \leq 1$$

As choice A, answers are appropriate.

12) Choice C is correct.

Rewrite as:

$x = (y^2 + 2y + 1 - 1) - 4 \to x = (y+1)^2 - 5 \to (x+5) = (y+1)^2.$

The equation $(x+5) = (y+1)^2$ is like the standard form of a left/right parabola, $(x-h) = 4p(y-k)^2$. Which means that it is a horizontal parabola.

13) Choice C is correct.

We can rewrite the given equation using the double angle identity for cosine:

$2(\sin^2\theta - \cos^2\theta) = -1 \to 2\big((1-\cos^2\theta) - \cos^2\theta\big) = -1$

$\to 2(1 - 2\cos^2\theta) = -1$

Simplify:

$2(1 - 2\cos^2\theta) = -1 \to 2 - 4\cos^2\theta = -1 \to -4\cos^2\theta = -3 \to \cos^2\theta = \frac{3}{4}.$

Therefore, $\cos\theta = \frac{\sqrt{3}}{2}$ or $\cos\theta = -\frac{\sqrt{3}}{2}$. Since θ is a positive acute angle, then the value of $\cos\theta$ is $\frac{\sqrt{3}}{2}$. Hence, the correct answer is C, $\theta = 30°$. Because $\cos 30° = \frac{\sqrt{3}}{2}$.

14) Choice A is correct.

Use the slope equation:

$m = \frac{y_2 - y_1}{x_2 - x_1} \to \frac{7-3}{-9+4} = \frac{4}{-5} \to m = -\frac{4}{5}.$

The slope of the line is $-\frac{4}{5}$.

15) Choice A is correct.

We know that π radians $= 180°$, so $1° = \frac{\pi}{180}$ radians. Therefore, $15° = 15° \times \frac{\pi}{180°} = \frac{\pi}{12}$ radians. Hence, the correct option is A, $\frac{\pi}{12}$.

16) Choice A is correct.

$f(x) = \cos x + 4$ will vary between 3 and 5. Because $-1 \leq \cos x \leq 1 \rightarrow 3 \leq \cos x + 4 \leq 5$.

$g(x) = 2 - \sin^2 x$ will vary between 1 and 2 since $\sin^2 x$ will vary between 0 and 1. So, we get: $-1 \leq -\sin^2 x \leq 0 \rightarrow 1 \leq 2 - \sin^2 x \leq 2$.

The maximum value of $f(x)$ is 5, which is not the same as the maximum value of $g(x)$ equals to 2. Two functions spread along the x-axis between the maximum and minimum values. Since the interval of the range of function does not have a common point, it does not intersect at any point. Therefore, the correct answer is A.

17) Choice C is correct.

Using the finite geometric series formula:

$S_n = \sum_{i=1}^{n} ar^{i-1} = a_1 \left(\frac{1-r^n}{1-r}\right)$.

Substitute $a_1 = 1$ and $r = 3$ in the previous formula.

$S_7 = 1\left(\frac{1-3^7}{1-3}\right) = \frac{1-2,187}{1-3} = \frac{-2,186}{-2} \rightarrow S_7 = 1,093$.

18) Choice D is correct.

Let's denote the height of the lighthouse as "h". The height h can be determined by observing that the two right-angled triangles formed by the lighthouse and the two boats.

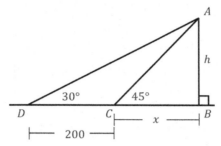

Find the tangent of the angles of the two boats. Let x be the distance of the closest boat to the lighthouse. Therefore, $tan\,45° = \frac{h}{x} \to h = x \times tan\,45° \to h = x$, and $tan\,30° = \frac{h}{200+x} \to h = (200+x)\,tan\,30° \to \frac{\sqrt{3}}{3} \times (200+x) = h \to 200\sqrt{3} + \sqrt{3}x = 3h$.

Now, substitute h instead of x into the second equation, we get:

$200\sqrt{3} + \sqrt{3}h = 3h \to h = \frac{200\sqrt{3}}{3-\sqrt{3}} \to h = 100(1+\sqrt{3})$.

Hence, the correct option is (D $100(1+\sqrt{3})$ meter.

19) Choice D is correct.

The equation of a line in slope intercept form is:

$y = mx + b$.

Solve for y:

$4x - 2y = 14 \to -2y = 14 - 4x \to y = \frac{(14-4x)}{-2} \to y = 2x - 7$.

The slope of the line is 2. The slope of the line perpendicular to this line is:

$m_1 \times m_2 = -1 \to 2 \times m_2 = -1 \to m_2 = -\frac{1}{2}$.

20) Choice D is correct.

Rewrite as: $x = \ln y^2$. Using, $y = \log_a x \to x = a^y$. This means that $x = \ln y^2 \to e^x = y^2$.

Then: $e^x = y^2 \to |y| = \sqrt{e^x}$.

Finally:

$y = \pm\sqrt{e^x} \to g^{-1}(x) = \pm\sqrt{e^x}$.

21) Choice A is correct.

Substitute a few points of the graph into the equations and check which equation passes through the points. First, evaluate the starting point (0,0). Therefore,

A. $0 = -9(0)^2 + 72(0) = 0$

B. $0 = -9(0)^2 - 72(0) = 0$

C. $0 \neq -9(0)^2 + 144(0) - 576 = -576$

D. $0 \neq -9(0)^2 - 144(0) - 576 = -576$

Now, evaluate the vertex point (4,144) for the remaining equations. So,

A. $144 = -9(4)^2 + 72(4) = -144 + 288 = 144$

B. $144 \neq -9(4)^2 - 72(4) = -144 - 288 = -432$

Finally, choice A is the correct answer.

22) Choice B is correct.

First, notice that the value of $\cos\theta$ is between -1 and 1 for any angle θ. This means that $x^2 - x + 1$ must also be between -1 and 1. If we try the options given in the problem one by one, we can check which one gives us a value for $x^2 - x + 1$ in the range $[-1,1]$.

Option A. -1: $(-1)^2 - (-1) + 1 = 1 + 1 + 1 = 3$, which is not in the range $[-1,1]$.

Option B. 0: $0^2 - 0 + 1 = 1$, which is in the range $[-1,1]$.

Option C. 1: $1^2 - 1 + 1 = 1$, which is in the range $[-1,1]$.

It turns out that all the given options are possible solutions. However, we need to check if they satisfy the given equation. Checking these values, we find:

For $x = 0$; $cos\left(\frac{\pi(0)}{2}\right) = cos\ 0 = 1$, which does equal $0^2 - 0 + 1 = 1$.

For $x = 1$; $cos\left(\frac{\pi(1)}{2}\right) = cos\left(\frac{\pi}{2}\right) = 0$, which does not equal $1^2 - 1 + 1 = 1$.

So, the only solution is B, 0.

23) Choice D is correct.

Firstly, we can rule out options A and C as they are secant and tangent functions respectively, and our graph shows a cosine function. Between options B and D, we can see that option D matches our graph perfectly. It's a cosine function (matching the shape of our graph), it has an amplitude of 2 (the graph oscillates between -1 and 3, a range of 4, and half of this range gives an amplitude of 2), and it's been translated 1 unit down (the midline of the graph is at $y = -1$). Therefore, the correct answer is: D, $y = 2\ cos(x) - 1$.

Effortless Math's CLEP Precalculus Online Center

... So Much More Online!

Effortless Math Online CLEP Precalculus Center offers a complete study program, including the following:

- ✓ Step-by-step instructions on how to prepare for the CLEP Precalculus test

- ✓ Numerous CLEP Precalculus worksheets to help you measure your math skills

- ✓ Complete list of CLEP Precalculus formulas

- ✓ Video lessons for CLEP Precalculus topics

- ✓ Full-length CLEP Precalculus practice tests

- ✓ And much more...

No Registration Required.

Visit **EffortlessMath.com/ CLEP-Precalculus** to find your online CLEP Precalculus resources.

Build Your Math Skills: Our Top Book Picks!

Download eBooks (in PDF format) Instantly!

Our Most Popular Books!

 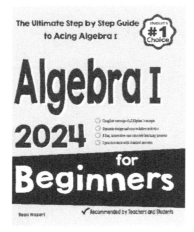 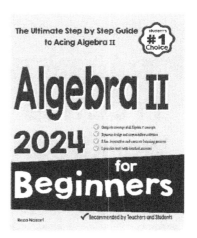

 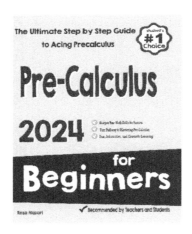 

 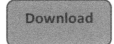   

Our Most Popular Books!

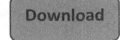

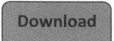

Receive the PDF version of this book or get another FREE book!

Thank you for using our Book!

Do you LOVE this book?

Then, you can get the PDF version of this book or another book absolutely FREE!

Please email us at:

info@EffortlessMath.com

for details.

Author's Final Note

I hope you enjoyed reading this book. You've made it through the book! Great job!

First of all, thank you for purchasing this study guide. I know you could have picked any number of books to help you prepare for your CLEP Precalculus test, but you picked this book and for that I am extremely grateful.

It took me years to write this study guide for the CLEP Precalculus because I wanted to prepare a comprehensive Precalculus study guide to help students make the most effective use of their valuable time while preparing for the final test.

After teaching and tutoring math courses for over a decade, I've gathered my personal notes and lessons to develop this study guide. It is my greatest hope that the lessons in this book could help you prepare for your test successfully.

If you have any questions, please contact me at reza@effortlessmath.com and I will be glad to assist. Your feedback will help me to greatly improve the quality of my books in the future and make this book even better. Furthermore, I expect that I have made a few minor errors somewhere in this study guide. If you think this to be the case, please let me know so I can fix the issue as soon as possible.

If you enjoyed this book and found some benefit in reading this, I'd like to hear from you and hope that you could take a quick minute to post a review on the book's Amazon page.

I personally go over every single review, to make sure my books really are reaching out and helping students and test takers. Please help me help CLEP Precalculus test takers, by leaving a review!

I wish you all the best in your future success!

Reza Nazari

Math teacher and author

Made in the USA
Coppell, TX
27 February 2025

46466836R00208